Educator's Companion
to Children's Literature,
Volume 2

Educator's Companion to Children's Literature, Volume 2

Folklore, Contemporary Realistic Fiction, Fantasy, Biographies, and Tales from Here and There

Sharron L. McElmeel

Drawings by
Deborah L. McElmeel

1996
Libraries Unlimited, Inc.

and its division
Teacher Ideas Press
Englewood, Colorado

LIBRARIES UNLIMITED, INC.
and its division
Teacher Ideas Press
P.O. Box 6633
Englewood, Colorado 80155-6633
1-800-237-6124

Production Editors: Tama J. Serfoss, Kay Mariea
Copy Editors: Dorothy Brandt, Tama J. Serfoss
Proofreader: Lori Kranz
Typesetter: Kay Minnis

Library of Congress Cataloging-in-Publication Data

McElmeel, Sharron L.
    Educator's companion to children's literature / Sharron L.
McElmeel ; illustrated by Deborah L. McElmeel.
    xiii, 157 p. 22x28 cm.
    Includes bibliographical references and index.
    Contents: v. 2. Folklore, contemporary realistic fiction, fantasy,
biographies, and tales from here and there
    ISBN 1-56308-330-2 (v. 2)
    1. Children's literature--Study and teaching (Elementary)--United
States. 2. Children--Books and reading. I. Title.
LB1576.M3975   1996
372.64'044--dc20   95-11608
                                                         CIP

For E. J., who is right.

Contents

2—FOLKLORE (*continued*)

Acknowledgments

Compiling the information included in this volume and its companion, *Educator's Companion to Children's Literature, Volume 1: Mysteries, Animal Tales, Books of Humor, Adventure Stories, and Historical Fiction,* would not have been possible without the enthusiasm, evaluations, suggestions, and help of many people.

Thanks to the many people who discussed books with me, recommended titles, and critiqued drafts as they were written and rewritten. Especially important were the help and support of those who assisted me with the research, locating and checking out books, returning books to libraries, and in general assisting with all the clerical tasks necessary in writing this kind of a book. I also wish to acknowledge the generosity of D. S. Tejmms, who graciously allowed me to use his poem, "High Adventures and Bright Dreams," to open chapter 6.

I appreciate the cooperation I received from the publicists, marketing directors, and editors of the many book publishing houses I contacted for information about books and authors. Credit goes to Fold-Pak resource specialists for contributing advice, information, and suggestions for ideas and books to use in each focus. Special thanks go to the reference staff of the Cedar Rapids Public Library, who not only helped verify facts but also assisted in locating elusive bits of information. And for her continuing inspiration and enthusiasm for good books of all types, my thanks to Nancy Jennings of O. G. Waffle Bookhouse in Marion, Iowa—she continues to know *all* the good books.

Introduction

This book provides information about books of folklore, contemporary realistic fiction, fantasy, biographies, and tales from here and there. To use this book, choose one of the five types of books for a class focus and, after reading chapter 1, which gives basic background and ideas about using a literature focus, read the chapter specific to that type of book.

After reading the appropriate chapters in this book, integrate the suggestions with your curriculum objectives and decide how the focus can be meshed with your goals and objectives. Collaborative efforts differ from one classroom to the next. Take the suggestions and weave them into your own curriculum.

Several read-aloud titles are proposed, but usually only one would be selected for any one focus. The other titles can be added to the lists of books that students can read independently; these are selective lists and are by no means exhaustive. Additional books in the various genres are published every year. Use the lists to locate some basic titles, but also consult your library's catalog to identify other titles available to your students.

At the end of each chapter are reproducible forms for you to duplicate and share with your students. The first form is a cover for the student reader's journal. However, some students may wish to design and produce their own covers. The pages following that cover include a response starter suggestion page, which could be displayed on a wall chart or by using an overhead projector; charts of books students have read and books they want to read, which are designed for individual accounting but could become class or group lists; and one-page posters featuring biographical information about authors who could be included in the specific focus.

An important point to remember is that one of the most valuable responses to a good book is to read another good book—fiction or nonfiction. Read, share, and enjoy.

1
Balancing Nonfiction and Fiction Reading

The most important thing to do is to read. Read like a wolf eats.
Read when they tell you not to read and read what they tell you not to read.
—Gary Paulsen, 1989

When Gary Paulsen, author of *Hatchet* and dozens of other adventure books, discusses his idea of reading, he suggests that young readers read everything and anything they can. They should not worry about what others might want them to read. He views "fiction as enhanced truth" and often puts incidents from his own life into his books.

Fiction and Nonfiction in the Literature-Based Classroom

The trend toward building literature-based classrooms and developing thematic units and inquiry models has put the emphasis on nonfiction. After years of including only fiction in our reading programs, nonfiction is quickly becoming an important part of many schools' reading plans. According to James Zarrillo, assistant professor of teacher education at California State University, Long Beach, "The question is no longer if their classrooms should be literature-based, but how to develop the best literature-based program possible."[1]

As more and more classrooms focus on themes that cannot be designated as purely social studies, science, or mathematics, information literature (nonfiction) is becoming a more integral part of classroom reading activities. We must be careful, though, as the pendulum swings toward encouraging young readers to make use of the many informational books available, that we do not leave behind fiction. Indeed, the techniques and content of fiction and nonfiction are not mutually exclusive. Many facts are embedded in fiction, and narrative structures are frequently used to further our understanding of the world. Folklore often contains facts about other cultures, times, and places; contemporary realistic fiction mirrors our society; fantasy is built on realistic details that are stretched into the realm of imagination; biographies are factual accounts of people who have left their mark on their community, and tales from here and there show the world to young readers.

Just as we must help children become aware that reading for information can be informative *and fun*, we also must help children remember that reading fiction is fun *and informative*.

A strong literature-based reading program includes all types of literature. J. Sanacore encourages the use of both fiction and nonfiction throughout the development of a theme-related topic. Reading both nonfiction and fiction will increase children's awareness and appreciation of both narrative and expository texts.[2] Just as we must plan thematic or inquiry-based units, we also must plan to focus on good literature of all types, including fiction. We must offer books in many different ways and for many different purposes. *McElmeel Booknotes: Literature Across the Curriculum* (Englewood, Colo.: Teacher Ideas Press, 1993) offers many suggestions for incorporating books of fiction and nonfiction into curriculum units. *The Latest and Greatest Read-Alouds* (Englewood, Colo.: Libraries Unlimited, 1994) describes books of fiction that are well-suited for reading aloud in the classroom or home. *Great New Nonfiction Reads* (Englewood, Colo.: Libraries Unlimited, 1995) describes wonderful new books of nonfiction that can be read aloud to foster children's curiosity and interest in information.

Author studies may focus on authors of fiction or nonfiction. Individual books can be introduced through booktalks. These methods, useful as they are, do not capitalize on the wealth of information classified by type. Many readers come to the library media center asking for a tall tale, a book about Benjamin Banneker, or a book like *Charlotte's Web*. By introducing fiction of various types to young readers, we help children build connections to other books of fiction (and nonfiction) and encourage them to look beyond the genre to the theme of the book to build their own connections with literature and to information or questions.

Few resources promote balanced literature-based reading program by highlighting the type of literature being read. This book, and its companion volume, *Educator's Companion to Children's Literature, Volume 1: Mysteries, Animal Tales, Books of Humor, Adventure Stories, and Historical Fiction*, do so. Each discussion provides for an immersion in reading and a spectrum of

involvement. Children's exploration of each type of book can take the reader into the work of many authors which can lead the reader to other reading and expressive activities.

This volume looks at four genres of books, but in addition, the final chapter, "Tales from Here and There," treats setting as the focus, discussing books set throughout the United States and in other parts of the world.

The Aesthetic and the Efferent Stances

The central goal of focusing on the type of book being read is to help students develop a love for reading and to make connections that will help them develop an inquiry approach to learning. The use of discussion helps readers become active participants in their own reading, whether or not they are reading from an efferent or an aesthetic stance. Writing in *Language Arts*, L. M. Rosenblatt describes an efferent stance toward reading as one where our main interest is in acquiring information and an aesthetic stance as one where we attend "mainly to what we are experiencing, thinking, and feeling during the reading."[3] The use of fiction in the reading program has most often focused on aesthetic readings. However, readers can adopt either an efferent or aesthetic stance toward a piece of writing, or even switch from one stance to the other during the same reading. For example, while enjoying a book of folktales aesthetically, we can also learn more about the culture from which the tales originated by taking an efferent stance.

Discussions can help students explore books of fiction and nonfiction from both the efferent and the aesthetic stances. For example, one activity might ask students to discuss a version of "Cinderella" in terms of feelings and emotions. Other activities might view the story from an efferent stance by asking students to compare different cultures' versions of the story and learn about the culture by comparing the variant details. For example, the glass slipper of the traditional French version of "Cinderella" is replaced by a silk brocade slipper in the Chinese version, reflecting the importance of silk to the Chinese culture. The bearer of the finery for the ball is a fairy godmother in the French version but is a magic fish in the Chinese variant—again, fish is an important food in China.

Discussion Groups and the Reader's Journal

Through discussion groups, students are motivated to become active participants in the reading process. They are encouraged to formulate their own questions, to take charge of discussions and analysis, and to learn from others: the teacher serves as guide and moderator, facilitating the discussions and response activities.

The link between reading, writing, and thinking is strengthened through the use of the reader's journal. The reading provides an opportunity for students to think, and the writing helps them clarify their thoughts. Students who read, and then respond to that reading by writing, build their reading comprehension. Discussions that build on what has been written provide an opportunity for students to listen, speak, compare, and evaluate.

Though the teacher may at times provide suggestions of points to discuss in relation to a selection that has been read, it is not the teacher's role to provide the questions, the topics to discuss, or the vocabulary words to discuss. The teacher guides and facilitates.

The Focus

In a literature focus based on the type of book being read, the main thread that ties the books together is how the reader classifies them. For example, a book such as *Johnny Appleseed: A Tall Tale* by Steven Kellogg (Morrow, 1988) could be considered both a tall tale and a biography. One person might include the book in a focus on folklore (which includes tall tales), while another might include it as a biography. Either classification would be appropriate. Often the study of a particular type of literature can be combined with an author focus, because many authors tend to write in the same general area. In the first four chapters in this book, suggestions will be given for collaborative focuses on authors who represent a specific

genre. The study of a genre can be enhanced by sharing information about specific authors and the writing techniques and research activities. In the final chapter the books cited will be based on the geographical location of the setting. An index within the chapter will assist in establishing a focus on setting.

Focusing on genre or books tied together by setting is just another way of sparking interest in reading and in sharing good books. Units emphasizing the type of literature being read should stand alongside author studies, thematic literature units, and inquiry units in the quest to immerse young readers in a balanced selection of literature of all types. The following information provides suggestions for getting started and implementing a literature focus. The term *genre* is used to refer to all five types of books, although books with specific settings are not technically a specific genre.

Introducing the Focus and Preparing the Surroundings

The beginning steps for introducing a type of book include creating a learning environment that focuses on the specific type of literature (including nonfiction) and that stimulates reading. That environment should consist of a focus center and writing and activity centers. Selecting picture books, short stories, and full-length books to read aloud will help acquaint readers with the type of literature to be studied and will provide the basis for introducing and implementing discussion.

Each focus unit should begin with an introductory activity. Specific suggestions for each genre in this book are given in the relevant chapters. There are, however, some general steps that should be taken. The most important component of any literature unit is a knowledgeable and interested facilitator (you!) who has in-depth knowledge of the literature to be discussed. The first step is to gather and read many titles in the selected genre and then read the general information in the appropriate chapter in this book. After you have read the background information, plan the specific introductory activities you will use to introduce the books to the students. Often picture books or short stories or selections can be read aloud. After the genre is introduced, readers will realize that they have already read books in the genre. A discussion about the books that students have already read can serve to identify the elements that make a book fit into the genre.

Focus Corner

In one corner of your room, set up a focus corner. A bulletin board with a ledge or table in front makes an ideal place to display material related to the focus genre. Include information about and pictures of authors who are known for writing in the genre, book jackets of popular books in the genre, terms associated with the genre, maps of settings, recommended book titles, activity cards, and other appropriate materials. Display many related books on the ledge or table in front of the display area. Space should also be available to display student-related work.

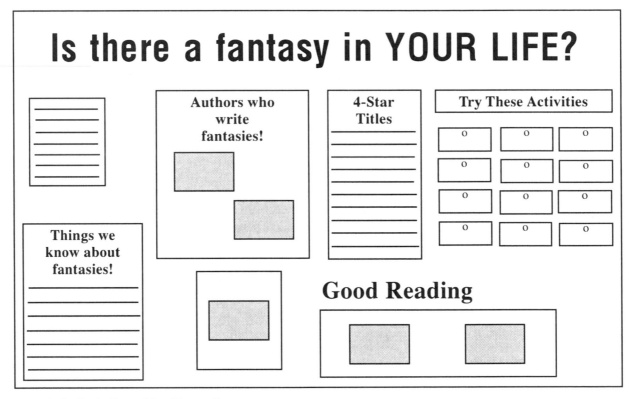

Is there a fantasy in YOUR LIFE?

Authors who write fantasies!

4-Star Titles

Try These Activities

Things we know about fantasies!

Good Reading

Sample Bulletin Board for Focus Center

Activity Cards

Write instructions for suggested activities for the focus genre on card stock, tagboard, or blank catalog cards. If a hole is not already in the card, punch one near the top edge. Put a pin in the bulletin board to serve as a hook on which to hand the cards. If displaying the activity choice cards on a bulletin board is not convenient, a chicken ring or a metal ring can be used to hold them together, and the packet of cards can be placed on the ledge or tabletop. Students

Activity Choice

Write activity suggestion in this space.

Activity Cards

can choose the activity they wish, remove the card, copy the instructions, and then replace the card before proceeding with the activity.

Creating a Writing and Activity Center

Provide table space in or near the focus center for children to concentrate on their reader's journal and other related extension and reaction activities. Make the center special by including colored writing paper (readers choose a color to match their reactions), special writing pencils, a box of crayons, waterpaints, scissors, art paper, and lined paper. If table space is limited, the center can be more like a cupboard for supplies needed to create visual or written responses to readings. Dictionaries, thesauri, and computers (several, if possible) should be available for student use.

Read-Alouds
and Discussions

Getting Started

After introducing readers to the focus genre, the teacher (or students) should choose a book to read aloud. Suggestions for specific titles are given in each chapter. The read-aloud book should establish a basis for the focus and should be selected to interest readers in exploring other titles in the focus genre on their own. Use the read-aloud book as a whole-class activity and reading experience to model the techniques for participating in discussion groups and journal writing.

Each student should be provided with a reader's journal. (Reproducible pages that can be used in the journal appear at the end of each chapter.) Each day, read a portion of the book and then model discussion groups. Suggested questions for discussion can be found on the "Response Starter Suggestions" page for the reader's journal at the end of each chapter (for example, see page 44). At first, questions should be oral. At the end of the discussion, model writing a reader's response to the day's selection. Ask students to jot down some of the main points in their journals for future reference, and give them a copy of the response you wrote. Every question will not be discussed every day, and often students' ideas will change as they find out more about the plot or characters. It is important to discuss special words, story elements, and other concepts associated with the focus genre. Dedicate a bulletin board to vocabulary and genre terminology.

Discussion Charts

After discussion groups and journal writing have been modeled as a whole-class activity, have students begin working in small discussion groups. Figure 1.1, page 6, is a chart to track discussion group participation. Although this chart has worked for many classroom groups, you may wish to adapt it or design your own chart to record discussion activity.

Discussions can certainly be held without using a chart. The basic, if not the only, reason for a chart is to give teachers a more concrete idea of what occurs in the discussion groups when they are not present. And the chart helps hold the students accountable for their attention to the reading selection during the discussion. However, after both students and the teacher are comfortable with student-led discussion groups, many teachers say that the need for the discussion chart diminishes, and progress becomes apparent as individuals and groups meet with other groups or with the teacher for direct instruction, evaluation, and other purposes. In the beginning, however, the discussion chart gives both the students and the teacher some confidence that what is expected to happen is indeed happening.

Date: _____

Name	Duty*	Participation Check**								
	L									
	S									
	V									
	Q									
	E									

　　*L=leader　　S=scribe　　　V=vocabulary person　　　Q=questioner　　E=encourager
　**Q=Question　　　　　　　R=Respond　　　　　　C=Comment

List at least two of today's discussion questions.

_____

_____

_____

Vocabulary discussed (interesting, unknown, unusual):

_____

_____

_____

Evaluation of group participation (circle one):　　　Good　　　　Fair　　　　Poor

Comments:

_____

_____

_____

_____

Plan for tomorrow:

_____

_____

_____

_____

Fig. 1.1. Discussion chart.

Reading Workshop Activities— Using the Reader's Journal and Discussion Groups

If students have not participated in reading workshops, the concept of the reader's journal and the self-directed discussion groups will need to be modeled. The steps will go from teacher-written response, to collaborative response writing, to individual responses, and finally, to self-directed discussion groups using the group's own questions and responses. The goal of the reader's journal and discussion chart is to help move the students to the point where they are responding to their reading and conducting discussions about that reading in their own student-led groups. This allows students to zero in on aspects of the reading that they feel are appropriate or that interest them, while the teacher is free to meet with small conference groups or individuals to provide direct instruction, evaluate progress, provide guidance for response activities, assist students with research strategies, and supervise other related language arts activities.

Modeling Daily Workshop Activities

In the following sequence only one day has been allowed for each step in the modeling process, but you may wish to stay at a particular step for more than one day. Often, providing for additional modeling or guided practice sessions is necessary to allow some young readers to grasp a concept. Before beginning, arrange for each child to have a reader's journal book available for responses. The reader's journal might be a special cover, a few prepared pages on which students can record their thoughts and record books they read and books they wish to read, and a blank back cover. (Suggestions for covers and reproducible prepared pages are provided at the end of each genre-oriented chapter.) The journals might be stapled, or a three-ring binder can be used so that additional pages could be added along the way. The reader's journal could also be as simple as a spiral notebook.

Begin the first session by introducing the book selected for reading aloud. Discuss the author and the students' prior knowledge of the book. If the book is a folklore tale or a realistic tale from another culture, locate the setting on a map, and discuss what the students know about that area of the world. If historical references are made in the book, discuss students' knowledge about those historical references. If a fantasy is going to involve elements of magic, discuss what students know about magic and magical happenings.

During the introductory session, read aloud the first chapter of the book. Introduce the reader's journal, explaining to students that each day they will be given an opportunity to respond to the selection that has been read. Their responses will be dated and written in their reader's journal. Any reactions to group discussions might be recorded there as well, along with notations of any words that the student wants to discuss or learn more about. Explain that during the first day or two you will model the response writing or the response will be written as a collaborative effort.

On this first day, personally compose a response to what was read. Try to be honest, responding not as a teacher, but as a reader genuinely interested in the book and its action. Discuss your written response with your students as you write it on chart paper or display it using an overhead projector. At this time students should be given their reader's journals. As soon as possible after writing the first day's entry as a model response for the students, provide the students with copies of the response you wrote and modeled for their journal. The entry in the journal should be dated.

The introductory session and the modeling of the response on this first day will depend on the length of time you read aloud. However, 20–30 minutes of reading aloud and an equal amount of time to model the response and distribute journals are usually sufficient. Subsequent days' activities will be accomplished during 30–40 minute periods.

Ask students to refresh their memory of the prior day's reading by reading, and then discussing, the reader's journal entry. Then read a second portion of the book. If you read for 20 minutes, allow half that time (10 minutes) for students to write their responses in their journals. Or hold a group discussion about the portions of the book that have been read and write a collaborative response. Allow students to generate discussion points and ask questions about the reading. Do not be too quick to fill gaps in the discussion with your own comments or questions. In the beginning students may be reluctant to share their thoughts or may think they need to copy the style of questions a teacher might ask in a traditional reading group. The goal is to provide an atmosphere that will allow students to share their own thoughts about the material read.

As soon as possible after the collaborative response is written, make copies and distribute them. Students should place the copy in their journal.

By the third day students may be asked to respond independently in their own journal. They may write spontaneously, or if they need a prompt, they may use the response starter suggestions listed in their journal. (The suggestions are included in the reproducible pages at the end of each genre-oriented chapter in this book.) The journal entries students create after each day's reading become the basis for discussion on the following day.

At the beginning of the third day, read the day's portion of the read-aloud selection and then ask students to respond to the reading in their journal. As students listen to the selection

(and later as they read independently), they should be encouraged to write down unfamiliar or interesting words from the reading. During the subsequent discussion, locate those words in the reading and discuss them in context. As the discussion activates their prior knowledge, some group members will have theories on the meaning of the new words. If the word makes sense in context, the group can decide to accept the definition as developed. Eventually, the definition will be refined as the word is encountered in additional readings. Each time a new word is discussed, an additional layer of meaning will be added. Readers who take note of meaningful words in context will develop their vocabulary while avoiding the less efficient and much less meaningful "word list—look up the definition routine."

After the response writing time has passed, students may stop or they might be allowed to finish up if necessary while their classmates go on to other reading workshop activities.

Ask students to reread their entries in their reader's journal and to be prepared to discuss them. This is the day the group discussion technique will be modeled. Use the discussion form (see fig. 1.1, on page 6) to record discussion activity. Select five students (vary the group in terms of ability and level of participation) to come to a table in the center of the room. (You may wish to preselect these students and brief them on the activity prior to this demonstration. A day or two before the demonstration, call the small group together and help practice the discussion procedure and the roles of the members.)

After several years of experimenting with the size of discussion groups, I have found five participants usually work best. If your numbers do not come out even, it is usually best to make the group smaller rather than larger. If the group is smaller than five, combine the roles of some participants so that all positions are covered.

The person designated as the *leader* helps keep the discussion moving and attempts to draw all members of the group into the discussion. The leader's role is *not* that of boss. (Some students equate the leader with the teacher.) In this discussion scheme no one is the teacher; each participant is an equal participant. Often, at the beginning of this process, the students will hesitate, expect the teacher to fill in the silence, to ask the questions, or to quiz over vocabulary words. Do not fall into the trap; let the silence hang and be patient. After a time students will begin the discussion and will make comments. In the process all participants must demonstrate genuine acceptance of the comments from each member of the discussion group.

The *scribe* is the person who writes the names of the participants on the discussion chart. (During the demonstration and modeling of this discussion procedure, ask the scribe to record the names of the five students in the first column of the chart.) Then as each person speaks and contributes to the discussion, the scribe makes a small check mark in the appropriate square. As students become acclimated to the discussion process and begin to contribute more easily to the discussion, checks can be made in the four corners of each square and a fifth check in the very center. As groups become more familiar with the chart, they can begin to use codes to indicate the type of comment or contribution made by each participant. For example, *Q* indicates a question, *R* indicates a response to someone else's comment, and *C* indicates a general comment. The same procedure for using the squares for the check mark can now be used to indicate the type of participation.

The person designated as *vocabulary person* should be a student who is especially alert to new, unusual, or interesting vocabulary words and who is willing to encourage others to share the words they consider new, unusual, or interesting.

The role of the *questioner* may be misleading if it is not carefully explained. All members of the discussion group are responsible for bringing up topics of interest, asking questions, and requesting clarification. However, it is the questioner who is to direct the attention of the group to dealing with questions and topics that require critical thinking. For example, if a participant says, "I really like the way the story ended," someone in the group should ask that person to elaborate on why the ending was satisfactory. If no one else asks, the questioner should do so. If a participant mentions that she or he thinks a specific event will happen next, the questioner should encourage that person to explain why.

The job of encouraging each other is part of every participant's responsibility, but the *encourager* should be especially alert, offering comments such as "That's an interesting observation," or "What do you think, John?" or "You have a good point." The encourager not only makes a special effort to encourage everyone to participate but also validates comments made by participants.

At the end of the day's discussion, ask the group to discuss and come to a consensus concerning which two questions addressed during the discussion received the most emphasis. Have the scribe record the questions in the area provided on the discussion chart. Because vocabulary is such an important element in adding to the students' schematic background and in their growth as readers, that topic is given a separate line on the discussion chart. Ask students to record any vocabulary words they discussed that day. The group should then evaluate the group participation, reaching a consensus on rating. Students should be encouraged not to point to any individual concerning participation in the discussion but to focus instead on the group. Finally, the group should determine its plan for the following day: for example, read another chapter or read so many pages. This discussion chart should be turned in to the teacher.

Read another selection from the book and ask students to respond in their reader's journal.

Ask students to review their response from the previous day and then convene a discussion group to again demonstrate the procedure for using the discussion chart and holding the discussion. Review the roles of the leader, scribe, vocabulary person, questioner, and encourager. Replace one or two students in the original demonstration group with other students. Read another selection from the book and ask students to respond in their reader's journal.

From this point on, read a selection from the book every day and schedule time for students to respond in their reader's journal. Every other day, convene a discussion group. Before the discussion ask students to read their journal entries for the two previous days. After the first day or two of the model discussion groups, each student should be assigned to a group. Try to include a member of the model discussion group in each discussion group. At first you may wish the groups to meet at different times so that you can observe how they are handling their responsibilities. If you do this, be particularly aware of your role as facilitator and participant rather than as authority figure and questioner. Eventually the groups can meet at the same time, and you can move from group to group or meet with individuals or small groups for other purposes.

It has been my experience that the sooner one can get to the point where the groups are meeting at the same time, the sooner the groups will assume responsibility for the quality of their discussions. As long as the teacher is present at every discussion, the students will tend to look to the teacher for direction. This is

especially true if this is the first experience students have had with student-led discussion groups. It is important that discussion groups be heterogeneous and that the groups change when a new book or a new focus is begun.

Once the read-aloud book and a complete cycle of reading and responding to a book have been completed, hold a culminating session in which the whole group discusses the entire book. What did they think of the book? How would they rate the book: poor, fair, good, or excellent? To whom would they recommend the book and why? Would they read other books by the same author?

Moving to Independent Reading

The reading and discussion techniques outlined above should be a major component in every classroom's reading workshop. A reading workshop is the scheduled time during a day when students focus on reading, become involved in reading conferences, or form flexible groups that meet to share books, learn reading strategies, and respond to what has been read. The reading workshop is scheduled in conjunction with the writing workshop and the content area workshop. The three workshops constitute the entire day's activities, and all direct instruction, project activities, and other curriculum-related activities are scheduled within the three workshop time blocks.

After modeling the reading, journaling, and discussion techniques through the use of a read-aloud book (as described in the previous section), the next and final step is to move to independent reading. Independent reading is an important component in building a genre focus because it provides an opportunity for immersion in the genre.

Students should be asked to select books within the focus genre to read during the reading workshop. The pattern of reading, responding, reading entries in the reader's journal, and discussion should be established as the pattern for the reading workshop experience.

Forming Discussion Groups

Students can be grouped into specific discussion groups based on various criteria, such as same book title, books in the same series, books by the same author, or books with a similar theme within a genre; or grouping can be based simply on personal compatibility.

If students are grouped on the basis of books by the same author, the discussion can center on similarities (and differences) in the author's writing style from book to book and the techniques the author used to build interest, to develop characters, plot, and so forth. If the group is composed of readers who are reading titles by various authors, the discussion might focus on the way the individual authors have developed their books in terms of the focus genre. Readers of fantasy, for example, might focus on common themes such as good versus evil, the influence of magic and imaginary beings on the story, or the nature of the main character's quest or problem.

Those reading the book from an efferent stance might discuss the facts about events and places in the book and the research that the author must have done; and they might ask their own questions surrounding the setting, events, and facts in the book. Using a timeline to sequence the events assists the logical, mathematical student in perceiving the flow of the plot. Such an activity also builds an awareness of the setting and its time period. Discussions could center on the historical facts in the book, how the author incorporated the historical facts into the story line, and other related topics.

Ways to Share Information About Books

In addition to the reader's journal and discussion procedure described in the preceding section, there are many other methods for sharing information about books. The reader's journal and discussion technique allow for the maximum use of the books in the focus genre within the reading program. Another technique is the literary triad. Still more techniques are listed in figure 1.2, on page 13.

 # Literary Triad

The procedure for this activity includes grouping participating students into groups of three. Group members are then asked to discuss the books they are reading. (They do not need to have finished the book, and ideally each individual in the group is reading a different title.) The discussion should not be of the round-robin type but should be structured more like the discussion of a good movie—it should be light and friendly. Allow the discussion to go on for three to five minutes. If it seems to be winding down sooner, end it immediately. The discussions should end while each participant still has something to say.

Number the students 1-2-3. At this time 1 should write a letter to 2, 2 should write to 3, and 3 should write to 1. The letter should follow up on the discussion just interrupted. After three to five minutes, stop the writing before all have finished. After students have read the letters written to them, 1 should write back to 3, 3 should write back to 2, and 2 should write back to 1. After three to five minutes, the writing should be halted, the letters passed back to the original writer, and the session ended. As the procedure is used more often, the discussions will become more involved and the writing more focused. The time span for each segment may need to be expanded to five to 10 minutes.

One Student's Progress

I was introducing the concept of the literary triads to a specific third-grade class and a member of the class resisted participating. This child seldom participated in any activity that involved interaction or cooperation within a group. He sought much attention and actually received quite a bit from some teachers through negative behavior. We discussed that choosing not to participate was not an option but that he, Alan, could of course choose what to say during the discussion and what to write in his letter. During the discussion he sat with his arms folded across his chest and did not enter into the conversation. No attention was given. Once the letter writing started, the class was told that their pencils must move on the paper but what they said was up to them. Alan wrote only a couple of words. He did not actively participate. When it came time to pass the letters to their recipients, Alan's letter went to Alisha.

Alisha was one of the most gifted third-grade students in the class. Alisha took one look at the letter and raised her hand and asked in a polite voice, "How can I answer Alan? Alan didn't write anything." My response was that I didn't know. "What do you think?" She immediately caught on and took up her pencil and began to write feverishly. When she was finished she had written almost an entire page. Each word nailed Alan for his lack of cooperation and told him that he was the one missing out by being stubborn. When she passed the letter back to Alan, he read it and stuffed the paper into his desk.

The next time the literary triads were attempted, Alan watched the teacher out of the corner of his eye to see if he was being watched. When he verified that he was not going to get any special treatment for his participation or nonparticipation, he began to contribute a few things in the discussion group. When the time came to write, he wrote. Somewhere between the fourth and fifth attempts at literary triads Alan became a full participant. He learned that his comments were going to be accepted by his peers, that he was going to get more attention for participating than for resisting, and he found out that he actually liked some of the books that others were talking about. He felt some degree of pride when other students began to ask him if they could have his book when he was finished with it. By asking this, the other students were validating Alan's choices for good books to read and their respect for his choices and for what he had to say about the books he was reading.

Alan continued to participate throughout that year, but the real payoff came during the following year. Alan had been assigned to a fourth-grade classroom where the teacher was using the reader's journal and discussion group activities, but Alan thought she should let the students also try the literary triads. The teacher did not know what he was referring to and dismissed his request, thinking that it would soon be forgotten. But Alan persisted over a period of two to three weeks; almost every day he asked his teacher if she had asked about the literary triads yet.

Finally, the teacher realized that Alan was serious and maybe she had better find out about the triads. She inquired and once she knew what was involved, she readily agreed to hold literary triads every other Friday. Alan helped introduce the concept to the students in the class who were not familiar with the concept, but for the most part the students who had been introduced to triads as third-graders were able to continue using the technique once the teacher agreed to facilitate the scheduling and allow time for them to take place. Once the students were involved in the literary triads, the teacher used the reader's journal and discussion technique for the class's reading workshop but utilized the literary triads to encourage the students to share the books they were reading during their daily free-choice independent reading time. Some people refer to this free-choice reading time with acronyms such as U.S.S.R. (uninterrupted silent sustained reading) or D.E.A.R. (drop everything and read).

More Ways to Share Books

 Have students create a video booktalk for the book. The Reading Rainbow® segments on public television use student booktalks at the end of each 30-minute segment. Use these booktalks as prototypes for student booktalks. Students should show the videotape they produce to their classmates.

Have students make an audio advertisement for the book. Record the advertisement on a cassette tape, and make the tape available in a listening center. Be sure to include where the book may be obtained: public library, school library media center, or classroom reading corner.

 Have students make a poster (similar to the movie posters displayed outside movie theaters) featuring the book. Display the poster in the library media center or in an appropriate spot in the room.

Have students develop a skit depicting a passage from the book that is funny or interesting or that in some way will interest others in reading the book.

 Have students conduct a mock interview with the author of the book. Discuss how the author came to write the book and why the author thinks that boys and girls will want to read the book. Researching the life of the author will help the mock author discuss her or his background.

Have students create a book display featuring interesting items related to the book. These might include a map of the book's setting, an illustration and brief profile of each of the main characters, a summary of the character's problem, and interesting or pertinent statements or questions that might lead another reader to want to explore what is in the book.

 Have students read the first chapter or two from the book onto an audiotape. Read as far into the book as it takes to really hook the listener. Then suggest that the listener get the book and finish it. This type of recording is called a cliffhanger. Put the tape and the book in a listening center.

Fig. 1.2. Seven activities to help students share the books they are reading.

From *Educator's Companion to Children's Literature, Volume 2: Folklore, Contemporary Realistic Fiction, Fantasy, Biographies, and Tales from Here and There*. © 1996. Libraries Unlimited. (800) 237-6124.

Culminating the Focus_____

Always attempt to bring closure to a focus on a particular genre by sharing a common activity. The culminating activity might be as simple as a final reading and sharing session, or students may decide to have a character day and come dressed as favorite characters from folk stories that had been shared during the focus on folklore. Throughout the day (or specific class period), the students would be "in character"— responding as the character would and alluding to events that happened to the character.

The students might also construct a folklore museum and offer tours to other groups in the school. Exhibits might include the three magic beans from "Jack and the Beanstalk," Cinderella's glass slipper (or silk slipper or footwear from another version of the tale); some of the unbroken eggs (both plain and jeweled) from "The Talking Eggs"; some of the straw, sticks, and bricks used to build the three little pigs' houses; or Red Riding Hood's cape or the basket she carried to her grandmother's house.

A focus on contemporary realistic fiction might culminate in a character day much like the one suggested for the folklore culmination. Students might dramatize episodes from selected books, or they might role-play other outcomes by changing the action of one or more of the characters.

Students might hold a reading fair, where each student would devise a way to share information about her or his favorite book of contemporary realistic fiction in a visual or oral presentation. The presentation might involve creating a jackdaw (a collection of objects representing characters, events, or objects in the story), role-playing one of the characters in the book, or simply talking about the book.

The focus on fantasy might be culminated with a fantasy day read-in or with a fantasy character museum containing models or pictures of fantasy characters created by the students. Allow students to make cassette tape recordings to introduce the fantasy creatures to those making the museum tour.

Culminating the focus on biographies could involve constructing a large-scale time line. Each reader would place the accomplishments and significant dates of a biographical subject on the time line. Discussions between the subject and one or more of his or her contemporaries about modern or past issues (as shown on the time line) could be constructed and dramatized.

An ethnic festival might help culminate a focus on tales from around the world. Readers might play games from different parts of the world (providing a wonderful opportunity to connect fiction with nonfiction titles about traditions and games from other countries), eat snacks (minties from Australia or bowls of rice from Japan) from story locations, and view displays of the settings from around the world.

One of the simplest and most effective focus culminations is simply to designate a time for each class member to share books he or she has read in the focus genre and to spend some additional time reading.

Notes_____

1. James Zarrillo. "Teachers' Interpretations of Literature-Based Reading." *The Reading Teacher* 43 (October 1989): 22-28.

2. J. Sanacore. "Expository and Narrative Texts: Balancing Young Children's Reading Experiences." *Childhood Education* 67 (1991): 211-214.

3. L. M. Rosenblatt. "Literature—S.O.S!" *Language Arts* 68 (1991): 444-448.

2
Folklore

Folklore comprises traditional creations of peoples, primitive and civilized. These are achieved by using sounds and words in metric form and prose, and include also folk beliefs or superstitions, customs, and performances, dances and plays. Moreover, folklore is not a science about a folk, but the traditional folk-science and folk-poetry.

—Jonas Balys as quoted in
Funk & Wagnalls Standard Dictionary of Folklore Mythology and Legend (1949)

Folklore books are the written versions of oral narratives that have been passed from generation to generation in various cultures. The storyteller is an important figure in oral cultures; storytellers tell of their people's history, explain the way the world was and how it originated, and preserve the lives, customs, beliefs, and emotions of the people whose story they are telling. In parts of Africa, storytellers are called *griots*. In the Pueblo communities in the southwestern United States, storytellers have been immortalized in traditional clay storyteller figures. Gail Haley created a storyteller, Poppyseed, as a literary device to tell the Appalachian tales of Jack.

From Folktales to Myths

The genre of folklore includes several major groupings: folktales, ballads, fairy tales, legends, fables, myths, folk songs, and tall tales. Most folklore is classified in the 398 section of the library media center. Myths, however, are most often found in the 291 section, because they reflect the religious beliefs of a civilization.

Myths

Myths explain how something came to be in the universe—how the sun was placed in the sky, the origin of the constellations, or why the moon shines at night. Myths refer to gods and beings greater than humans and reflect the religious beliefs of their cultures.

Legends

Legends are very much like myths in that they often explain how something came to be. Unlike myths, though, legends deal more with earthly things such as how the bear got its stumpy tail and how the jaguar got its spots. Because legends are often stories of historical figures who are put into fictional situations and given fictional traits, a reader who is not familiar with the truth about these historical characters may have difficulty distinguishing tall tales or legends from biography.

Tall Tales

Tall tales are fictional glorifications of historical figures. Tall tales stretch those facts to the point of incredibility. Tall tales are a variant on folktales that seems to be unique to the United States. The majority of tall tale heroes are male, although there are fantastic female heroes in some tall tales. One of these women, Sally Ann Thunder Ann Whirlwind, Davy Crockett's wife, is featured in Mary Pope Osborne's *American Tall Tales* (Knopf, 1991). Other legendary female heroes are featured in Robert D. San Souci's *Cut from the Same Cloth: American Women of Myth, Legend, and Tall Tales* (Philomel, 1993).

Fables

Fables such as "The Hare and the Tortoise" and "The Fox and the Crow" are stories for which Aesop and La Fontaine are well known. These tales most often have talking animals with single traits, and the tale is brief with a clear moral message to provide instruction in proper actions and thinking. Fables are straightforward, didactic, and moralizing.

Although the animals are often considered to have been personified (made to have traits of people), they do, for the most part, retain their animal characteristics. Most fables actually play on the traits of the animal, for example, the slowness of the tortoise in "The Hare and the Tortoise," and the long beak of the stork in "The Fox and the Stork."

Fairy Tales

Fairy tales, or nursery tales, often begin with "Once upon a time," and conclude with "And they lived happily ever after." Between those phrases are giants, fairies, pixies, elves, and magic. Often the numerals 3 and 7 are significant; for example, the three little pigs, seven dwarfs, and in "Rumpelstiltskin" there are three rooms of straw to be spun into gold and three guesses for each of three days. Stock characters show up in fairy tales: wicked stepmothers, fairy godmothers, people who transform themselves, and members of royalty. Often the characters in a tale indicate the country of the tale's origin. Giants often appear in English tales; fairy godmothers in French tales of princes and princesses; Welsh tales include talking animals, hills, and valleys and people who transform themselves; and leprechauns populate Irish tales.

Ballads and Folk Songs

Many folk songs and ballads in the United States originated from stories about such legendary characters as John Henry and Paul Bunyan. In Europe and other countries, ballads have been sung about legendary heroes such as Robin Hood and Dick Whittington.

Simple fairy tales such as "Little Red Riding Hood," "Jack and the Beanstalk," and "The Three Billy Goats Gruff" are more popular in the primary grades, while the older students enjoy the somewhat lengthier and more romantic stories. The separation is not based in any historical designation—originally all folk literature was intended for adults.

Fairy tales and folktales often have themes that implicitly or explicitly focus on justice. Actions move rapidly and reach a climax relatively quickly. The tone of these tales is seldom didactic although some readers will perceive a message meant to be learned.

Fairy tales are sometimes gruesome: a wolf eats a pig or a little girl, parents leave children to die in the woods, and the woods are full of bears and goblins. Fairy tales are often perceived as sexist, as well, showing girls as weak victims. Sometimes retellers change details of the original oral story, so that Red Riding Hood flees into the woods rather than being eaten by the wolf, Hansel and Gretel's parents lose their children rather than abandoning them in the woods, and the female characters are stronger and more self-sufficient. However, part of the value of folk literature is its reflection of the values and thoughts of the times during which they were written. Studying folk literature in this context can be a valuable activity for older readers.

Folktales in Today's Culture

Folk literature is clearly a part of our culture's heritage. Poetry and modern stories often allude to Greek myths, Aesop's fables, and other folk literature. For example, a character in Carol Gorman's *Jennifer-the-Jerk Is Missing* (Simon & Schuster, 1994) is known for "crying wolf"— a reference to the fable "The Boy Who Cried Wolf," and Tomie dePaola uses a visual allusion to "The Three Billy Goats Gruff" when he includes a troll under the bridge with three goats in *Helga's Dowry: A Troll Love Story* (Harcourt, 1977). Many of the words and references we use today come from myths (see Isaac Asimov's *Words from the Myths*, illustrated by William Barss [Houghton, 1961]). For example, *cereal*; is derived from Ceres, the goddess of grain or agriculture, and the god Mercury, known as a speedy messenger, has become the logo for a worldwide floral service and the brand name of an automobile.

Literary Folk Stories

In addition to referring to folk literature, many authors mimic the style of folk literature in their own original tales. Hans Christian Andersen is perhaps the best known of these authors. His many fairy tales emulate the form and elements of the older, traditional tales.

Paul Goble is well known for his literary tales featuring the Plains Indian trickster Iktomi. Because these tales are not retold from the oral tradition, but only mimic the form, they are considered "literary" folk stories. Andersen's tales are "literary fairy tales." Goble's original stories are "literary legends."

Another popular author, David Wisniewski, researches the folk literature of a culture and then uses selected elements in an original tale about that culture. His literary legends include *Elfwyn's Saga* (Lothrop, 1990), set in Iceland; *Rain Player* (Clarion, 1991), set in the ancient Maya culture of middle America; *The Warrior and the Wise Man* (Lothrop, 1989), set in Japan; and *The Wave of the Sea-Wolf* (Clarion, 1994), set in the Tlingit culture of the Pacific Northwest.

Connections for Readers

As a young boy in England, Paul Goble was fascinated by Native American culture, reading whatever he could find on the subject. His interest continued throughout college and military service, and even though he became an industrial engineer his interest in the Native American culture soon became his vocation rather than just his avocation. After searching for books about Native Americans for his children, Richard and Julia, Paul Goble decided that someone needed to write accurate accounts of historical events from the Native American perspective. Goble spent several summers on reservations in South Dakota and Montana, and he and his first wife, Dorothy, co-authored several books about Native Americans before Goble moved to the United States in 1977.

In 1978, Goble married Janet Tiller, and for 13 years they lived in the Black Hills of South Dakota where his studio, a small room in his house, faced pine trees, the meadow, and the forest wildlife. Goble continued to study Native American culture, meeting with people on reservations, attending ceremonies, and visiting historical museums to study paintings and beadwork. For a few years in the early 1990s, the Gobles lived in Lewiston, New York, before moving in 1992 to Montana where Paul continues to write stories about Native Americans. Some of his tales are retellings of traditional legends, while others, particularly the Iktomi tales, are literary legends.

Connections for Readers

David Wisniewski creates literary folktales and is featured in the chapter focusing on fantasy. (See index.) His extensive author notes at the end of each of his books detail the research and the folklore motifs that he used in creating his tales.

Elements of Folktales

Cultural Variations of Similar Tales

Folk literature from many cultures contains variations of similar tales, motifs, or patterns. These stories and their motifs are referenced in Stith Thompson's six-volume reference work, *Motif-Index of Folk-Literature* (Indiana University Press, 1955-1958). The most common motifs include a long sleep or enchantment, magical powers, magical transformation, magic objects, wishes, and trickery.

Folklorists theorize that these similar stories originated in one region of the world and were spread to other regions as people traveled or traded. Other folklorists believe that, as people's concerns seem to focus on similar topics regardless of the culture, their original stories tend to focus on explaining the same phenomena and values. The details, which help to flesh out the story, reflect the animals, flora, and traditions of the culture that originated each version of the story. Porridge in one version of a tale might become cornmeal mush in another version in another country—representing the type of food in that culture. In the nature of oral literature, each time a tale is retold, it is re-created to reflect the current surroundings and incorporate local changes and embellishments.

A great deal of variation is possible both from oral retellings and from printed versions. Retellers make their own storytelling voice heard. They may change the setting, add a character, insert dialogue, or enhance a specific element of the tale—all in an effort to create their own unique story, a story that will fit the needs of the retellers and their audience.

Tricksters

Tales from many cultures feature a trickster character. The primary West African trickster is Anansi (sometimes spelled Ananse), a lovable rogue, portrayed as either a spider or a spider-like man. Whichever form he takes, though, Anansi displays vulnerable human qualities. Stories that feature Anansi show how small, seemingly defenseless people or animals use their brains to outwit others who are more powerful. Eric A. Kimmel has retold several Anansi tales, including *Anansi and the Moss-Covered Rock* (Holiday, 1988), *Anansi and the Talking Melon* (Holiday, 1994), and *Anansi Goes Fishing* (Holiday, 1991).

Connections for Readers

For many years Eric A. Kimmel taught at Portland State University in Oregon during the day and told stories whenever he got a chance. He has been a writer of children's stories since 1969, but it wasn't until 1986 that his book *Hershel and the Hanukkah Goblins* (Holiday, 1989) was published. Since then Kimmel has retold stories he recalled from his own childhood, stories encountered in his reading and travels, and stories from university acquaintances. The stories Kimmel retells are not chosen for their value to a folklorist, but because there is something in the story that attracts his attention. He wants something funny, unusual, surprising, even weird in his stories, and he makes some changes to put something of himself into each story.

In Germany, the trickster is often a wolf, and in Japan, as well as France, it is a fox. Japanese author and illustrator Mitsumasa Anno uses a fox character to help tell the stories in *Anno's Twice Told Tales: The Fisherman and His Wife and the Four Clever Brothers* by the Brothers Grimm and *Mr. Fox* (Philomel, 1993).

In the southern United States, Anansi has become "Br'er Rabbit," and "Aunt Nancy" in some versions of the adapted tales, but more frequently the trickster in southern tales is "Jack," a pivotal character in many Appalachian tales. Richard Chase popularized many Appalachian tales in his collections *The Jack Tales* (Houghton, 1943) and *Grandfather Tales* (Houghton, 1948).

Folklore—Then and Now

Grimm's Fairy Tales

One well-known body of folklore is the work of Jacob and Wilhelm Grimm. The Grimm brothers collected folklore from their native Germany. Later the brothers began to develop a new German dictionary in addition to their work collecting folk literature.

Jacob Ludwig Carl Grimm (b. 1785) and Wilhelm Carl Grimm (b. 1786) were born in Hanau, Germany, near Frankfurt. Both studied historical law and German folk poetry at Marburg University. They were philologists and collectors, and recorded a collection of local stories, "Nursery and Household Tales," attempting to record the stories exactly as they were told to them. The two brothers were never willingly separated during their lifetime. Jacob never married. Wilhelm married a childhood friend, Dorothea (Dortchen) Wild, and they had three children. Dorothea contributed to the brothers' folklore collection, which included popular fairy tales like "Little Red Riding Hood" and "Hansel and Gretel."

The *Grimm's Household Tales* (1812) are among the enduring tales from the nineteenth century. The tales have been retold and regrouped into hundreds of collections including: *Popular Folk Tales: The Brothers Grimm*, translated by Brian Alderson, illustrated by Michael Foreman (Doubleday, 1978); *Favorite Tales from Grimm*, retold by Nancy Garden, illustrated by Mercer Mayer (Four Winds, 1982); and Virginia Haviland's *Favorite Fairy Tales Told in Germany* (Little, Brown, 1959; Beech Tree Books, 1994).

English Fairy Tales

Joseph Jacobs collected popular tales told in England. An Australian by birth (b. 1854), he was educated at London University and

Cambridge. He became a noted historian and for a time was an editor of the *Jewish Encyclopedia*. Later he became a professor of English at the Jewish Theological Seminary in New York. Jacobs retold the stories he collected in a manner that emulated the technique of a nanny or grandmother telling stories. Jacobs's collections of English fairy tales, *English Fairy Tales* (1890) and *More English Fairy Tales* (1894), are still much used today. He also collected three other volumes of folk literature: *Celtic Fairy Tales* (1892), *Indian Fairy Tales* (1892), and *A Book of Wonder Voyages* (1896). *A Book of Wonder Voyages* is a collection of Aesop fables. Joseph Jacobs became known as a folklorist and storyteller.

French Fairy Tales

More than 100 years before the Brothers Grimm collected stories from the German peasants and more than 200 years before Jacobs's work in England, Charles Perrault was collecting the fairy tales of France. Perrault was born in Paris in 1628. He studied law but later turned to writing verse. Perrault is credited with being the first to set down the collection of fairy tales that included "Bluebeard," "Cinderella," "Diamonds and Toads," "Little Red Riding Hood," "Puss in Boots," and "The Sleeping Beauty." Many believe that Charles Perrault's son, Pierre (1678-1700), had some part in collecting the verses for the 1696 prose collection *Contes de ma mère l'oye* ("The Tales of Mother Goose") but concede the credit for the collection to Charles Perrault. Pierre Perrault died at the age of 22 in 1700; Charles died three years later at 75.

Southern Folktales

Richard Chase collected southern American folklore from various parts of North Carolina, Virginia, and Kentucky that he retold in *The Jack Tales* and *Grandfather Tales*. In contrast to the Brothers Grimm, who attempted to record the precise words of the local tellers of their fairy tales, Chase acknowledges that his retellings are composites of several versions. "I have put each tale together from different versions, and from my own experience in telling them. I have told the tales to all kinds of listeners, old and young; and only then, after many retellings, written them down."

Illustrated Fairy Tales

For the most part, early collections of folklore were not illustrated. The original collections, although written, were intended to promote the sharing of the stories through storytelling. However, once the picture book became popular, so did the illustrated folktale.

Much information about people and cultures can be gleaned from illustrated folk stories and collections of tales. Pictures of flowers and animals represent those of the culture the tale represents. For example, *Mufaro's Beautiful Daughters* by John Steptoe (Lothrop, 1987)—a tale with many of the same motifs as the traditional Cinderella tale—takes place in Zimbabwe. The illustrations show the flora and fauna of that region of the world. Another version of Cinderella, Shirley Climo's *The Egyptian Cinderella*, illustrated by Ruth Heller (Crowell, 1989), shows the flora and fauna of Egypt.

The details of a story can also assist in tracing the story to its origins. Gail E. Haley was living in the Caribbean Islands in the late 1960s and became interested in the local stories. One story, in particular, interested her because it told of a jaguar, an animal that did not inhabit the islands. The story tells how Anansi the spider (in this story a spiderlike man) earned the sky god's golden box of stories that he then scattered to the far corners of the earth. Haley's illustrated version of *A Story, A Story* (Atheneum, 1970) cited its origins as West Africa. The Africans brought their stories to the Caribbean with them, and in this case, the retellers did not change the animals to reflect the new setting. Haley's book became one of the first picture books to show a black god.

Many traditional tales, especially fairy tales such as "Beauty and the Beast," "Snow White and the Seven Dwarfs," and "Rumpelstiltskin," are set in a romantic time gone by. The medieval era is a popular setting. Kings and queens, emperors, and pharaohs rule empires populated by both rich and noble and common folk, whose interactions become the subject of many folktales.

Connections for Readers

Gail E. Haley's first book was printed in 1962 with illustrations she created using pine block prints. She used the book to promote her artistic ability to publishers. Three years later she was offered a book to illustrate. In 1971 she earned the Caldecott Award for *A Story, A Story*. Some of her more recent titles include *Jack and the Bean Tree* (Crown, 1986), *Jack and the Fire Dragon* (Crown, 1988), and *Mountain Jack Tales* (Dutton, 1992), a collection of traditional tales told in North Carolina where Haley and her husband, David Considine, reside. They share their Blowing Rock, North Carolina, home with several cats and a finch or two—the cats often appear in Haley's illustrations. Haley even put her husband on the last page of *Birdsong* (Crown, 1984). Haley and Considine are associated with Appalachian State University in North Carolina.

Thirty years ago the folklore our children heard most often originated in Europe. Gradually the folklore of other nations, specifically the tales from Asia and those told by Native Americans, came into the mainstream. In general, the folk literature shared with young people reflects the makeup of today's society. As our culture has become increasingly diverse, so too has our folklore.

Over the years, traditional characters such as the Jiza and Oni of Japanese tales and the animal characters in African and Native American legends began to change the images seen in folk literature.

There are still some distinctions, though. Usually the tales of France, Germany, England, and other northern European cultures are considered fairy tales, while Native American and African stories are often designated as legends. Several tales from Asia are considered legends or fables, for example, Marcia Brown's retelling of *Once a Mouse: A Fable Cut in Wood* (Scribner, 1961), a tale originating from the Panchatrantra tales from India. However, Asian variants of European fairy tales such as *Lon Po Po: A Red Riding Hood Story from China*, translated and illustrated by Ed Young (Philomel, 1989), and *Yeh-Shen: A Cinderella Story from China*, retold by Ai-Ling Louie, illustrated by Ed Young (Philomel, 1982), are also called fairy tales.

Connections for Readers

Ed Young was born in Tientsin, China, and grew up in Shanghai and Hong Kong. Young came to the United States on a student visa and studied at the Los Angeles Art Center and later taught at Pratt Institute, Yale University, Naropa Institute, and the University of California at Santa Cruz. During his career Young has illustrated dozens of books for children, a few of which he also wrote. His painting reflects the philosophy of the Chinese, which he describes by saying, "Chinese painting and words are complementary. There are things that words do that pictures can not, and likewise, there are images that words can never describe." Young and his wife live in Hastings-on-Hudson, New York.

Folklore—Changing Times

Because folk and fairy tales originated from the oral tradition, they often reflect the values and ideas of an older time. However, some tales can still deal with today's issues; for example, some people believe "The Three Little Pigs" teaches that anything worth doing (as in building a house) is worth doing well. "Red Riding Hood" could remind children not to talk to strangers.

Sometimes, though, the roles of men and women in the historic folk literature defy contemporary values of female equality. There is a contemporary trend to "rewrite" many fairy tales or nursery rhymes in nonsexist language and remove the references to the female characters' dependence on men. To alter the traditional tales changes the history of their origin and the situation under which they evolved; however,

some retellings have managed to create strong women characters without substantially changing the original or the representation of the original culture. Still, in many cases, these retold tales are more suitable for sharing with a contemporary audience and in effect have evolved as true folk literature is supposed to evolve—changing with the reteller to reflect the situation and culture in which they are retold.

One example of a traditional tale retold to reflect today's values is Eric A. Kimmel's *Four Gallant Sisters* (Holt, 1992). Kimmel combined and "reformulated" two Grimm Brothers' tales to tell of female heroes who are active, powerful, and good. The four sisters disguise themselves as men, learn skills, and prove that they are intelligent, insightful, and wise as well as courageous. Together they rescue a princess and her four brothers and must decide whether they want to continue their charade now that they have met four handsome princes. In this story, the female characters determine their own fate and manage to live "happily ever after" based on their own courage and actions. While the retelling retains some female stereotypes, it dispels others.

Variations on a Theme: The Three Little Pigs

Another trend in today's folklore study is to uncover variations on the familiar version of the tale. Traditional variations include Gavin Bishop's *The Three Little Pigs* (Ashton Scholastic, 1989), illustrated by the author, which in addition to the familiar huffing and puffing, tells of the wolf's attempts to trick the pigs out of the brick house by arranging to visit the turnip patch, apple orchard, and the fair. Finally, the wolf decides to come down the chimney at which point he meets his demise at the hands of the third little pig. Erik Blegvad has retold a similar version of the tale in his *Three Little Pigs* (Atheneum, 1980). Other retellers have shortened the tale to conclude prior to the visits to the turnip patch, apple orchard, or the fair. One example of the shortened version is Paul Galdone's *Three Little Pigs* (Clarion, 1970).

However, contemporary authors have also retold the story of the three little pigs with a variety of twists. James Marshall retells the tale in his book, *The Three Little Pigs* (Dial, 1989), with many humorous details in both the text and the illustrations. Marshall's tale, while inserting phrases that update the tale and projecting humor through the illustrations, does follow the full version of the tale. Susan Lowell tells a southwestern adaptation in *The Three Little Javelinas* (Northland, 1992; Scholastic, 1992), which takes place in the Sonoran Desert, where Native American, Mexican, and Anglo cultures blend together. *Javelina* is a Spanish word for wild pigs. In this version it is the trickster, Coyote, who attempts to blow down the javelinas' houses.

Humorous Twists

Another trend seems to be to take a well-known folktale and add humorous twists that give the tale a different flavor. Steven Kellogg has done this masterfully in his retellings of Paul Bunyan, Johnny Appleseed, and Pecos Bill tales.

Another author/illustrator, Tony Ross, has also created some humorous "updated versions" of traditional stories. Among his retellings are *The Three Pigs* (Pantheon, 1983); *Puss in Boots: The Story of a Sneaky Cat* (Delacorte, 1981); *The Pied Piper of Hamelin* (Lothrop, 1978); *The Boy Who Cried Wolf* (Dial, 1985); and *Foxy Fables* (Dial, 1986). Ross adds modern touches to each of these retellings. In *The Three Pigs,* the wolf shows up in a gray flannel topcoat to pursue pigs who have moved to the country to escape an overcrowded high-rise apartment in the city. In Ross's version of "The Fox and the Crow" in *Foxy Fables*, the conceited crow steals a piece of mozzarella cheese and returns home to her third-story apartment. Ross's retelling of "The Hare and the Tortoise" has the two sharing a quiet moment of sports talk with beverage in hand. When the traditional challenge takes place, the hare stops for a nap and the tortoise goes by. When the hare realizes the tortoise has passed by, he jumps up and hits his head on a low-hanging branch, causing him to lose the race.

In addition to nontraditional versions, in which the basic premise of the tale is maintained

and only the details are changed to provide humor or a modern view of the tale, some authors create parodies of traditional tales. A parody is an original tale that mimics the form of the traditional tale but provides a variation on the basic story elements. Often the parody involves retelling the tale from a completely different perspective. For example, Jon Scieszka's *True Story of the Three Little Pigs by A. Wolf* (Viking Childrens Books, 1989) tells the story from the wolf's perspective.

Other parodies reverse the characters' roles, as in *The Three Little Wolves and the Big Bad Pig* by Eugene Trivizas, illustrated by Helen Oxenbury (McElderry, 1993)—in which it is the "Big Bad Pig" who attempts to enter the house of the wolves—and *Bad Egg: The True Story of Humpty Dumpty* by Sarah Hayes (Little, Brown, 1987). Another example is Jane Yolen's *Sleeping Ugly* (Putnam, 1984), which reverses some of the concepts in the traditional "Sleeping Beauty" tale. Attempts to eliminate stereotypes can also result in parodies as in Bernice Myers's *Sidney Rella and the Glass Sneaker* (Macmillan, 1985), a modern-day parody of "Cinderella."

Beginning a Focus on Folklore

Begin a unit focusing on folklore with a general introduction. This general introduction might include a brief discussion of the characteristics of folk literature and will often include reading a folk story aloud.

Picture books can be used as part of the general introduction. It is often effective to introduce each type of folklore by reading aloud a book that falls into different categories of folklore, such as fables, fairy tales, or another folklore type. Often it is difficult to clearly distinguish between the different types of folklore. For example, legends and myths can both explain elements in nature, though myths often refer to gods or deities. However, the ability to distinguish each type of folklore from one another is not as important as realizing that there are different categories and that sometimes they may overlap. Appreciation of the stories is the most important goal at all levels.

Read-Alouds and Discussions

The read-aloud book should be carefully chosen to interest listeners in reading more books of folklore, such as those listed on pages 26-34.

It is important that students become familiar with the terms and techniques folklore retellers use so that, during discussions, the students will recognize the techniques and be able to discuss those techniques using common terms. A bulletin board could be dedicated to new words and to the terms.

- motifs
- themes
- variant forms
- setting
- attempts at resolution
- solution
- climax
- parody

During the read-aloud sessions, continue to discuss students' perceptions about different variations of folklore. Identify the basic elements (skeleton or story grammar) common to all versions. Once students are familiar with the basic story grammar of a particular tale, they will be able to generate their own literary versions of the tale.

After group discussion and journal writing have been modeled to the whole class, break the students into smaller discussion groups as outlined in the "Reading Workshop Activities" and "Moving to Independent Reading" sections of chapter 1 (see pages 7-13). Since individual folk stories are often much shorter than a novel, it would be advantageous to organize groups for discussion based on those reading variants of the same tale, tales retold by the same reteller, or those reading stories with similar motifs. The focus would be on comparing and contrasting the tales.

Collections of Traditional Tales to Read Aloud

Aesop. **Aesop's Fables**. Selected and illustrated by Michael Hague. Holt, 1985. Read-aloud audience: grades 3-7; ages 8-12.
Contains 13 of Aesop's most familiar fables, each illustrated with Hague's detailed paintings in muted tones.

Asbjørnsen, Peter Christian, and Jørgen E. Moe. **Norwegian Folk Tales**. Illustrated by Erik Werenskiold and Theodore Kittelsen. Pantheon, 1982; Deyer, 1990. Read-aloud audience: grades 3-7; ages 8-12.
Contains many of the most familiar Norwegian tales—tales populated by trolls, and animals and people who use their wit to achieve their goals.

Bierhorst, John, ed. **Black Rainbow: Legends of the Incas and Myths of Ancient Peru**. Farrar, 1976. Read-aloud audience: grades 3-7; ages 8-12.
The introduction gives background information on the Inca land and culture, including the religion of ancient Peru. The collection includes modern tales in addition to the historical tales that have survived. Among the stories included are "The Serpent," "The Condor Seeks a Wife," "The Rainbow," and "The Mouse Husband."

Bryan, Ashley. **Beat the Story Drum, Pum-Pum**. Illustrated by Ashley Bryan. Atheneum, 1980. Read-aloud audience: grades 3-7; ages 8-12.
Five tales from Nigeria: "Hen and Frog," "Why Bush Cow and Elephant Are Bad Friends," "The Husband Who Counted the Spoonfuls," "Why Frog and Snake Never Play Together," and "How Animals Got Their Tails."

Chase, Richard. **The Jack Tales**. Illustrated by Berkely Williams Jr. Houghton, 1943. Read-aloud audience: grades 3-7; ages 8-12.
Includes tales from the Appalachians. One of the tales, "Jack and the Robber," is a variant version of the Grimm Brothers' *Bremen Town Musicians*.

Cohn, Amy L., compiler. **From Sea to Shining Sea: A Treasury of American Folklore and Folk Songs**. Illustrated by Molly Cone et al. Scholastic, 1993. Read-aloud audience: grades 3-7; ages 8-12.
A collection of familiar folk literature from various locations within the United States. Popular folk songs are featured.

d'Aulaire, Ingri, and Edgar Parin d'Aulaire. **Ingri and Edgar Parin d'Aulaire's Book of Greek Myths**. Doubleday, 1962. Read-aloud audience: grades 3-7; ages 8-12.
Traditional Greek myths that explain the origin of the world, day and night, evil in the world, and other phenomena for which we now have scientific explanations.

deWit, Dorothy, ed. **The Talking Stone: An Anthology of Native American Tales and Legends**. Illustrated by Donald Crews. Greenwillow, 1979. Read-aloud audience: grades 3-7; ages 8-12.
Twenty-seven tales of Native Americans from nine geographic regions of North America.

Ehrlich, Amy, adapter. **The Random House Book of Fairy Tales**. Illustrated by Diane Goode. Random, 1985. Read-aloud audience: grades 3-7; ages 8-12.
Nineteen of the best-known fairy tales, including "Rapunzel," "Beauty and the Beast," "Thumbelina," and "Hansel and Gretel."

Grimm, Jacob, and Wilhelm Grimm. **The Complete Brothers Grimm Fairy Tales**. Edited by Lily Owens. Catham River Press/ Crown, 1981 (1984). (Originally published in *Grimm's Household Tales*, 1812.) Read-aloud audience: grades 3-7; ages 8-12.
A collection of 215 tales by the Brothers Grimm including "Cinderella," "Rapunzel," "Sleeping Beauty," and less familiar tales such as "Willful Child" and "Lucky Hans."

Hamilton, Virginia. **Her Stories: African American Folktales**. Illustrated by Leo Dillon and Diane Dillon. Blue Sky Press, 1995. Read-aloud audience: grades 3-7+; ages 8-12+.
From hundreds of years of oral tradition, these tales tell of the strength and courage of the many women who fought to keep their families together, who provided leadership in the fight for (and flight to) freedom, and who helped others cope with the harsh realities of their lives.

———. **The People Could Fly: American Black Folktales**. Illustrated by Leo Dillon and Diane Dillon. Knopf, 1985. Read-aloud audience: grades 3-7+; ages 8-12+.
Retellings of African American folktales of animals, fantasy, and the supernatural and of the desire for freedom, born of the sorrow of slaves and passed on in hope.

Haviland, Virginia. **Favorite Fairy Tales Told Around the World**. Illustrated by S. D. Schindler. Little, Brown, 1985. Read-aloud audience: grades 3-7; ages 8-12.
Tales gleaned from Haviland's popular series that featured favorite tales from many different parts of the world: England, France, Germany, Russia, Italy, and several other countries.

Hitakonanu'laxk. **The Grandfathers Speak: Native American Folk Tales of the Lenape People**. Interlink Books, 1993. Read-aloud audience: grades 3-7; ages 8-12.
Hitakonanu'laxk, chief of the Lenape Nation (sometimes known as Delaware Indians), tells 25 tales of the Lenape people. An introductory section explains the history of the Lenape people and discusses their customs and lifestyle. Each of the stories is two or three pages long and can be easily read or told to children. The stories attempt to explain creation, the origin of the constellations, the discovery of fire, and other natural phenomena.

Livo, Norma J., and Dia Cha. **Folk Stories of the Hmong: Peoples of Laos, Thailand, and Vietnam**. Libraries Unlimited, 1991. Read-aloud audience: grades 3-7+; ages 8-12+.
The oral tradition among the Hmong has existed for hundreds of years. The written language did not even exist until 1950. Livo and her Hmong co-author retell 27 authentic Hmong tales. The tales are categorized as beginnings, how/why stories, and stories of love, magic, and fun. Sixteen pages of color photographs depict traditional Hmong dress and needlework. All of the stories

are appropriate for older readers; selected stories are appropriate for younger listeners.

McNeil, Heather. **Hyena and the Moon: Stories to Tell from Kenya**. Illustrated by Joan Garner. Libraries Unlimited, 1994. Read-aloud audience: grades 3-7+; ages 8-12+.
Stories include "The Boy Who Went to Heaven," "Rabbit and Lion," "Peace and Quiet," "Monkey's Feast," "Rabbit's Drum," "Ripe Fruit," "Good Luck, Bad Luck," and "Hyena Moon." Ethnic groups represented are the Kikuyu, Turkana, Akamba, Kipsigis, Taita, Luhya, and Samburu. Includes cultural and historical background information on the ethnic groups, notes on the stories, further resources, and tips for sharing the stories with young readers/listeners. Color photos of Kenyan storytellers and animals portrayed in the story are included.

Onassis, Jacqueline, ed. **The Firebird and Other Russian Fairy Tales**. Illustrated by Boris Zvorykin. Viking, 1978. Read-aloud audience: grades 3-7; ages 8-12.
Retells four Russian folktales: "The Firebird," "Vassilissa the Fair," "Maria Morevna," and "The Snow Maiden."

Pelton, Mary Helen, and Jacqueline DiGennaro. **Images of a People: Tlingit Myths and Legends**. Illustrated by Jennifer Brady-Morales (Ts'anak). Libraries Unlimited, 1992. Read-aloud audience: grades 3-7+; ages 8-12+.
"Before there was a North or South, when Time was not, Klingaton-kla, the Earth Mother, was blind and all the world was dark." These are the beginning words of the first Tlingit myth in Pelton and DiGennaro's collection of 22 tales from the Tlingits of the northwestern region of the United States. The illustrator is a traditional Tlingit artist.

Perrault, Charles. **The Complete Fairy Tales of Charles Perrault**. Illustrated by Sally Holmes; translated by Neil Philip and Nicoletta Simborowski. Clarion, 1993. Read-aloud audience: grades 3-7; ages 8-12.
Includes the most popular of Perrault's tales as well as several less familiar tales. The tales are populated with magic, fairy godmothers, and people and animals that transform themselves. Included are "Cinderella," "Sleeping Beauty," and less familiar tales such as "Tufty Ricky" and "The Fairies," among others.

Philip, Neil, ed. **The Spring of Butterflies and Other Folktales of China's Minority Peoples**. Translated by He Liyi. Illustrated by Pan Aiqing and Li Zhao. Lothrop, 1986. Read-aloud audience: grades 3-7; ages 8-12.
Fourteen tales from the Tibetan, Thai, Vighur, Bai, and other non-Chinese peoples living in China.

Tashjian, Virginia. **Once There Was and Was Not: Armenian Tales Retold**. Illustrated by Nonny Hogrogian. Little, Brown, 1966. Read-aloud audience: grades 3-7; ages 8-12.
Armenian tales that tell of people who outwit others or deliberately misinterpret actions to provide an advantage for themselves. Tales have a gentle humor and reinforce values of honesty and hard work.

Vathanaprida, Supaporn, reteller. **Thai Tales: Folktales of Thailand**. Edited by Margaret Read MacDonald. Libraries Unlimited, 1994. Read-aloud audience: grades 3-7+; ages 8-12+.
Twenty-eight tales showing many aspects of the Buddhist worldview. Vathanaprida draws on her memories of childhood in northern Thailand. She shares her tales and comments to help readers become acquainted with the world of Thai folklore and culture. Humorous tales of Buddhist monks and tales of amazing magical events that entertain the Thai imagination are included in the collection.

Vigil, Angel. **The Corn Woman: Stories and Legends of the Hispanic Southwest**. Libraries Unlimited, 1994. Read-aloud audience: grades 3-7+; ages 8-12+.
Forty-five folk stories and legends from the Hispanic Southwest are retold. The collection includes ancient creation myths of the Aztecs and the traditional tales of Spanish colonialists—obscure and well-loved stories. Among the tales retold are religious stories; stories of magic, transformation, and wisdom; and short comic

tales. Fifteen of the stories are also told in Spanish. Illustrated with pictures of original paintings and sculpture by contemporary Latino artists.

Moving to a Multitude of Books

After listening to folklore stories being read aloud, young readers will be ready to move on to reading workshops, discussed in "Moving to Independent Reading" (pages 10-13). Two of the most popular retellers of folktales are Jan Brett and Paul Galdone. Other authors that would make excellent author focus subjects include Verna Aardema, Marcia Brown, Demi, Tomie dePaola, Beatrice Schenk de Regniers, Paul Goble, Michael Hague, Nonny Hogrogian, Eric A. Kimmel, and Janet Stevens.

More Folklore to Read

The following folklore suggestions are categorized in two ways. The first section categorizes tales by their title or theme. This section provides basic critical reading lists that promote comparing and contrasting versions of tales. These tales do not indicate a target audience as they may be used by students from primary to middle grades (and above). The second section lists newer folklore titles that may provide new perspectives on some old and new tales.

"Beauty and the Beast"

In the traditional tale of "Beauty and the Beast," a kind and beautiful young woman grows to love the beast in whose castle she is held and through her great love she releases him from the spell that has turned him from a handsome prince into an ugly beast. Compare/contrast the portrayal of the beast in each of the illustrated versions and note some of the refinements the tale has undergone over time. In some versions the beast is portrayed as a wild boar, bear, or monsterlike figure. Both Charles Perrault and Madame Leprince de Beaumont are credited with early versions of this tale.

Apy, Deborah. **Beauty and the Beast**. Illustrated by Michael Hague. Holt, 1983.
Traditional version based on the retelling of Madame Leprince de Beaumont's version. Originally published by Green Tiger Press in 1980.

Brett, Jan. **Beauty and the Beast**. Illustrated by Jan Brett. Clarion, 1989.
A version inspired by Sir Arthur Quiller-Couch's 1910 edition. The beast is a wild boar, deliberately modeled on Walter Crane's rendition of over 100 years ago.

Gerstein, Mordicai. **Beauty and the Beast**. Illustrated by Mordicai Gerstein. Dutton, 1989.

Goode, Diane, translator. **Beauty and the Beast**. Illustrated by Diane Goode. Based on the French tale by Madame Leprince de Beaumont. Bradbury, 1978.

Hautzig, Deborah. **Beauty and the Beast**. Random, 1995. Step 3 of the Step into Reading series.

Hearne, Betsy Gould. **Beauty and the Beast: Visions and Revisions of an Old Tale**. University of Chicago Press, 1989.
A scholarly examination of a multitude of versions of "Beauty."

Howard, Richard, translator. **Beauty and the Beast**. Illustrated by Hilary Knight. Simon & Schuster, 1990.

Mayer, Marianna. **Beauty and the Beast**. Illustrated by Mercer Mayer. Four Winds, 1978.
Traditional version based on Madame Leprince de Beaumont's version.

McKinley, Robin. **Beauty**. HarperCollins, 1978.
A modern expanded version of the traditional tale.

Perrault, Charles. **Beauty and the Beast**. Illustrated by Charles Moore. Rizzoli, 1991.

Willard, Nancy. **Beauty and the Beast**. Illustrated with wood engravings by Barry Moser. Harcourt, 1992.
A retelling of the original tale set in the early 1990s in New York City.

"Cinderella" and Variant Forms from Around the World

The Cinderella tale is of an "ash-girl" who with the aid of a benefactor appears at a dance, festival, or (in later versions) a church, and wins the admiration of a prince, then disappears. Later, when the prince finally locates her, he is able to verify her identity with a ring or slipper test. The Cinderella tale is generally regarded as one of the best known folktales in the world—many believe there are more than 500 variants. The earliest known version dates from ninth-century China. It was carried by traders to other parts of Asia and to Europe. Perrault is generally credited with its circulation in Europe, although his version omitted several motifs found in variants elsewhere in the world.

In the Chinese version it is the bones of a magical fish that give Yeh-Shen golden slippers and an azure blue dress with a cloak of kingfisher feathers. In the climax of the tale Yeh-Shen marries the king, and her stepmother and stepsister are crushed in a shower of stones. The Brothers Grimm version retains many of the original motifs: a tree planted on Cinderella's mother's grave brings the finery for the ball. In many other versions told throughout the world, it is Cinderella's mother, who as a cow, goat, or other domestic animal assists Cinderella in her quest to attend the ball or festival. In the Grimm version, when the prince searches for the true owner of the golden slipper, one of the stepsisters chops off her heel in order to make the slipper fit, and the other chops off her toe. But the dripping blood reveals each as the wrong woman, and Cinderella marries the prince. On their wedding day, birds fly down and peck out the eyes of the wicked stepmother and stepsisters. The punishment meted out to the stepmother and stepsister in many versions (including the Grimm version) is in direct contrast to the more congenial climax in Perrault's version.

Perrault also seems to have added the element of the fairy godmother (a traditional character in French tales). The magic hour of midnight seems to be new with the Perrault version as well as the substitution of the glass slipper for the traditional gold one. In Perrault's version, the prince and Cinderella marry but the stepmother and stepsisters are treated much more kindly; the stepsisters marry lords of the court and the stepmother is invited to live on the palace grounds. Marcia Brown remains faithful to the Perrault version, portraying the stepsisters more kindly than most retellers; in Brown's retelling the stepsisters are portrayed as haughty and homely but not particularly cruel.

Walt Disney's film *Cinderella* (and the book based on the movie) is more similar to the Perrault version of the tale than to any of the other versions. The fairy godmother makes her appearance, but, instead of transforming a large rat and lizard into the coachman and footmen, Disney transforms an old horse and dog into Cinderella's escorts.

Climo, Shirley. **The Egyptian Cinderella**. Illustrated by Ruth Heller. Crowell, 1989.

———. **The Korean Cinderella**. Illustrated by Ruth Heller. HarperCollins, 1993.

Ehrlich, Amy. **Cinderella**. Illustrated by Susan Jeffers. Dial, 1985.

Galdone, Paul. **Cinderella**. McGraw-Hill, 1978.

Greaves, Margaret. **Tattercoats**. Illustrated by Margaret Chamberlain. Clarkson N. Potter, 1990.

Grimm, Jacob, and Wilhelm Grimm. **Cinderella**. Translated by Anne Rogers. Illustrated by Svend Otto S. Larousse, 1978. (Original title: *Aschenputtel*)

———. **Cinderella**. Illustrated by Nonny Hogrogian. Greenwillow, 1981.

Huck, Charlotte. **Princess Furball**. Illustrated by Anita Lobel. Greenwillow, 1989.

Jacobs, Joseph. **Tattercoats**. Illustrated by Margot Tomes. Putnam, 1989.

Kha, Dang Manh. **In the Land of Small Dragon**. Told to Ann Nolan Clark. Illustrated by Tony Chen. Viking, 1979.

Louie, Ai-Ling. **Yeh-Shen: A Cinderella Story from China**. Illustrated by Ed Young. Philomel, 1982.

Martin, Rafe. **The Rough-Face Girl**. Illustrated by David Shannon. Putnam, 1992.

Perrault, Charles. **Cinderella**. Illustrated by Marcia Brown. Scribner, 1954.

San Souci, Robert D. **Sootface: An Ojibwa Cinderella Tale**. Illustrated by Daniel San Souci. Doubleday, 1994.

Steel, Flora Annie. **Tattercoats: An Old English Tale**. Illustrated by Diane Goode. Bradbury, 1976.

Steptoe, John. **Mufaro's Beautiful Daughters: An African Tale**. Illustrated by John Steptoe. Lothrop, 1987.

Vuong, Lynette Dyer. **The Brocaded Slipper**. Illustrated by Vo-Dinh Mai. Lippincott, 1985 (1982).

Wilson, Barbara Ker. **Wishbones**. Illustrated by Meilo So. Bradbury, 1993.

Connections for Readers— Parodies, Poems, and Other Connections to "Cinderella"

Brooke, William J. "The Fitting of the Slipper." In **A Telling of the Tales: Five Stories**. Illustrated by Richard Egielski. HarperCollins, 1990.

Jackson, Ellen B. **Cinder Edna**. Illustrated by Kevin O'Malley. Lothrop, 1994.

Livingston, Myra Cohn. "Look Cinderella." In **A Song I Sang to You**. Harcourt, 1984.

Minters, Frances. **Cinder-Elly**. Illustrated by G. Brian Karas. Viking, 1994.

Myers, Bernice. **Sidney Rella and the Glass Sneaker**. Illustrated by Bernice Myers. Macmillan, 1985.

Silverstein, Shel. "In Search of Cinderella." In **A Light in the Attic**. HarperCollins, 1981.

Viorst, Judith. "... And Then the Prince Knelt Down and Tried to Put the Glass Slipper on Cinderella's Foot." In **If I Were in Charge of the World and Other Worries**. Atheneum, 1981.

"Hansel and Gretel"

Retellers have, through both text and illustrations, changed the mood of the traditional tale of "Hansel and Gretel" by portraying the characters in various ways—the parents as either cold and harsh or loving but poor; the witch as a menacing hag or a wicked witch. Anthony Browne brings the traditional tale into a contemporary setting by showing the stepmother in a fur coat and high heels, smoking a cigarette. On the stepmother's dresser is a bottle of Oil of Olay® and a television is among the family's sparse furnishings. Paul Zelinsky uses somber but lush oil paintings to create the dense dark forest and the interior of the poor woodcutter's cottage, suggesting a more traditional setting. Lisbeth Zwerger's brown wash gives her illustrations the feeling of long ago. Susan Jeffers, whose illustrations are very detailed, is one of the artists to pictorially suggest that the stepmother and the witch are one and the same. Jeffers wraps the stepmother in a shawl identical to the one the witch wears in later scenes. Anthony Browne suggests this dual identity by placing a mole on each woman's cheek. Throughout his illustrations Browne presents triangular shapes (suggestive of the witch's hat) and symbols of cages and flight. Browne's version has been criticized as bringing the tale too close to the present and in the process making it more threatening to the younger reader. But the retelling provides an interesting variation for critical reading by older students.

Black, Fiona, reteller. **Hansel and Gretel**. Illustrated by John Gurney. Ariel/Andrews and McMeel, 1991.

Grimm, Jacob, and Wilhelm Grimm. **Hansel and Gretel**. Illustrated by Adrienne Adams. Translated by Charles Scribner Jr. Scribner, 1975.

———. **Hansel and Gretel**. Illustrated by Anthony Browne. Adapted from the translation by Eleanor Quarrie, 1949. Julia MacRae Books/ Franklin Watts, 1981.

———. **Hansel and Gretel**. Illustrated by Susan Jeffers. Translated from the German by Mrs. Edgar Lucas and included in the collection *Fairy Tales of the Bros. Grimm* (Lippincott, 1902). Dial, 1980.

———. **Hansel and Gretel**. Adapted and illustrated by Arnold Lobel. Delacorte, 1971.

———. **Hansel and Gretel**. Illustrated by Lisbeth Zwerger. Translated from the German by Elizabeth D. Crawford. Morrow, 1979.

Marshall, James, reteller. **Hansel and Gretel**. Illustrated by James Marshall. Dial, 1990.

Ross, Tony, reteller. **Hansel and Gretel**. Illustrated by Tony Ross. Overlook Press, 1994.

"Mouse Husband"

The emergence of power is the theme in the "Mouse Husband" tales. In each of the stories, mouse parents seeking a powerful spouse for their lovely and intelligent daughter view almost anything else as more suitable as a husband than the insignificant mouse. But in the search they come to realize that all beings are powerful in some manner, including the lowly mouse. Versions of the traditional stonecutter tale, such as Gerald McDermott's *The Stonecutter:*

A Japanese Folk Tale (Viking, 1975; Harcourt, 1995), also deal with the concept of power.

Bulatkin, I. F. "The Match-Making of a Mouse." In **Eurasian Folk and Fairy Tales**. Illustrated by Howard Simon. Criterion, 1965.

Dupré, Judith. **The Mouse Bride: A Mayan Folk Tale**. Knopf, 1993.

Gackenbach, Dick. **The Perfect Mouse**. Illustrated by Dick Gackenbach. Macmillan, 1984.

Kimmel, Eric A. **The Greatest of All: A Japanese Folktale**. Illustrated by Giora Carmi. Holiday, 1991.

Morimoto, Junko. **The Mouse's Marriage**. Viking Kestrel, 1986 (1985).

Uchida, Yoshiko. "The Wedding of the Mouse." In **The Dancing Kettle and Other Japanese Folk Tales**. Illustrated by Richard C. Jones. Harcourt, 1949.

"The Stonecutter"

Power is the theme in the tales of the stonecutter. In each story the stonecutter seeks to be someone more powerful, only to realize that he once held the power he seeks. Several Asian countries have versions of these tales. Demi has illustrated a version of the tale from China, and others have retold versions from India and Japan.

Demi. **The Stonecutter**. Illustrated by Demi. Crown, 1995.

McDermott, Gerald. **The Stonecutter: A Japanese Folk Tale**. Illustrated by Gerald McDermott. Viking, 1975; Harcourt, 1995.

Newton, Patricia Montgomery. **The Stonecutter: An Indian Folktale**. Illustrated by Patricia Montgomery Newton. Putnam, 1990.

"The Three Billy Goats Gruff"

The tale of the three goats who trip-trap across the bridge on their way to greener pastures has been retold many times. Under the bridge is a troll, typically a character in Norwegian tales. Essential elements in the Norse tale are the appearance of the troll as the three goats cross the bridge, the repetition of "trip, trap, trap," the troll's demands, and the goats' responses. The illustrated versions of this tale present variations on the theme. Janet Stevens, for example, depicts the biggest billy goat in the leather jacket she herself would have liked to own. In the Appalachian version, it is a bear that eats members of a human family making their way across a bridge to obtain sody sallyraytus (baking soda). In this version, the family members are rescued when the squirrel comes back from the store and lures the bear into chasing him up a tree. When the bear attempts to jump from one limb to another, he falls and devoured characters emerge from his split belly. This element in the tale make the story a "swallow" story as well as a variant of "The Three Billy Goats Gruff."

Arnold, Tim. **The Three Billy Goats Gruff**. Illustrated by Tim Arnold. Macmillan, 1993.

Asbjørnsen, Peter Christian, and Jørgen E. Moe. **The Three Billy Goats Gruff**. Illustrated by Marcia Brown. Harcourt, 1957; 1991.

Chase, Richard. "Sody Sallyraytus." In **Grandfather Tales**. Houghton, 1948.

Galdone, Paul. **Three Billy Goats Gruff**. Illustrated by Paul Galdone. Seabury, 1973; Houghton, 1987.

Langley, Jonathan. **The Three Billy Goats Gruff**. Illustrated by Jonathan Langley. HarperCollins, 1995.

Rounds, Glen. **The Three Billy Goats Gruff**. Illustrated by Glen Rounds. Holiday, 1993.

S., Svend Otto. **The Three Billy Goats Gruff: A Retelling of a Classic Tale**. Illustrated by Svend Otto S. D. C. Heath, 1989.

Stevens, Janet. **The Three Billy Goats Gruff**. Illustrated by Janet Stevens. Harcourt, 1987.

Ziefert, Harriet. **The Three Billy Goats Gruff**. Illustrated by Laura Rader. Tambourine, 1994.

"The Wolf and the Seven Little Kids"

In this Brothers Grimm tale, when the nanny goat leaves her children she warns them not to open the door to the big bad wolf. They are tricked into doing so and are eaten, all except the youngest, who hides and helps the nanny goat find the others when she returns from the market. Some of the versions are very traditional in both text and illustration, but other versions, such as those illustrated by Janet Stevens and Tony Ross, bring the tale into contemporary times by showing the kids being pushed in a stroller, wearing cowboy boots and hat, listening to a Walkman®, or riding a tricycle.

Grimm, Jacob, and Wilhelm Grimm. **The Wolf and the Seven Kids**. Illustrated by Kinuko Craft. Troll, 1979.

———. **The Wolf and the Seven Kids**. Illustrated by Felix Hoffman. Harcourt, 1957.

———. **The Wolf and the Seven Little Kids**. Translated by Anne Rogers. Illustrated by Svend Otto S. Larousse, 1977.

Kimmel, Eric A., reteller. **Nanny Goat and the Seven Little Kids**. Illustrated by Janet Stevens. Holiday, 1990.

Ross, Tony. **Mrs. Goat and Her Seven Little Kids**. Illustrated by Tony Ross. Atheneum, 1990.

Connections for Readers— A Literary Version to Compare

Wood, Audrey. **Heckedy Peg**. Illustrated by Don Wood. Harcourt, 1987. Weston Woods® has available a video version of this story of a mother who leaves her seven children at home while she goes to the market. When she returns she finds that a witch has taken them and turned them into food.

"Goldilocks and the Three Bears"

One of the earliest versions of "The Three Bears" was Robert Southey's version, who told the story of an old woman who peeked into the house of the bears. The intruder in Joseph Cundall's 1850 retelling in his *Treasury of Pleasure Books for Children* was a little silver-haired girl. In Joseph Jacobs's version retold in *More English Fairy Tales* (1894), the intruder was a fox. It wasn't until 1904, in *Old Nursery Stories and Rhymes,* illustrated by John Hassall, that the intruder became a little girl called Goldilocks. In some versions the bears are referred to as great, huge bear; middle-sized bear; and wee, little bear while in other versions they are Papa Bear, Mama Bear, and Baby Bear. Illustrations of the amenities in the bears' home range from simple bowls, chairs, and furnishings to elaborately carved objects with symbolic motifs. The illustrations for Jan Brett's version are ornate and depict a Ukrainian setting. Common to most settings are the wooded surroundings, but time period and location are usually indicated by the style of the house and the characters' clothing. The bears in Paul Galdone's version do not wear clothing, whereas Steven's version dresses the bears in homey clothes: Papa in plaid shirt, suspenders, and pants; Mama in high heels, a dress, and a pearl necklace; and baby bear in overalls and tennis shoes. Ross's version shows a television set in the bears' home and Goldilocks in jeans.

Brett, Jan. **Goldilocks and the Three Bears**. Illustrated by Jan Brett. Putnam, 1987.

Cauley, Lorinda Bryan. **Goldilocks and the Three Bears**. Illustrated by Lorinda Bryan Cauley. Putnam, 1981.

Galdone, Paul. **The Three Bears**. Illustrated by Paul Galdone. Clarion, 1972.

Jacobs, Joseph. "The Three Bears." In **Tomie dePaola's Favorite Nursery Tales**. Edited and illustrated by Tomie dePaola. Putnam, 1986.

Langley, Jonathan. **Goldilocks and the Three Bears**. Illustrated by Jonathan Langley. HarperCollins, 1993.

Marshall, James, reteller. **Goldilocks and the Three Bears**. Illustrated by James Marshall. Dial, 1988.

McPhail, David. **Goldilocks and the Three Bears**. Illustrated by David McPhail. Scholastic, 1995.

Rockwell, Anne. **The Three Bears and 15 Other Stories**. Illustrated by Anne Rockwell. Crowell, 1975; Harper Trophy, 1984.

Ross, Tony. **Goldilocks and the Three Bears**. Illustrated by Tony Ross. Overlook Press, 1992.

Spowart, Robin. **The Three Bears**. Illustrated by Robin Spowart. Knopf, 1987.

Stevens, Janet. **Goldilocks and the Three Bears**. Illustrated by Janet Stevens. Holiday, 1986.

Watts, Bernadette. **Goldilocks and the Three Bears**. Illustrated by Bernadette Watts. Holt, 1988.

Ziefert, Harriet. **Goldilocks and the Three Bears**. Illustrated by Laura Rader. Tambourine, 1994.

Connections for Readers— A Parody to Use

Brinton Turkle has created a wordless book, *Deep in the Forest* (Dutton, 1976), that features a bear who intrudes into the cabin home of three humans—a tale that will be immediately recognized as a reverse of the "Goldilocks and the Three Bears" story. Create a text to accompany the illustrations, and use the book as a model to write reversal tales for other familiar folktales.

"Rumpelstiltskin"

"Rumpelstiltskin" (German), "Tom Tit Tot" (English), and "Duffy and the Devil" (Cornish) all involve a young woman who is asked to use her spinning skills to create something requested by a king, squire, or other dignitary. In return the woman is given an honored status in the household or kingdom. But to accomplish the spinning or knitting tasks, the woman makes a deal with a strange little creature who will aid her if she promises to give him her firstborn child. When it comes time to relinquish the child, the woman is given the opportunity to keep the child by guessing the creature's name.

Galdone, Paul. **Rumpelstiltskin**. Illustrated by Paul Galdone. Clarion, 1985.

Grimm, Jacob, and Wilhelm Grimm. **Rumpelstiltskin**. Illustrated by Diane Diamond. Holiday, 1983.

Jacobs, Joseph, ed. "Tom Tit Tot." In **English Folk and Fairy Tales**. Putnam, n.d.

Langley, Jonathan. **Rumpelstiltskin**. Illustrated by Jonathan Langley. HarperCollins, 1992.

Ness, Evaline. **Tom Tit Tot**. Illustrated by Evaline Ness. Scribner, 1965.

Tarvoc, Edith. **Rumpelstiltskin**. Illustrated by Edward Gorey. Four Winds, 1974 (1973).

Zelinsky, Paul O. **Rumpelstiltskin**. Illustrated by Paul O. Zelinsky. Dutton, 1986.

Zemach, Harve. **Duffy and the Devil**. Illustrated by Margot Zemach. Farrar, 1973.

"Star Husband"

The Native American tale of "The Star Husband" combines religious beliefs, how-and-why explanations, and references to Native American customs. In the basic tale, a woman wishes for a star husband. When her wish is granted, she bears a boy child. She ignores a warning not to dig in the floor of the sky and is banished from her husband. When she dies she is allowed to rejoin her husband and son (the moon) in the sky. In some versions her son is banished with her. He is marked with a facial scar and becomes known as Scarface. He must journey to the Sun to have the scar removed. To commemorate the Sun's removal of the scar, the Blackfeet celebrate the Sun Dance. Star Boy becomes another star with his father, Morning Star, and his mother, Evening Star.

Esbensen, Barbara Juster. **The Star Maiden: An Ojibway Tale**. Illustrated by Helen K. Davie. Little, Brown, 1988.

Goble, Paul. **Star Boy**. Illustrated by Paul Goble. Bradbury, 1983.

Grinnell, George B. **North American Legends**. Edited by Virginia Haviland. Illustrated by Ann Strugnell. Collins World, 1979.

Mobley, Jane. **The Star Husband**. Illustrated by Anna Vojtech. Doubleday, 1979.

San Souci, Robert D. **The Legend of Scarface: A Blackfeet Indian Story**. Illustrated by Daniel San Souci. Doubleday, 1978.

Wyss, Thelma Hatch. **Star Girl**. Illustrated by John Pimlott. Viking, 1967.

"Runaway Tales"

Cookies, buns, and rolling cakes attempt to elude their makers. In each of these runaway tales, a series of other animals or people attempt to catch and eat the runaway. The character chants a refrain that makes him or her known as the fastest or cleverest of all. In most of the tales, the animals or people who take up the chase abandon it when the next group enters the story. In the end the runaway character meets his or her match when a crafty animal gobbles up the character.

Brown, Marcia. **The Bun: A Tale from Russia**. Harcourt, 1972.

Cauley, Lorinda Bryan, reteller. **The Pancake Boy**. Illustrated by Lorinda Bryan Cauley. Putnam, 1988.

Cook, Scott. **The Gingerbread Boy**. Illustrated by Scott Cook. Knopf, 1987.

Galdone, Paul. **The Gingerbread Boy**. Illustrated by Paul Galdone. Clarion, 1975.

Haviland, Virginia. "Johnny Cake." In **Favorite Fairy Tales Told in England**. Little, Brown, 1959.

Kimmel, Eric A. **The Gingerbread Man**. Illustrated by Megan Lloyd. Holiday, 1993.

Lobel, Anita. **The Pancake**. Illustrated by Anita Lobel. Morrow, 1978.

Rockwell, Anne. "The Gingerbread Man." In **The Three Bears and 15 Other Stories**. Crowell, 1975; Harper Trophy, 1984.

Schmidt, Karen. **The Gingerbread Man**. Illustrated by Karen Schmidt. Scholastic, 1985.

Steel, Flora Annie. "The Wee Bannock." In **English Fairy Tales**. Illustrated by Arthur Rackham. Macmillan, 1962 (1918).

Connections for Readers— A Literary Tale and a Poem to Connect

Bennett, Rowena. "The Gingerbread Man." In **Sing a Song of Popcorn: Every Child's Book of Poems**. Edited by Beatrice Schenk de Regniers et al. Scholastic, 1988.
This poem is a rhyming version of the tale.

Sawyer, Ruth. **Journey Cake, Ho!** Illustrated by Robert McCloskey. Viking, 1953. Also available in non-print form from Weston Woods®.
This literary tale provides a variant ending to the traditional tale.

"The Frog Prince/Princess"

In these tales, a young member of royalty who treats a frog badly is admonished to keep his or her promise to marry the frog. All turns out well when a kiss changes the frog into a handsome spouse and the newlyweds live happily ever after. Or so it seems.

Berenzy, Alix. **A Frog Prince**. Illustrated by Alix Berenzy. Holt, 1989.

Black, Fiona. **The Frog Prince**. Illustrated by Wayne Parmenter. Andrews and McMeel, 1991.

Cecil, Laura. **The Frog Princess**. Illustrated by Emma Chichester Clark. Greenwillow, 1994.

Galdone, Paul. **The Frog Prince**. Illustrated by Paul Galdone. McGraw-Hill, 1974.

Isele, Elizabeth. **The Frog Princess**. Illustrated by Michael Hague. Crowell, 1984.

Lewis, J. Patrick. **The Frog Princess: A Russian Folktale**. Illustrated by Gennady Spirin. Dial, 1994.

Ormerod, Jan. **The Frog Prince**. Illustrated by Jan Ormerod. Lothrop, 1990.

Connections for Readers— Literary Tales That Connect

Gwynne, Fred. **Pondlarker**. Illustrated by Fred Gwynne. Simon & Schuster, 1990.
At the last minute, the frog changes his mind and chooses to remain a frog.

Scieszka, Jon. **The Frog Prince Continued**. Illustrated by Steve Johnson. Viking Childrens Books, 1991.
After being kissed and transformed into a handsome prince, the young man finds that life is not what he thought it might be. In order to find a happier life, the frog prince asks a witch to transform him. The kiss of his princess again works its magic. This time both turn into frogs and hop away.

"The Month Brothers"

"The Month Brothers" tale, which contains motifs from several other traditional tales, is said to have originated from Czechoslovakian folk literature. In Beatrice de Regniers's retelling, *Little Sister and the Month Brothers*, the orphan girl, who is responsible for most of the household drudgery, is referred to as Little Sister. In both de Regniers's and Samuel Marshak's versions, the stepsister sends the kind and good little sister out on a cold winter day to gather some flowers (in de Regniers's version it is violets, in Marshak's version it is snowdrops). As the young girl searches for the flowers, she comes to a clearing where she meets the Month Brothers. Because of her kindness and humble behavior, the Month Brothers pass their staff from one to the other until the correct month rules and the flowers blossom. Upon her return home the girl is sent out again, this time to gather fruit. Predictably the little sister's success encourages the cruel stepsister to set forth on her own. Her abrasive nature and rude behavior prompt the Month Brothers to produce a swirling snowstorm to prevent her returning home. The stepmother sets out to find her daughter and meets a similar fate. The young girl now has the cottage to herself, where she lives until her handsome "prince" arrives to marry her. In de Regniers's version the prince is an honest farmer, thus reflecting the rural emphasis of the Slavs. The little sister and her honest farmer husband live together in harmony. The Month Brothers do not forget them, ensuring that spring comes early to their meadow and that in the wintertime the snow drifts around their cottage to protect them from the cold wind.

Diane Stanley's illustrations for the Samuel Marshak version bring a richness to the tale that is not present in Tomes's illustrations for the de Regniers version. However, Tomes's technique of illustrating with many small sequential pictures provides an element of humor and a layer of meaning not present in the Marshak version. Marshak's version is longer and more detailed than de Regniers's.

"The Month Brothers" story shares the motifs of the wicked stepsister and stepmother imposing duties on the orphan and of magic with "Cinderella." However, another motif, that of accomplishing an impossible task, is also shown in "The Month Brothers." The motif of greediness punished and innocence rewarded is also strongly presented in "The Month Brothers" tales; less so in the "Cinderella" variants.

de Regniers, Beatrice Schenk. **Little Sister and the Month Brothers**. Illustrated by Margot Tomes. Clarion, 1976; Mulberry, 1994.

Marshak, Samuel. **The Month Brothers: A Slavic Tale**. Translated by Thomas P. Whitney. Illustrated by Diane Stanley. Morrow, 1983.

Nathan, Dorothy. **The Month Brothers**. Illustrated by Uri Shulevitz. Dutton, 1967.

Additional Folklore Selections

Bruchac, Joseph. **Flying with the Eagle, Racing the Great Bear: Stories from Native North America**. Bridgewater, 1993. Target audience: grades 5-7; ages 10-12.
Sixteen Native American rite-of-passage tales that tell of boys participating in traditional rituals or achieving their tribal status through the accomplishment of Herculean tasks.

Knutson, Barbara. **Sungura and Leopard: A Swahili Trickster Tale**. Little, Brown, 1993. Target audience: grades 3-5; ages 7-10.
In this Tanzanian tale, a leopard and a hare inadvertently choose the identical building site and unknowingly build a house together. Once the foes recognize the situation, neither will budge. In the battle of wits that follows, poor Leopard loses to the clever trickster, Sungura.

Lester, Julius. **John Henry**. Illustrated by Jerry Pinkney. Dial, 1994. Target audience: grades 3-5; ages 7-10.
A fresh new look at a familiar legend about an African American folk hero. John Henry pulverizes boulders and smashes rocks to smithereens in a race against a steam drill.

Rodanas, Kristina, adapter. **Dance of the Sacred Circle: A Native American Tale**. Illustrated by Kristina Rodanas. Little, Brown, 1994. Target audience: grades 3-5; ages 7-10.
This Blackfeet legend tells the magical tale of a young boy, whose tribe is on the brink of starvation, who journeys far from home in search of the Great Chief. The Great Chief calls together a sacred council of birds, trees, and animals to help him create a new creature that will bring renewed hope to the Blackfeet people.

Author! Author!

Jan Brett

Jan Brett began filling notebooks with sketches of her horses and other pets when she was a young child growing up in Hingham, Massachusetts, where she was born in 1949. One of her pets was a chicken that often rode on her shoulder.

When Jan Brett was in her early twenties she attended art school, including the Boston Museum of Fine Arts School. There were beautiful images all around her. Now when she illustrates her stories, Brett often uses borders to tell another part of the story and get as many images as possible on a page. She travels and does a great deal of research to authenticate her settings. To gather images and information to help her illustrate *The Mitten*, she visited the Ukrainian section of New York and talked to several people, including a Ukrainian woman who helped her learn about the customs in Ukraine. She used images from northern Europe in her version of *Goldilocks and the Three Bears,* as well as many bear motifs and hidden images of the hedgehog—an animal she often includes in her books.

Brett lives with her husband, Joseph Hearne, a member of the Boston Symphony, in Norwell, Massachusetts, and in the Berkshire Mountains near the symphony's summer festival home in Tanglewood. Their mountain home is near a shimmering lake, surrounded by birds and wild animals, which sometimes show up in Brett's books.

From *Educator's Companion to Children's Literature, Volume 2: Folklore, Contemporary Realistic Fiction, Fantasy, Biographies, and Tales from Here and There.* © 1996. Libraries Unlimited. (800) 237-6124.

Jan Brett

Jan Brett was born December 1, 1949, in Hingham, Massachusetts, where she grew up. She enjoyed reading and drawing and often drew the many animals around her. She especially liked horses and drew them over and over again—trying to make them perfect. The illustrations she now creates for picture books often include some of the animals she had when she was growing up: horses, dogs, cats, guinea pigs, rabbits. One of her pet chickens, Delly, used to ride on her shoulder.

In the late 1960s, Brett enrolled in the New London Academy (now Colby-Sawyer College), and in 1970, she attended the Boston Museum of Fine Arts School. Her detailed illustrations are the result of the many images she has collected during extensive research and travels. Many of her books also come from people she meets or places she has been. For example, Brett knew immediately that someday she would put Miriam, a little girl she considered unusual and filled with curiosity, in a book. When she retold her version of *Goldilocks and the Three Bears,* Miriam seemed the perfect model for Goldilocks. Brett's pet mouse, Little Pearl II, was the model for the mouse that appears in *Goldilocks* and in *The Mitten.*

Brett retold *The Mitten* at the suggestion of three teacher friends who thought she would enjoy drawing the animals and snowy scenery that are part of the story. Because the tale originated in Ukraine, Brett enlisted the aid of Oxana Piaseckyj to translate original versions into English. One of the versions she found had animals squeezing into an old pot, which broke into bits when too many animals crawled in. Some versions had violent endings. One had a hunter blasting away at the mitten because he needed to feed his family. Drawing on the several versions she found, Jan Brett created her own retelling, which includes important aspects of the tale and gives it a new twist at the end. Brett researched the culture by visiting the Ukrainian section of New York City. She found out what a Ukrainian house looked like and a guide at the Ukrainian Museum told her that the children's clothes should look somewhat oversized, as clothes were often handmade and had to last a long time. Brett also learned that Ukrainians often hung a water jug so those passing by could help themselves to a cool drink. A stork's nest on the roof was thought to be good luck.

A neighbor boy, Tad Beagley, became the model for Nicki in *The Mitten.* He climbed trees, jumped walls, and leaped into the air so that Brett could take pictures, which she used to create the images of the boy in the book. Her mother was the model for Baba, the grandmother in the story. Brett changed her mother's shiny brown hair to a silver gray and created a long braid to hang down her back. However, Brett did not think that Baba looked very friendly wearing the traditional scarf worn by Ukrainian women, so she hung it on a peg instead. Later, she learned that wearing a scarf had become a sexist stereotype, so she was glad that she had placed the scarf on the peg.

Stories Retold and Illustrated by Jan Brett

Beauty and the Beast. Retold and illustrated by Jan Brett. Clarion, 1989. Target audience: grades 3-7; ages 7-12.
A lovely maiden uses her kindness and beauty to release a handsome prince from the spell that has imprisoned him in the body of an ugly beast. Brett's retelling is faithful to the traditional tale first retold by Madame Leprince de Beaumont.

Goldilocks and the Three Bears. Retold and illustrated by Jan Brett. Putnam, 1987. Target audience: grades PreK-3+; ages 4-8+.
Brett uses her creative art to feature unusual designs and intricate patterns in her illustrations for this traditional retelling. Small acorns adorn the bedposts, and other pieces of furniture feature carved bear figures. Floral endpapers are another of the book's distinctive design elements.

The Mitten: A Ukrainian Folktale. Retold and illustrated by Jan Brett. Putnam, 1989. Target audience: grades PreK-3+; ages 4-8+. Nicki's grandmother knits him snow-white mittens, but when he wears them on his walk in the snowy countryside, he loses one. While he is separated from the mitten, several animals squeeze inside until it is so stretched out that when the small mouse sits on the bear's nose and causes him to sneeze, the mitten flies off and the animals scatter in all directions. The mitten flies into the air and Nicki recovers it— but both he and his Baba are left to wonder how the mitten became so big. A retelling based on an old Ukrainian folktale.

Town Mouse, Country Mouse. Retold and illustrated by Jan Brett. Putnam, 1994. Target audience: grades PreK-3+; ages 4-8+. A classic retelling embellished with Brett's detailed and intricate illustrations. The town mouse visits the country mouse and learns to view its own home as more desirable. The town mouse invites the country mouse to its home and subsequently the country mouse decides that the country is a most desirable place to live.

Author! Author!

Paul Galdone

In the early 1900s, Paul Galdone arrived in the United States at the age of 14 from Budapest. He lived with his family in New Jersey and took three English classes a day to learn English. He was often embarrassed in English class but felt more at home in biology. He drew animals for other class members and discovered that he was proficient at drawing grasshoppers.

Eventually Galdone's family moved to New York City, and while attending art school, Paul Galdone began to work for the art department of Doubleday. He designed book jackets and became interested in book illustration. Later, when with his wife, Jannelise, and their two children he settled in Rockland County, New York, he began to do more and more freelance illustration work. After illustrating several books by other writers, he began to retell stories in his own books. He became known for the nursery tales that he put into single books.

Many of the images Paul Galdone put into his books came from the woods, vegetable gardens, fruit orchards, and trout streams that surrounded the Galdones' Rockland County home and their Tunbridge, Vermont, farm. Galdone enjoyed hiking around his farm and sketching the animals he saw.

In his later years, Paul Galdone illustrated some of his daughter Joanna's stories, as well as his own. He died of a heart attack in 1986.

Paul Galdone

Paul Galdone was born in Budapest, Austria-Hungary (now Hungary) in the early 1900s, though sources differ on whether the actual year was 1907 or 1914. Several sources agree that he was 14 years old when he immigrated with his family to the United States. An aunt who lived in New Jersey had arranged for him to enroll in high school upon his arrival. At the time he could not speak English so he took three English classes every day.

The family eventually moved to New York City where Galdone studied at night and attended the Art Students League and worked as a busboy, an electrician's helper, and a fur dyer. Eventually, Galdone landed a job working in the art department of Doubleday, where he first became involved with children's books as a book jacket designer. Vacations in Vermont were often spent drawing and painting the rural countryside. After four years in the U.S. Army Corps of Engineers, he settled in Rockland County in New York State. He took up freelance work and began illustrating books. At the time of his death in 1986, Galdone had illustrated almost 200 books over four decades.

Galdone is best known for his retelling of traditional nursery rhymes and folktales for the primary and early intermediate reader. He contributed to the trend of devoting an entire book to a single Mother Goose nursery rhyme, fable, or folktale. He retold tales from the Grimm Brothers, Charles Perrault, and Joseph Jacobs, as well as from lesser-known sources. Although he simplified the tales and successfully used rhyme and repetition, his retellings generally reflected their tales' origins faithfully—with the exception of the endings, which he often tempered to reflect his own kindness and sense of humanity.

Galdone often used pen and watercolor illustrations in conjunction with black-and-white sketches to produce meticulously researched settings, ranging from Antarctica to medieval Europe to, most commonly, rural America.

At the time of his death, Galdone was dividing his time between a farm in Tunbridge, Vermont, and a rambling house in Rockland County. His house was surrounded by wooded areas, fruit trees, streams, and gardens. He and his wife, Jannelise, had a daughter, Joanna, and a son, Paul Ferencz. Joanna is a teacher and writer; her father illustrated some of her books. Paul is an architect.

Stories Retold and Illustrated by Paul Galdone

Cinderella. Retold and illustrated by Paul Galdone. McGraw-Hill, 1978. Target audience: grades 2-6; ages 7-11.

A classic retelling of the French version of the Cinderella tale. This retelling includes a conciliatory ending in which Cinderella forgives her two less-than-kind sisters.

Elves and the Shoemaker. Retold and illustrated by Paul Galdone. Clarion Books, 1984. Target audience: grades 2-6; ages 7-11.

The tale of a poor shoemaker and his wife who were so poor that they could not afford any more shoe leather to continue in their trade. Late at night elves come and use the last pieces of leather to create the most exquisite pair of shoes—shoes that sell for enough to buy more leather. After several nights the shoemaker and his wife make a set of clothes for each of the elves.

Hansel and Gretel. Retold and illustrated by Paul Galdone. McGraw-Hill, 1982. Target audience: grades 2-6; ages 7-11.

A woodcutter and his wife leave their children in the woods because they can no longer afford to care for them. When the children find their way to a cottage made of candy, they encounter a wicked witch who wants to eat them for supper.

Henny Penny. Retold and illustrated by Paul Galdone. Clarion, 1968. Target audience: grades PreK-3; ages 4-8.

Led by the misguided Henny Penny, five fowl march down the road to tell the king that the sky is falling. When the hapless five meet the clever

Fox, he leads them into his cave—and they disappear, never to return.

Jack and the Beanstalk. Retold and illustrated by Paul Galdone. Clarion, 1974. Target audience: grades PreK-6; ages 4-11.
Originally published as *The History of Mother Twaddle and the Marvelous Achievements of Her Son Jack*, this tale recounts the journey of Jack up the beanstalk, where he obtains riches that will make his mother and him comfortable for the rest of their lives. On his final trip up the beanstalk, he is chased back down by the giant, from whom Jack has been taking the riches.

Little Bo-Peep. Retold and illustrated by Paul Galdone. Clarion, 1968. Target audience: grades PreK-3; ages 4-8.
A traditional nursery rhyme is told through classic text and simple but expressive illustrations.

The Little Girl and the Big Bear. Retold by Joanna Galdone and illustrated by Paul Galdone. Clarion, 1980. Target audience: grades PreK-6; ages 4-11.
A retelling of a traditional Slavic tale, a variant of the "Little Red Riding Hood" tale. The little girl is lost in the forest, captured by a big bear, and forced to work as his servant. After an unsuccessful attempt to escape, she outwits the bear by hiding in a basket of apple pies that she has convinced the bear to deliver to her grandparents.

Little Red Hen. Retold and illustrated by Paul Galdone. Clarion, 1973. Target audience: grades PreK-2; ages 4-8.
Three friends refuse to help their housemate gather the wheat, grind it, make the flour into bread, and bake it. When the tasks are completed, the red hen asks who will help her eat the bread. All her friends volunteer, but she declines their help and eats it alone.

Little Red Riding Hood. Retold and illustrated by Paul Galdone. McGraw-Hill, 1974. Target audience: grades PreK-3; ages 4-8.
Little Red Riding Hood packs her basket with bread and wine and sets out to visit her grandmother. Detracted by the clever wolf, Little Red Riding Hood is delayed in getting to her grandmother's house until after the wolf has taken her place. The woodcutter, in classic fashion, rescues both Little Red Riding Hood and her grandmother.

The Magic Porridge Pot. Retold and illustrated by Paul Galdone. Clarion, 1968. Target audience: grades PreK-6; ages 4-11.
A hungry girl is given a magic pot that provides porridge for her and her mother. One day, the mother uses the pot and is unable to make the pot stop producing porridge, which keeps boiling out of the pot. A similar theme appears in *Strega Nona* (Prentice-Hall, 1975), the popular Italian version of the tale told by Tomie dePaola.

Puss in Boots. Retold and illustrated by Paul Galdone. Clarion, 1976. Target audience: grades 2-6; ages 7-11.
In this retelling of one of Perrault's French folktales, clever and ingenious Puss uses his mischief-making to obtain a fortune for his master.

Rumpelstiltskin. Retold and illustrated by Paul Galdone. Clarion, 1985. Target audience: grades PreK-6; ages 3-11.
A poor miller brags that his beautiful daughter can spin straw into gold. The king takes her to his castle and instructs her to spin three rooms full of straw into gold. The only way she can accomplish this is with the help of a little man who demands jewelry and the woman's first child. When after a year the strange man returns for her child, he agrees to release her from her promise if the woman, who is now a queen, can tell him his name.

Three Little Kittens. Retold and illustrated by Paul Galdone. Clarion, 1981. Target audience: grades PreK-1; ages 4-6.
The classic verse is illustrated with charming paintings of the kittens interacting with their mother.

The Three Little Pigs. Retold and illustrated by Paul Galdone. Clarion, 1970. Target audience: grades PreK-3; ages 4-8.
An adaptation of Joseph Jacobs's tale of three little pigs who set off to find their way in the world. A straw house and a stick house are not sturdy enough to withstand the wolf's huffing and puffing, but the brick house is and the wolf

meets his demise when he attempts to enter through the chimney.

The Town Mouse and the Country Mouse. Retold and illustrated by Paul Galdone. McGraw-Hill, 1971. Target audience: grades PreK-3; ages 4-8.

In this tale, two mice each find that they prefer their own home. The town mouse does not like the plain and simple food of the country mouse, preferring instead his more elaborate menu in the city. The country mouse likes the rich and bountiful food available at the city mouse's abode but the increased dangers make the offerings less attractive.

The Turtle and the Monkey: A Philippine Tale. Retold and illustrated by Paul Galdone. Clarion, 1983. Target audience: grades PreK-4; ages 4-9.

A greedy monkey tries to cheat a turtle out of bananas that rightfully belong to her.

What's in Fox's Sack? An Old English Tale. Retold and illustrated by Paul Galdone. Clarion, 1972. Target audience: grades PreK-2; ages 4-7.

The sly fox plays on people's curiosity to get a better and better deal. When his greediness has him taking a boy in a trade, a crafty woman substitutes a bulldog that gives the fox his due.

Going Beyond

The focus on folklore will result in students reading many versions of narrative tales that grew from the oral traditions of the various cultures throughout the world community from which they originated. Identify the basic motifs in the different versions and compare and contrast them. As the various stories are read and retold among class members, recognize that there is no one correct version. Each time a tale is retold, it is re-created and it becomes a story of its own. A great deal of variation is possible both from oral retellings and from printed versions. Retellers make their own voices heard. They may change the setting, add a character, insert dialogue, and enhance a specific element of the tale—all in an effort to create their own unique story, a story that will fit their needs. The following are some suggestions for collaborative activities involving folk literature.

Folklore Activity

- Script a folktale and use the script as the basis for a readers theatre presentation.

- Discuss how the setting or location of a tale is reflected in the details of each version read. Locate the setting on a map of the world.

- Retell your own version of a specific folktale.

- Celebrate the birthdays of Wilhelm Grimm (February 24, 1786) and Jacob Grimm (January 4, 1785) by holding a Grimm storytelling festival. (Designate a date for a one-day festival sometime between Jacob's and Wilhelm's birthday, or begin the festival January 4 and culminate it February 24.) Read tales from the Grimm Brothers' collections, illustrate a favorite part or a favorite tale, record a reading on a cassette tape recorder, create story puppets, or make a full-scale model of one of the Grimm characters.

- Read stories from the Brothers Grimm every day from Jacob's birthday on January 4 to Wilhelm's birthday on February 24. On a map locate the origins of the tale and pinpoint any specific locations mentioned, such as the Black Forest or Bremen Town.

- Research Black folk heroes. A collection of 16 tales of High John is contained in Steve Sanfield's *The Adventures of High John the Conqueror*, illustrated by John Ward (Orchard, 1989). Other tales from the oral tradition are retold in Virginia Hamilton's *The People Could Fly: American Black Folktales* (Knopf, 1985) and *Many Thousands Gone: African Americans from Slavery to Freedom* (Knopf, 1992).

- Write a literary letter to a folktale character. As a model read *Dear Peter Rabbit* by Alma Flor Ada (Atheneum, 1994). The tale includes letters from the literary character Peter Rabbit to folklore characters: the three little pigs, Goldilocks (who, it is revealed, is the daughter of old Mr. McGregor), the big bad wolf from "The Three Little Pigs," and Little Red Riding Hood.

- Create a "new" version of a favorite tale. Be sure that some original details are included. For example, in a version of the Slavic tale commonly known as "The Month Brothers," Beatrice Schenk de Regniers, while maintaining the essence of the story, added some details that corresponded to events in her life. In *Little Sister and the Month Brothers* de Regniers had Little Sister being sent in February to obtain strawberries, instead of apples, because de Regniers recalled her mother serving strawberries in February. Little Sister is sent to pick violets, de Regniers's favorite flower.

- Continue the story of a folklore character. For example, how was Cinderella's marriage to the Prince? What happened to the three little pigs after they took care of the wolf? Did the king ever find out about the deceptive behavior of his queen in "Rumpelstiltskin"? (Model: *The Frog Prince Continued* by Jon Scieszka [Viking Childrens Books, 1991].)

- Retell a tale from the point of view of a character who is not the hero of the tale. (Model: *The True Story of the Three Little Pigs by A. Wolf* by Jon Scieszka [Viking Childrens Books, 1989].)

- Plan and hold a Folklore and Flapjack celebration. Invite parents and others from the community to an early-morning celebration of folklore. Serve flapjacks, display folklore-related materials (such as pâpier-maché characters), perform readers theatre productions, or share other visual representations of folklore.

- After reading any of the tall tales or legends, change the gender of the main characters and retell the tale. If the tale is told in a nonsexist manner, not much about the character's actions will change, since males and females are able to do the same things. In most cases, however, the exercise should uncover some perceptions you and your students might have.

Culminating the Focus on Folklore

The purpose of a culminating activity is to bring closure to a specific focus. General ideas for culminating activities are discussed in chapter 1 (page 14). More specific suggestions for a culminating activity for this focus on folklore include holding a "folklore character" day during which participants would dress as and play the role of a folklore character, a reading hour during which snacks connected with folklore would be served (apples [from *Snow White and the Seven Dwarfs*], peanut brittle [a food invented by tall tale character Joe Macarac], and so forth), or a showcase of dramatic presentations sharing favorite scenes from various folklore tales. Any of the suggestions for folklore activities on pages 41-42 might be parlayed into a culminating activity. The following four pages may be reproduced for student use in conjunction with this folklore focus.

Folklore
Reader's Journal

My Name: _____

From *Educator's Companion to Children's Literature, Volume 2: Folklore, Contemporary Realistic Fiction, Fantasy, Biographies, and Tales from Here and There.* © 1996. Libraries Unlimited. (800) 237-6124.

Response Starter Suggestions

Your folklore reading journal is where you record your ideas, thoughts, questions about vocabulary, and questions and comments about the plot and characters in the book or chapter you have just read. Sometimes it is difficult to get started, so the following questions might provide you with an idea to help you begin. These questions are only suggestions; the journal is yours and should contain questions and comments about the parts of the book that interest you.

- What are some of the major motifs in this tale?

- What do you know about the characters?

- What is the basic story grammar of the story? (Main characters, conflict, attempts at resolution [often three], solution, and climax)

- What details in this story stretch the elements/events beyond belief?

- Were there any surprises in the story?

- How did the author introduce you into the setting?

- If the tale is illustrated, how did the illustrator give you more information about the setting?

- Did the author foreshadow any events to come?

- How is this story similar to any other stories (particularly other folk stories) that you have read or heard?

- If this story is similar to others you have heard or read, how has the reteller changed the details to create the variant?

Date each of your journal entries. Responses mean more later if you use complete sentences.

Have fun and enjoy your reading.

Folklore Tales I Have Read

Title	Reteller/illustrator
1.	
2.	
3.	
4.	
5.	
6.	
7.	
8.	
9.	
10.	
11.	
12.	
13.	
14.	
15.	
16.	
17.	
18.	
19.	
20.	

Folklore Tales I Want to Read

Title	Reteller/illustrator
1.	
2.	
3.	
4.	
5.	
6.	
7.	
8.	
9.	
10.	
11.	
12.	
13.	
14.	
15.	
16.	
17.	
18.	
19.	
20.	

3
Contemporary Realistic Fiction

Children need books that reflect the antics of heroes and heroines as naughty as they are. Children need characters like Max in Sendak's *Where the Wild Things Are*, or Tom Sawyer, Huck Finn, or Pinocchio— certainly not to cheer on bad behavior but to cheer on books.

—Judith Viorst (1978)

Several years ago I read a book by M. E. Kerr, *What I Really Think of You* (Harper, 1982), and although I thought it was a good read, I decided that the plot was pretty farfetched for a contemporary realistic story. The story centered on the daughter of a charismatic Christian and the son of a television evangelist who struggle to come to terms with their situations in life and their families. I was raised on an Iowa farm in a conventional environment, so the situations the teenagers encountered in the book were far removed from any experiences I (or anyone I knew personally) had had. Several days after I had finished the novel, a teenage reader came up to me and declared that the book was one of the best she had ever read—"That story could have been about me. My family is just like that." Well, so much for my opinion. That was my first solid realization that what may be real for one reader may not be real for another, and vice versa.

Contemporary Realistic Fiction— An Introduction

Contemporary realistic fiction must present many facets of life and accurately reflect life as it is lived today. But because there are many different lifestyles, there must also be diversity in the selections on our library media center shelves. Everything in a story of contemporary realistic fiction must conceivably be able to happen to real people living in today's world. There are no talking animals, no trips into another time period, and no magic or improbable happenings; and the action must be realistic in

terms of events that might happen today or might have happened in the recent past. But while many of us would view some books as reflecting our own experience, many other books present situations foreign to us. Unfamiliar situations create in readers a level of awareness that expands their experience base.

Contemporary realistic fiction allows young readers to identify with problems and situations they share with others like themselves. For example, children dealing with fractured families may find some solace in the stories of Mavis Jukes, whose books are described as dealing with "mending families." Children having problems with peer relationships may see something of themselves in the characters of Barbara Park, who writes about bullies and exclusive groups. Realistic fiction also provides for escapism. For example, children who dream of adventure will enjoy books by Gary Paulsen. Realistic fiction allows young readers to read for pleasure and for escape. They can find comfort in situations that are similar to their own or wonder at situations they can only imagine.

For much of today's society, there are no topics that can't be treated by realistic fiction if the author portrays the necessary facts of the situation while being careful not to sensationalize the story. Conflicts must be dealt with in a realistic manner and allow readers to view each situation from varying perspectives. Serious topics must not be dealt with superficially; "heavy" topics must be approached in a sensitive and honest manner to help readers develop their own perspective of a situation.

Topics in Contemporary Realistic Fiction

The topics of emerging maturity, death, our pluralistic society, friendships, and experiences of diverse cultural groups all belong to the genre of contemporary realistic fiction. Realistic fiction consists of tales of everyday living that emerge from family interactions, school situations, and relationships between generations and friends.

Families

"Traditional" family values are evident in stories by Beverly Cleary, Eleanor Estes, and Carolyn Haywood. Originally written as contemporary novels, these stories now represent a reality of decades ago and have given way to tales by Lois Lowry and Judy Delton. The families Cleary, Estes, and Haywood created are in general traditional two-parent families. Lois Lowry retains a two-parent family in her books about Anastasia and Sam, but Judy Delton's books about Maggie feature a family separated by divorce, with the grandmother playing a large role in Maggie's upbringing. In Delton's series about Angel, she must deal with the fact

that her single mom dates, remarries, and brings a new sibling into the family.

Other types of family relationships are drawn into the books of Betsy Byars, Patricia MacLachlan, Katherine Paterson, and Cynthia Voigt. Mavis Jukes writes stories about blended families and mending the fractures caused by divorce. Paula Danziger writes in a humorous vein about divorce and parent-child relationships.

Coming-of-Age Stories

Judy Blume examines some of these same family situations as well as coming-of-age problems. While Blume has long been recognized as the novelist who deals with the sensitive topics of adolescence, she wrote her books in the early 1970s, an era that is history for today's young readers. The need for coming-of-age novels for today's intermediate/middle-grade readers is being met by new writers, such as Carol Gorman, who has written a wonderful new coming-of-age novel, *The Miraculous Makeover of Lizard Flanagan* (HarperCollins, 1994).

Connections for Readers— Carol Gorman

Carol Gorman has written many books, embedding in each bits and pieces of her own life. Her characters, such as Jennifer in *Jennifer-the-Jerk Is Missing* (Simon & Schuster, 1994), often live in houses from Gorman's neighborhood. The tunnels under schools that appear in some of her stories are much like those under the high school she attended. The idea for a character in a wheelchair for *Chelsey and the Green-Haired Kid* (Houghton, 1987) came from the University of Iowa hospitals where she worked with handicapped children.

Friends and School

Johanna Hurwitz and Patricia Reilly Giff have contributed many titles about friends and school situations. Hurwitz's Aldo series blends humor with situations that many readers can identify with. Giff's series about the kids at Polk Street School focuses on a classroom of children and follows them through the school year. Giff's other books deal with children in other school situations.

Death

Those who have never experienced the death of someone they care about might gain some insight by reading Katherine Paterson's *Bridge to Terabithia* (Crowell, 1977), Doris Buchanan Smith's *A Taste of Blackberries* (Crowell, 1973), or a more recent title, a novel based on a popular movie, *My Girl*, by Patricia Hermes (Archway/Pocket, 1991).

Connections for Readers— Books About Death

For many years death was a taboo topic in books for young readers, but in recent years authors (and publishers) have come to regard books that treat such topics as useful in helping young readers develop resilience in dealing with serious problems and events in their lives. The theme of many of Patricia Hermes's books is loss. Generally categorized as problem novels, Hermes's books feature characters who face obstacles that test their courage and ingenuity. Adult readers might question whether a youngster could cope all that well in many of the situations Hermes's characters face—but young readers view the characters as believable and the situations as realistic. To affect young readers, the stories must present many types of characters, both good and bad, who can help readers assess their own feelings toward events in their lives. Among Patricia Hermes's novels are *Nobody's Fault* (Harcourt, 1981), *You Shouldn't Have to Say Good-Bye* (Harcourt, 1982), and *A Solitary Secret* (Harcourt, 1985).

Problem Novels

Contemporary realistic fiction must present the real world as it is today, with today's problems and issues. It should allow children to identify with characters with similar interests and problems but also help them expand their awareness of others who live in situations different from their own. Because books often deal with problems common to both the fictional characters and the readers, a subclass of fiction has emerged. Those books are referred to as "problem novels."

Realistic Fiction— Then and Now

By some standards, one could consider the fiction of Beverly Cleary, Eleanor Estes, and Judy Blume contemporary realistic fiction— and at the time the books were written, they were both contemporary and realistic. But those stories no longer fit snugly into the contemporary realistic genre. Realistic fiction stories, by our definition, are stories of young people who experience events in "today's world." The incidents in the earlier books by Cleary and Haywood would be closer to those the parents of today's young readers might have experienced, and even then one wonders if all the past generation lived in quiet suburban neighborhoods in single-family homes. In today's society, young readers have moved away from a narrow view of the world, and their concerns have blended with the concerns of the society in which they live. Today's families are often single-parent families; children are being raised by grandparents, foster parents, and other adults who become significant in their lives. Families live in quiet suburban neighborhoods, inner cities, large cities, small rural towns, apartments, sprawling ranch homes, and townhouses. Children confront peer pressure, gangs, drugs, divorcing parents, illnesses, and many other situations children may not have encountered in earlier times.

Defining Contemporary Realistic Fiction

Humor, adventure, animal stories, and mysteries are considered by some to be in the realistic fiction genre. However, those topics can also be clearly placed in other categories, because most real-life young readers do not get involved in survival situations, mysterious happenings, or exciting animal tales.

Realistic Fiction and Realism

Some readers are confused by the term *contemporary realistic fiction*—noting that *realistic* is perhaps a contradictory term when used with the word *fiction*. The events in realistic fiction must be realistic in terms of being within the realm of possibility, although they might not actually have occurred. Events can be based on things that happened in real life but details can be changed in the retelling.

Connections for Readers— Judy Delton

The four children Judy Delton raised in the St. Paul, Minnesota, area provided her with many incidents she could include in her books. In *Angel's Mother's Boyfriend* (Houghton, 1986), Delton relates an incident about dyeing some clothing green. When the roasting pan that had been used for the dyeing was later used to bake a ham, the ham turned green. That incident came from a real-life incident in which a similar chain of events in Delton's family produced a purple Thanksgiving turkey. An incident in *Kitty in the Middle* (Houghton, 1979) was based on the time Delton's preteenage daughter and a friend decided to spend the afternoon eating candied mints and little sandwiches at a stranger's wedding.

Realistic Fiction and Fantasy

Readers further confuse contemporary realistic fiction with modern fantasy, because fantasy writers often attempt to build more identification with their plots, characters, and settings by creating those elements realistically before allowing the text and the reader to ease into fantastical realms. Supernatural attributes, magic, unexplained events, and mysterious beings move the story from contemporary realistic fiction into the imaginary world of modern fantasy. The major and most definitive characteristic of realistic fiction is that the situations are well within the realm of possibility. Problems in realistic fiction are not solved through magical powers. Toys are not personified, animals do not talk or behave as people, and there are no little people, supernatural beings, or real people who have supernatural experiences.

Realistic Fiction and Animal Stories

Realistic animal stories are sometimes included in the genre of realistic fiction. However, while animal stories can present realistic situations if the preponderance of action relies on the animal characters, the stories are best classified, I believe, as animal stories.

Realistic Fiction and Historical Fiction

The activities referred to in contemporary realistic fiction should refer to the activities of youngsters today. An evening out with friends will most likely involve attending a movie or school dance, hanging out on a street corner, or going to a teen center or mall. Books such as those by Laura Ingalls Wilder, while realistically representing the time about which they were written, are now best considered historical fiction. In fact, those books should be dealt with as such, especially considering some of the prejudicial comments about "Indians" that are made in the stories. Books written in and reflecting a particular time period are valuable in that they give us a sense of the past—the feelings, the attitudes, and the events that brought us to where we are today. But those stories reflect the society of a time past and should be appreciated in that light.

Contemporary realistic fiction must not take us back in time or bring an imaginary world to our doorstep. The setting must be realistic and current in both time and place. For the most part, the books discussed in this chapter are set in the United States, the location with which most young Americans can best identify. Titles that would fit in the realistic fiction category, but are set in other places around the world, are in general dealt with in chapter 6, "Tales from Here and There."

Contemporary Realistic Fiction and the Reader_____

Many believe that reading about others experiencing problems or caught up in an adventure can help young readers develop new interests and learn new ways of handling conflicts in their own lives. Coping and critical thinking are behavior traits that are often modeled through the actions of characters in books of realistic fiction.

It is important to remember that what might seem realistic to one reader may not seem realistic to another. A reader living on a farm in Iowa will very likely have a different view of everyday life than a child growing up in the inner city of Chicago or New York. Similarly, a child who has already experienced fleeing from Vietnam, surviving in a refugee camp, and coming to a strange new land will have a decidedly different view of life than a child born in the community where she or he still lives. A wide range of characters and ideas will bring a diversity of perspectives and experiences to realistic fiction. Use this diversity to help readers expand their own view of the world and the society in which they live.

According to Alleen Pace Nilsen and Kenneth L. Donelson in their *Literature for Today's Young Adults*, 4th edition (HarperCollins, 1993), realistic fiction in the 1990s tends to focus less on shock and titillation and more on excitement, romance, and optimism. Realistic fiction in the 1990s presents a wider worldview and less

stereotyping. Parents are dealt with in a more balanced and convincing fashion, and a diversity of approaches to problems connected with racism and ethnic identification are routinely presented.

A renewed focus on contemporary problems has some critics pointing to a new realism in children's books and openly worrying about books that have an agenda to promote rather than a story to tell. One participant in an Internet forum on censorship quipped, "We need to involve readers with books that tell a good story, not books that have a 'message.' If someone has a message to send, they should use Federal Express." Others cite concerns about the characterization of minorities, the stereotyping of women, problems in contemporary society, and profane language. Some question whether realistic fiction is really reflecting society or contributing to the way society is developing. Calls for censorship of realistic fiction abound. What one group views as constructive and valuable, others consider controversial.

Contemporary Issues and Contemporary Realistic Fiction

In contemporary realistic fiction the major concerns center on sexism, sexuality, violence, profanity, racism, and family problems. *Harriet the Spy* by Louise Fitzhugh (Harper, 1964) is often credited with being one of the first children's books to present a strong young female character. Harriet is outgoing, assertive, and bright. What she does is interesting and compelling. Boys and girls alike enjoy reading about her escapades. Before Harriet came along, those choosing books to read aloud or those recommending books to young readers often felt that girls would read (or listen to) books about boys, but boys did not want to read (or listen to) books about girls. In books before about 1980, male characters tended to engage in activities that were more interesting than those of female characters, so boys and girls both enjoyed reading or having books with male characters read to them.

In reality the gender of the main character has little if anything to do with the books young people want to read. They identify less, it seems, by gender than by role. Girls want to read about someone who does interesting things, and so do boys. Whether the character is male or female seems to have less to do with choice of book than the plot or what the book has to say.

Ramona Frasher has examined the sexual stereotyping of characters and the occurrences of female and male characters in literature for young readers. Her findings and conclusions were published by the International Reading Association in *Sex Stereotypes and Reading: Research and Strategies* (1982). Frasher suggests that stereotyping of roles was so prevalent that prior to 1980, male characters were featured three to one over female characters in children's books; it will be many years of book publishing before a random selection of books will provide a balance of good literature for children to read. In and of itself a well-written book is not stereotypical if it represents a female in a "traditional" mother role. However, it is the lack of balance that brings about stereotyping, that is, when most children's books present women only in the traditional mother role. Over an extended period of time, as more and more books are published, the balance should become more in line with reality. Children should be able to select a book and find not only females in a great diversity of roles, but also males shown filling roles once thought to be traditionally female, such as nurses, elementary school teachers, and homemakers.

In choosing any book of realistic fiction for children, keep in mind how you will use that book. Some books suitable for elementary students as part of a classroom discussion or examination of an author's overall body of work might not be appropriate for independent reading at that level. Good books, if they are chosen for the story, not the controversy or the message, will allow young readers to assess real problems, ideas, and events in genuine situations and to think clearly about them.

Censorship and Contemporary Realistic Fiction

Katherine Paterson, author of the Newbery Award book *Bridge to Terabithia* (Crowell, 1977), frequently relates information about the letters she received in response to *The Great Gilly Hopkins* (Crowell, 1978). Those letters often criticized Paterson for Gilly's language in the book. Paterson relates that she receives few comments about the abuse and injustice Gilly receives, and muses that if readers only knew the effort it took to clean up Gilly's language enough to get her into the book, they would have a different view of the situation. In this instance it is clear that many were more concerned about Gilly's bad language than they were about what prompted it. The letter writers were more concerned about language than about child abuse or the lack of a loving, stable family for a child. However, I believe that shielding our children from bad language will not make it or the situation behind it go away.

In 1994, one elementary school in an urban city was asked to reconsider using a realistic mystery title with grades 2 and 3. The book, a murder mystery with teenage drinking and murder at the center of the story, was being used as part of an overall author focus (in conjunction with a planned visit by the author). The complainants did not consider the context in which the book was being used, but only their own sense of values and experiences. The teachers had considered the context and felt that the use of the book was appropriate. However, they agreed to cease using it to spare the child of the complainants from being singled out in any way. That turned out to be a mistake, because the complainants quickly expanded their campaign to exclude the use of the book in all classrooms in all elementary schools in the district—more than 25 schools. Several other parents expressed disdain at having an "outsider" decide what their child could or should be able to read or have read to them.

Ironically, this was all happening during the same month children were hearing about a young mother who drowned her two children by pushing her car into a river while they were restrained in their car seats. Children were also being exposed to all the details of the public murder trial of O. J. Simpson. During the period when the use of the book was being reconsidered, a national talk show featured teenage alcoholics and their stories. Some of them had begun to drink as young as nine years old.

Is a book about drinking and murder appropriate for late primary readers? There is probably no right answer to that question. But it does behoove teachers, parents, librarians, and all of those who work with young readers to know them and to realize that they need to have books that will help them think. Information is bountiful; it is the thinking that we need to develop. What one does with information is the key to its value. If children can read (or listen to) a book dealing with teenage drinking and other troublesome situations and discuss those situations with peers and adults who might provide some additional insight, then the book has helped those children. If, on the other hand, youngsters have not had an opportunity to think through certain situations in advance, their real-life responses to them might be inappropriate.

Choosing Contemporary Realistic Fiction

When choosing a book to use with children, consider the following questions: 1) Does the book have literary merit in terms of quality of writing and use of language; does it have a well-drawn plot, redeemable characters, a theme readers will care about, and interesting action? 2) Will students understand the situations presented in the book? 3) What factors support the use of this particular book rather than another title of comparable plot, theme, or topic?

Overall, books of contemporary realistic fiction should be selected based on the conflicts they draw from the real world. A conflict should be integral to the theme and overall plot of the story. In addition, the plot, characters, and setting must be well developed and credible. Books should be chosen because they have literary merit, not because they are controversial; nor should books be avoided because of someone's perceived notion of what might be objectionable. Gray censorship occurs when teachers and library media specialists back off from using a book they otherwise would have used, for fear that a controversy might arise.

Because children confront a wide range of issues in real life, they should be given an opportunity to choose from books that represent a wide range of issues, plots, and themes. The topics of single-parent families, child abuse, spousal abuse, foster homes, alcoholic parents, peer relationships, stepparents, the physical and emotional changes of adolescence, the struggle to survive in dangerous neighborhood situations, death, a parent's remarriage, a mother's surrogate pregnancy, school problems, sibling rivalry, incest, intergenerational relationships, and many others that affect young people are legitimate topics. Being able to gather, ponder, and discuss ideas about how to deal with situations will enhance readers' ability to deal with those situations in real life and empathize with others who are in circumstances different from their own.

As demonstrated in this chapter with the anecdote about the book by M. E. Kerr, readers cannot assume that just because their experiences do not match those presented in a book, the book is not realistic or relevant to other readers. That is why children must be able to choose among many different titles with diverse plots, themes, and characters.

Beginning a Focus on Contemporary Realistic Fiction _____

Begin the unit focusing on contemporary realistic fiction with a general introduction. This general introduction might include a brief discussion of the characteristics of realistic books, especially when compared to books of fantasy and books in other related genres: humor, mysteries, and sports stories. The early stages of this focus on realistic fiction often include the reading aloud of a book that deals with situations in the contemporary world.

Read-Alouds and Discussions

The book selected for reading aloud should be carefully chosen to interest listeners in reading more realistic fiction. Among my favorite titles are those about Anastasia by Lois Lowry and those about Angel by Judy Delton. These authors generally write books that are both realistic and humorous, which is why they are my personal choices. Other favorites include Avi, Marion Dane Bauer, Judy Blume, Bruce Brooks, Betsy Byars, Matt Christopher, Carol Carrick, Beverly Cleary, Vera Conford, Barbara Corcoran, Paula Danziger, Paula Fox, Lynn Hall, Virginia Hamilton, Patricia Hermes, Suzy Kline, E. L. Konigsburg, Nicholasa Mohr, Walter Dean Myers, Barbara Park, Katherine Paterson, Gary Paulsen, Cynthia Rylant, Susan Shreve, Doris Smith, Cynthia Voigt, and Mildred Pitts Walter. Though no one recommendation can be identified as the best novel for reading aloud to a specific group, many titles are fast paced enough to capture the interest of listeners and to keep them interested as the book progresses chapter by chapter over a series of days. Several suggestions are listed in the following section.

The general procedures for using a read-aloud book to initiate and model discussions are outlined in chapter 1 (see pages 5-6) and are appropriate to any genre, including contemporary realistic fiction.

During the discussion of the read-aloud title and subsequent readers' discussion groups, encourage a focus on the author's techniques for bringing the reader into the plot by appealing to the reader's schematic background regarding the setting and the universal characteristics and personality traits that are held by the characters. Identify the specific nature of the story. How did the author inject a sense of realism into the plot?

After group discussion and journal writing have been modeled to the whole class, break the class into smaller discussion groups as outlined in the "Reading Workshop Activities" and "Moving to Independent Reading" sections of chapter 1 (see pages 7-13).

Some Great Contemporary Realistic Fiction Books to Read Aloud

Byars, Betsy. **Bingo Brown's Guide to Romance**. Viking Childrens Books, 1992. Read-aloud audience: grades 3-5; ages 7-10.
Melissa, Bingo's "lost love," moves from Bingo's hometown to Bixby, Oklahoma. They correspond at first, but when Melissa receives a photocopy instead of the original of a letter from Bingo, their correspondence abruptly stops.

When Melissa returns home, Bingo arranges to visit her at her cousin's house, but fails to regain Melissa's favor. Through the episodes in the book, Bingo records his questions and answers regarding the situation, which eventually become his "Guide to Romance, a Record of the Personal Ups and Downs of Bingo Brown. Dedicated to My Brother, Jamie, as a Guide and Comfort to Him When He Finds Himself, as He Surely Will, upon the Roller Coaster of Life."

Cleary, Beverly. **Muggie Maggie**. Illustrated by Kay Life. Morrow, 1990. Read-aloud audience: grades 3-5; ages 7-10.
Maggie does not want to write in cursive nor does she care if she ever learns to read it. She reasons that she will not need that skill since she knows how to use the computer. Besides, learning to read cursive is of little use when adults often write very messy cursive. But the real reason Maggie does not want to try to read cursive is because her classmates laughed at her the first time she tried. When "Maggie" looked more like "Muggie," her classmates dubbed her Muggie Maggie. Maggie doesn't want to take another chance. But Mrs. Leeper has an idea— an idea that is sure to work.

Fox, Paula. **Monkey Island**. Orchard, 1991. Read-aloud audience: grades 5-7; ages 10-12.
Before all of Clay's troubles began he lived in a home with both his mother and father. He was a normal 11-year-old boy going to school, playing with friends, and doing all the things other boys his age did. Then his father loses his job and his mother goes to school and is trained for a computer job. Unable to deal with the fact that his wife is supporting the family and that he still does not have a job, Clay's father leaves the family. And things go downhill from there. The mother discovers she is pregnant and soon is unable to work. Social services tries to help out by providing an apartment and food, but when Clay's mother disappears he is left alone to face the world. He fears that if others in the apartment building learn that he is alone, he will end up in a home. After several days Clay finds himself on the streets of New York with no place to live. He is a homeless child in a big city, roaming the city streets and parks. He finds

friends among the homeless and in their way they help him survive. Then Clay contracts pneumonia and must be taken to the hospital for treatment. Social services places him with kind foster parents—but it is his mother and baby sister that he really wants. All ends happily when the three are reunited.

Hamm, Diane Johnston. **Second Family**. Scribner, 1992. Read-aloud audience: grades 3-5; ages 7-10.

As a widower living alone, Mr. Torkelson (Mr. T.) welcomes the chance to have someone live with him. Through a home-sharing agency, he is matched with a 12-year-old boy and his mother. Rodney will attend school across the street, and his mother, Catherine, will attend classes at the university. The challenges that face this arranged family go beyond the household arrangements; Rodney is dealing with his parents' divorce, his move from California to Washington State, and the changes his mother makes to distance herself from the rejection she feels. Rodney finds that his classmates are not always kind to him and his mother, and when his own retaliation causes him to be suspended from school, Mr. T. finds it hard to help Rodney understand. After much effort the three feel like a family, but all does not end there. Rodney's mother decides that she will quit college and return to California. Rodney is pleased except for the fact that the two of them will be leaving Mr. T. behind. But maybe there is hope that Mr. T. and Mrs. Lacy will become better friends now that Mr. T. is more aware of how to keep himself from being lonely.

Irwin, Hadley. **The Original Freddie Ackerman**. McElderry, 1992. Read-aloud audience: grades 3-5; ages 7-10.

Trevor Frederick Ackerman has a mother and an "other dad Charlie." Before that he had an "other dad Norman." He even has a real dad, but at his dad's house he is plagued by stepsiblings and half-siblings. When Freddie's mother decides to go with Charlie on a summer trip to Bermuda, Freddie is faced with going to his dad's house or planning his own trip to his great-aunts' house on Blue Isle, Maine. His aunts, Calla and Louise, are eccentric but more perceptive than Freddie realizes. When Freddie

discovers some information about a valuable book, he also learns that there are plenty of family secrets to keep, and the secrets make the days more exciting—almost too exciting.

Kline, Suzy. **Herbie Jones and the Dark Attic**. Illustrated by Richard Williams. Putnam, 1992. Read-aloud audience: grades 3-5; ages 7-10.

Herbie Jones is ready for fourth grade, and most of his classmates will be those he was with in third grade; even his teacher, Miss Pinkham, has moved from third grade to fourth grade. But things have changed. Miss Pinkham has changed the way she organizes reading groups, and Herbie is placed in a group with his friend, Raymond, and the smartest girl in class, Annabelle. They have to select a book, read it, and then do projects based on the book. And Herbie's grandfather is coming to visit for two weeks. Herbie has often wanted to sleep in the attic, but once he volunteers to move up there for the two weeks, he begins to have second thoughts, dreading what might be there. On the first night he convinces his friend, Raymond, to stay with him. At first it is exciting, but when the raccoon comes to visit they decide that sleeping in the attic is not much fun. Herbie's story ends happily when his friends help to make the attic *the* (scary) place to be. The "Fanattics" even play hide-and-seek and hold their club meetings there.

Myers, Walter Dean. **The Mouse Rap**. HarperCollins, 1990. Read-aloud audience: grades 5-7; ages 10-12.

A story of friendship between 14-year-old Mouse and his friend. Mouse and his friend fall in and out of love as they search Harlem for a hidden treasure from the days of Al Capone. A major portion of the story is told in rap.

Namioka, Lensey. **Yang the Youngest and His Terrible Ear**. Illustrated by Kees de Kiefte. Little, Brown, 1992. Read-aloud audience: grades 3-5; ages 7-10.

Nine-year-old Yingtao Yang is the youngest in a family that has arrived in Seattle, Washington, from China. All members of the Yang family are talented musicians, except Yingtao. He must struggle to learn English and is being pressured to learn to play the violin for a major recital that may bring more students to his father, a music teacher. More students will mean that his father will be better able to support his family. Yingtao, who knows that his talent lies not in music but in baseball, has a good friend who would be a much better choice to play in the quartet at the recital. How can Yingtao convince his friend to take Yingtao's place, and how can Yingtao convince his father that his friend would be a much better choice for the recital?

Pettit, Jayne. **My Name Is San Ho**. Scholastic, 1992. Read-aloud audience: grades 3-5; ages 7-10.

San Ho's story begins in a small village in Vietnam where he and his family must dig trenches in which to hide. Later San Ho is taken to Saigon to live with a friend. While he is in Saigon, his mother meets an American serviceman who marries her and takes her with him to the United States. A few years pass while San Ho's mother arranges for him to join her. Once in the United States, he must learn to speak English, to like new foods, and to get along with his stepfather. The story follows San Ho's ups and downs and his struggles to deal with the racism he and his family face.

Radin, Ruth Yaffe. **Carver**. Illustrated by Karl Swanson. Macmillan, 1990. Read-aloud audience: grades 3-5; ages 7-10.

A short, moving story of a 10-year-old boy, Jon, who is blinded at the age of two in a car accident. In that same accident Jon's father is killed and his mother moves to Washington State to escape the memories. Later, when Jon has to attend a regular public school, his new teacher doesn't want a blind student any more than Jon wants to be there. Soon, though, he makes a friend, Matt, who agrees to help him obtain a cherished goal—to become an accomplished carver like his father. Through Matt, Jon meets a local sculptor named Carver, a grouchy old man who has stayed to himself ever since his wife died. The two youngsters manage to get him to help Jon learn his skill.

Rylant, Cynthia. **A Fine White Dust**. Bradbury, 1986. Read-aloud audience: grades 5-8; ages 10-12.

Thirteen-year-old Pete, struggling with his religious beliefs, becomes involved with a traveling evangelist who is less than honest. In light of his experiences with this evangelist, Pete finds that he is questioning his own sense of religion. But in the end, Pete realizes that "the Preacher man is behind me. But God is still right there, in front" (page 106).

Moving to a Multitude of Books

After listening to a contemporary realistic fiction book, the class will be ready to move on to reading workshops, discussed in "Moving to Independent Reading" (pages 10-13). Two of the most popular writers are Betsy Byars and Mavis Jukes. Either one of these authors would make an excellent subject for an author focus for the intermediate and middle school reader. Authors that might be considered for other author focus units include Beverly Cleary, Patricia Hermes, Suzy Kline, Walter Dean Myers, Katherine Paterson, Jerry Spinelli, and Cynthia Voigt.

More Contemporary Realistic Fiction to Read

Cleary, Beverly. **Strider**. Morrow, 1991. Target audience: grades 3-5; ages 7-10.

Through a series of diary entries, Leigh tells how he comes to terms with his parents' divorce. He even acquires joint custody of an abandoned dog and becomes involved in the track team at school.

Conford, Ellen. **Get the Picture, Jenny Archer?** Illustrated by Diane Palmiseiano. Little, Brown, 1994. Target audience: grades 3-5; ages 7-10.

Jenny Archer's grandparents give her a used camera, which she doesn't regard as special until she finds out that her favorite magazine is running a photo contest. She decides to enter the contest, certain she is going to win. She begins to take pictures of everything in her neighborhood. But when she takes a picture of someone she feels is attempting to harm a dog, things begin to get complicated.

Cooper, Ilene. **Trick or Trouble**. Viking, 1994. The Holiday Five series. Target audience: grades 5-7; ages 10-12.

Lia, Maddy, Kathy, Jill, and Erin become good friends at camp and agree to stay in touch when the summer ends. They decide to keep the good times going by meeting on holidays and to help each other out when times get bad. This first book in the series features Lia who, although popular at camp, has few friends at home. Her one friend, Scott, suddenly becomes interesting to all the other seventh-grade girls. But Lia knows she can count on her "holiday five" friends, who will be coming to town for the big Halloween party. But the party turns out to be tricky for everyone. The second book in the series is *The Worst Noel* (Viking, 1994).

DeClements, Barthe. **Tough Loser**. Viking, 1994. Target audience: grades 3-5; ages 7-10.

Jenna falls in love with a puppy she probably won't be allowed to keep, and Mike is ruining his hockey career with his volatile temper. It's hard to be the only good player on the worst team in the region—and Mike is a poor loser.

Greenwald, Sheila. **Rosy Cole: She Walks in Beauty**. Illustrated by Sheila Greenwald. Little, Brown, 1994. Target audience: grades 3-5; ages 7-10.

Rosy Cole notices how much attention her model friend is getting. Rosy vows that she is going to become beautiful as well, so she decides to get a makeover at the department store beauty counter. But the only attention she gets is giggles and stares. Later Rosy's friend's brother helps her find her new look at, of all places, the art museum. A humorous realistic story that deals with society's obsession with beauty.

Hermes, Patricia. **Nothing but Trouble, Trouble, Trouble**. Scholastic, 1994. Target audience: grades 3-5; ages 7-10.

Alex wants to be allowed to babysit, but her parents do not feel that she is responsible enough. In an effort to show how responsible she is, Alex agrees to stay out of trouble for two weeks. But with a class assignment to care for a pet, and a sister who is allergic to all the pets Alex can

borrow, keeping out of trouble is going to be difficult. Alex learns in the process that telling the truth is a major part of being responsible.

Kline, Suzy. **Herbie Jones and the Monster Ball**. Putnam, 1988. Target audience: grades 3-5; ages 7-10.

Herbie Jones's uncle decides to coach a baseball team. When he asks Herbie to join the team, Herbie is sure his summer is ruined.

———. **Song Lee and the Hamster Hunt**. Illustrated by Frank Remkiewicz. Viking, 1994. Target audience: grades 3-5; ages 7-10.

Song Lee is back in room 2B and with his friends at school. This time his hamster escapes from its cage and becomes the object of a schoolwide search.

Konigsburg, E. L. **T-Backs, T-Shirts, COAT, and Suit**. Atheneum, 1993; Hyperion, 1995. Target audience: grades 5-8; ages 10-12.

Twelve-year-old Chlöe's stepfather's sister operates a meals-on-wheels van in Florida. During a visit, Chlöe becomes involved in a controversy surrounding the wearing of T-back bathing suits.

Lowry, Lois. **Attaboy, Sam!** Illustrated by Diane deGroat. Houghton, 1992. Target audience: grades 3-5; ages 7-10.

Sam helps his older sister, Anastasia, create a birthday poem for their mother, but his own efforts to create a very special perfume as a gift have disastrous results.

MacLachlan, Patricia. **The Facts and Fiction of Minna Pratt**. Harper, 1988. Target audience: grades 3-5; ages 7-10.

Eleven-year-old Minna Pratt sometimes wonders about her eccentric family and her own ability as a cellist. She learns a lot about life from her family, her first boyfriend, and Mozart.

Mauser, Pat Rhoads. **A Bundle of Sticks**. Illustrated by Gail Owens. Atheneum, 1982; Aladdin, 1987. Target audience: grades 3-5; ages 7-10.

Fifth grade is not a pleasant experience when a class bully decides that you are his target. A martial arts school teaches techniques for defense and a philosophy that helps develop an awareness that one does not have to fight to defeat a bully.

Nelson, Theresa. **The Beggars' Ride**. Orchard, 1992. Target audience: grades 5-7; ages 10-12.

A 12-year-old flees from an unhappy home life and attempts to survive on the streets of Atlantic City. He hooks up with a small gang of homeless children, who all have their own reasons for distrusting society. Each of their stories presents a new perspective on the topic of homelessness.

O'Dell, Scott. **Black Star, Bright Dawn**. Houghton, 1988. Target audience: grades 5-7; ages 10-12.

Set against a backdrop of the fabled Iditarod Trail Sled Race from Anchorage to Nome, this story tells of a young Eskimo girl who enters the race and drives her dogsled team to the far north of Alaska. Her experiences teach her to trust herself and her dogs and help her discover her own inner strength. She also learns to value her Eskimo heritage, her values, and her beliefs.

Paterson, Katherine. **Flip-Flop Girl**. Dutton, 1994. Target audience: grades 3-5; ages 7-10.

When five-year-old Mason and nine-year-old Vinnie are uprooted because of the death of their father, the two find themselves at a loss and cope as best as they can—one in complete silence. In their new surroundings, no one seems to care much for the unkempt girl who always wears flip-flop shoes. Not even Vinnie or Mason realize how important the flip-flop girl will be to their adjustment to their new life.

Paulsen, Gary. **Dogsong**. Bradbury, 1985. Target audience: grades 5-7; ages 10-12.

A young Eskimo boy, Russell, leaves behind the more modern world where his people now hunt seal and caribou with snowmobiles to travel by dogsled 1,400 miles across the ice. During the journey he comes to terms with his own beliefs and fears. He is challenged by nature and discovers the power of the ways of his ancestors.

Peck, Richard. **Remembering the Good Times**. Delacorte, 1985. Target audience: grades 5-7; ages 10-12.

Three friends share everything: their worries, their high points, and their ambitions. Or so it seems. Trav, Kate, and Buck are a trio—supposedly sharing with one another every aspect of their lives—that is, until pressures cause Trav to commit suicide. Kate and Buck begin to wonder about their own self-worth and try to face the future by "remembering the good times."

Philson, Joan. **Hit and Run**. Atheneum, 1985. Target audience: grades 5-7; ages 10-12.

Sixteen-year-old Roland could be characterized as spoiled by some. He seems only to care about himself and his fast life. During a reckless evening he has a serious accident in a borrowed car. The realization of what he has done sends him fleeing into the wild Australian countryside, where he struggles to survive and to gain self-respect.

Radley, Gail. **The Golden Days**. Macmillan, 1991. Target audience: grades 3-5; ages 7-10.

Cory's security in his third foster home seems to be threatened when Michele and Dan, his foster parents, announce that they are going to have a baby. Cory's social worker encourages him to visit the local nursing home as a "foster friend." There he meets 75-year-old Carlotta, who dislikes her own situation as much as Cory dislikes living in foster homes. Together the two of them run away, but when Carlotta gets ill and Cory's foster parents track him down, the two seem destined to be put back into not-so-pleasant circumstances. But when Michele and Dan suggest that Carlotta come back to live with them along with Cory, he realizes that he really is wanted—and that going back may be just the thing to do.

Sachs, Marilyn. **What My Sister Remembered**. Dutton, 1992. Target audience: grades 3-5; ages 7-10.

Molly and Beth are biological sisters who now each have a different set of parents and very different memories of their past. Molly's adoptive parents are her aunt and uncle; Beth's parents are not related to her. The girls have not seen one another for eight years. Beth's adoptive mother is a nurse who helped care for her when she was young and in the hospital. Her parents, the Lattimores, are well off and are raising her in California. Molly lives with her parents in a small apartment on the East Coast. Secrets of the past have caused Beth to be resentful, and Molly feels that Beth is simply ungrateful. Until all the facts are revealed, neither can understand the feelings of the other. Once the secrets are out, there are signs that the girls may eventually heal their wounds and become friends as adults.

Taylor, Theodore. **Tuck Triumphant**. Doubleday, 1991. Target audience: grades 3-5; ages 7-10.

Fourteen-year-old Helen and her blind dog, Friar Tuck, are true companions. Both face identity problems when a Korean child is adopted into the family. But the real crisis comes when Helen and Tuck find out that the young boy is deaf. The book is a sequel to *The Trouble with Tuck* (Doubleday, 1981).

Voigt, Cynthia. **When She Hollers**. Scholastic, 1994. Target audience: grades 5-7; ages 10-12.

Tish has lived with her mother and adoptive stepfather since she was a small child. She is now a teenager and realizes that what her stepfather has done to her from the time she was little must end. Tish's decision is a difficult one, but she knows she must stop him.

Author! Author!

Betsy Byars

Betsy Byars never dreamed she would grow up to write children's books. She believed that writers of children's books were elderly men and women, absentminded, and slightly dotty. Now she has written more than 30 books for young readers, and she is still not elderly, absentminded, or dotty.

Byars was born in North Carolina the same year that bubble gum, Mickey Mouse, and Maurice Sendak made their debut into the world. During her growing-up years Byars had her own goat, rabbit, rooster, and dog. She wanted to work in a zoo and take care of baby animals whose mothers had rejected them. She still likes animals. A favorite dog appeared in *The Computer Nut* and sits under her desk when she writes. Other favorite things include Snickers® candy bars, popcorn, pizza, the beach, and fireworks on the Fourth of July.

Many of Byars's stories begin with incidents from her own life. She and her husband, Ed, live in South Carolina. Their four children, Laurie, Betsy, Nan, and Guy, now grown, all have appeared in their mother's books. One daughter, Betsy Duffey, also writes books for young readers.

Betsy Byars

In 1971, the American Library Association awarded Betsy Byars the Newbery Award for *The Summer of the Swans* (Viking Childrens Books, 1970). She had been writing for a little more than 10 years when that major award marked her emergence as one of the most popular authors of children's books. The idea for *The Summer of the Swans* came when Byars read an article in a college magazine, about swans on the university lake that persisted in flying away to less desirable ponds. From that seed evolved the book's plot, which centers on a 14-year-old girl and her mentally retarded brother. When Byars was notified of the award, one of her first thoughts is said to have been, "Now my books will be read." And they have been.

Betsy Byars was born Betsy Cromer on August 7, 1928, in Charlotte, North Carolina; that was the same year that brought the world Mickey Mouse, Maurice Sendak, and bubble gum. She grew up in South Carolina, attended college there, and in 1950 met Edward Byars, whom she married in 1960. During the years her husband attended graduate school, Betsy began to write articles for magazines such as *Look*, *Saturday Evening Post*, and *TV Guide*. During the next 10 years she became the mother of four children, and as they began to read, she began to write books for children. Her first nine books were turned down by publishers. Her 10th book, *Clementine* (Houghton), was published in 1962, and her second published book, *The Dancing Camel* (Viking), was released in 1965. Her 30th published book, *The Burning Questions of Bingo Brown* (Viking), was published in 1988. Among her more recent titles are *The Dark Stairs: A Herculeah Jones Mystery* (Viking, 1994) and *The Joy Boys* (Yearling First Choice Chapter Books, 1995), books that appeal to children who are emerging as readers of "chapter" books.

Byars often cites *The Midnight Fox* (Viking, 1968) as one of her favorite books. She spent a lot of time researching information about foxes before writing the book, which tells the story of a young boy's encounter with a fox, an animal

Byars portrays as rare and beautiful. This was something of a breakthrough book—Byars had found her niche. When she discusses her writing at conferences and during presentations, she often refers to this book as "the first thing I wrote that was what I really wanted."

Another milestone came with the publication of *The Computer Nut* (Viking, 1984). It was the first book Byars wrote on her new computer. During a 1986 interview with Richard F. Abrahamson, Byars stated that word processing has "taken all of the work out of writing." And "it is absolutely ideal, if you develop the habit of backing up everything and printing out what you have written for the day."[1]

Byars collects ideas for her books from the real, everyday world that surrounds her and her family. In fact, she still writes or thinks about her writing almost anywhere and while she is doing almost anything. She might make notes about her characters and plots while washing dishes or while waiting, as part of the ground crew, for her husband's glider to reach its destination. The opening scene in *Good-Bye, Chicken Little* (HarperCollins, 1979) came from an article Byars read about an intoxicated man who attempted to walk across an ice-covered river. In *The Pinballs* (HarperCollins, 1977), she included elderly twin sisters. While much of the twins' characterization came from Byars's imagination, the idea for creating the Benson sisters came from seeing elderly twins, dressed identically, shopping in a neighborhood grocery store. Her own childhood encounter with two bullies, the menacing Fletcher brothers, inspired the composite character Marv Hammerman in *The Eighteenth Emergency* (Viking, 1973).

For a time Byars lived in Morgantown, West Virginia, which provided the seeds for many books. A newspaper article about a man (and his goats) who were being put off their land to make way for an interstate highway inspired the story in *After the Goatman* (Viking, 1974). Harold, whose fat and miserable existence is uplifted by the goat man, is also a character in this story. Another article about a lost sandhill crane resulted in *House of Wings* (Viking, 1972). The idea for her award-winning *Summer of the Swans* (Viking, 1970) came during tutoring sessions for a learning-disabled student.

There are some common elements in Byars's books. Many of the children in her stories are being cared for by someone other than biological parents. Most of her characters are boys—partially because her three daughters, while they were growing up, made it clear that they did not want to be in her books. But most of her characters are highly individualized. And each of her four now grown children—even her dog—has appeared in her books. Byars herself appreciates individuality and admires other writers who bring unique characters into their books.

Byars often spends two years on a book, doing most of her writing during the winter. She and her husband spend their summers at their cabin on a lake enjoying their hobby of gliding. Both Byarses have their pilot's licenses, and in the summer of 1987 they flew a 1940 J-3 Cub airplane coast to coast. That experience provided the background for yet another book, *Coast to Coast* (Delacorte, 1992), which tells the story of Birch and her grandfather, who decide that they should take his Piper Cub on one last flight before he moves to a retirement community. The adventure takes the two on a dream trip from Charleston, South Carolina, across Alabama, Mississippi, and Texas. They finally reach California after flying across the Colorado River, Joshua Tree National Monument, and the San Gabriel Mountains. The plane trip is one last hurrah for Grandfather but it is just the beginning for Birch, who has a first date with a young man who helps tie down their plane when they are forced to land because of strong winds.

In 1986 the first book of Byars's Blossom Family quartet was published. Byars had not previously written sequels to her titles, even though there were requests for more books about specific characters; by the time that requests for sequels came in, for example in the case of *The Pinballs* (HarperCollins, 1977), she

had already written several other titles and found it difficult to get back into the characters from the earlier book. But in the case of the Blossom Family books, she wrote *The Not-Just-Anybody Family* (Delacorte, 1986) and "just went right on to write the sequel." The sequel evolved into a total of four titles about the Blossom family. Following close behind was another series, this one featuring Bingo Brown, a sixth-grader who constantly finds himself in and out of interesting situations.

Byars has also begun to write for the early chapter readers. In 1988, as part of the Vermont Migrant Education Program, she wrote and published an early reading title, *The Smallest Cow in the World*. An edition of that book, with illustrations by Jane Clark Brown, was published as an "I Can Read"® book in 1991 by HarperCollins. More recently (1995), *The Joy Boys* by Byars was published by Dell as a Yearling First Choice Chapter Book. Byars has also embarked on creating a series of mysteries featuring the intrepid Herculeah Jones.

The Byarses' four children—Laurie, Betsy, Nan, and Guy—are now grown with children of their own. Daughter Betsy Duffey has also become a children's book writer. Duffey's books include *A Boy in the Doghouse* (Simon & Schuster, 1991) and *Wild Things* (Viking, 1993). Betsy and Edward Byars live in Clemson, South Carolina.

Books by Betsy Byars

After the Goat Man. Illustrated by Ronald Himler. Viking, 1974. Target audience: grades 3-5; ages 7-10.
Figgy and his grandfather are evicted from their cabin when it is condemned to make room for a new interstate highway. They move into Harold and Ada's neighborhood, but Figgy's grandfather, known as the Goat Man, refuses to stay away from the cabin where he has lived all of his life. Harold, fat and bored from a summer of playing Monopoly®, is not anxious to be a hero but finds himself forced into that role when the Goat Man attempts to hold off the bulldozers with the use of a gun.

The Animal, the Vegetable, and John D. Jones. Illustrated by Ruth Sanderson. Delacorte, 1982. Target audience: grades 3-5; ages 7-10. Clara, Deenie, and their divorced father are going on a two-week vacation. Just before the family arrives at their destination, father announces that they will be joined by his friend and her son. The three children—Clara, Deenie, and John D.—spend most of the first week trying to make each other miserable. Then Clara floats out to sea on a plastic raft, John D. discovers that she is missing, and he sets into motion efforts to rescue her.

Bingo Brown and the Language of Love. Viking Childrens Books, 1989. Target audience: grades 3-5; ages 7-10.
Twelve-year-old Bingo Brown finds that he must face the "Trials of Today" and finds that there are few "Triumphs of Today." Throughout the novel Bingo survives his summer ordeals and the move of his girlfriend to another city. At the end Bingo has not only gained emotional maturity but is now able to write "none" in the trials list and finds he even has several entries in the triumphs section.

Bingo Brown, Gypsy Lover. Viking Childrens Books, 1990. Target audience: grades 3-5; ages 7-10.
Now in sixth grade, Bingo finds that he must face the prospect of a new baby brother and a long-distance relationship with his girlfriend, who has moved to another city. But it is the long-distance romance that makes him the authority on matters of the heart. Tough guy Billy Wentworth is even asking Bingo for dating tips. Another girl, Boots, is sure that Bingo is her soul mate—the mere thought of which makes Bingo a little dizzy. But Bingo returns to earth when his parents give him a new title: Bingo Brown, Big Brother.

Bingo Brown's Guide to Romance. Viking Childrens Books, 1992. Target audience: grades 3-5; ages 7-10.
Bingo and Melissa, his old girlfriend, have not corresponded for the past three months and now she is back in town. Bingo must move into action if he hopes to see Melissa again. (See full annotation in the Read-Aloud section of this

chapter.) The first book about Bingo Brown was *The Burning Questions of Bingo Brown* (Viking Childrens Books, 1988).

The Cartoonist. Illustrated by Richard Cuffari. Viking Childrens Books, 1978. Target audience: grades 3-5; ages 7-10.
Alfie loves to draw cartoons. In many ways he is like Jeff in *Bridge to Terabithia*, enjoying the solitude and quiet of an imaginary world. Alfie responds to people and events around him by creating cartoons and envisioning himself as a famous cartoonist. Because he has an abrasive mother and no friends at school, Alfie spends much of his time drawing in the attic of his ramshackle house. But when his world is threatened by the return of his older brother and his wife, Alfie finds that he must reconcile his real and imaginary worlds. Humorous dialogue keeps a serious topic from being too somber.

Coast to Coast. Delacorte, 1992. Target audience: grades 5-7; ages 10-12.
Birch's grandfather, who is about to move to a retirement home, fantasizes about taking one last ride in his Piper Cub plane before selling it. Thirteen-year-old Birch encourages him to take the coast-to-coast journey and then convinces him that she should go along. The two of them set off from Charleston, South Carolina, and fly across the southern states until they reach California. A mystery involving a poem Birch's grandmother had written on the day Birch was born is solved by the time they return from their flight.

The Glory Girl. Viking, 1983. Target audience: grades 5-7; ages 10-12.
Anna Glory attempts to cope with her family, the Glory Gospel Singers, even though she cannot carry a tune. Tensions, vicious pranks, and Uncle Newt (a misfit uncle) all contribute to the plot of this novel, but by the end, Anna realizes just what is most important.

The Golly Sisters Ride Again. Illustrated by Sue Truesdell. HarperCollins, 1994. Target audience: grades 3-5; ages 7-10.
May-May and her sister Rose share more adventures as they venture west with their traveling show. This book continues the adventures

begun in the early-to-read chapter books *The Golly Sisters Go West* (Harper, 1985) and *Hooray for the Golly Sisters!* (Harper, 1990).

Growing-Up Stories. Edited by Betsy Byars. Illustrated by Robert Geary. Kingfisher, 1995. Target audience: grades 5-7; ages 10-12.

A compilation of short stories and excerpts from novels about the growing-up years and turning points in life. Selections represent work from 26 authors including Judy Blume, L. M. Montgomery, and Roald Dahl.

The Joy Boys. Illustrated by Frank Remkiewicz. Yearling First Choice Chapter Books, 1995. Target audience: grades 3-5; ages 7-10.

Riding cows, making mud bombs, and hunting for wild animals are among the adventures shared by two brothers and their dog on the family farm.

The Night Swimmers. Illustrated by Tony Howell. Delacorte, 1980. Target audience: grades 5-7; ages 10-12.

Retta, Johnny, and Roy are three children who are left alone to take care of themselves while their father goes off at night to perform as a country and western singer. The story centers on Retta's personal growth as she moves through her grief after her mother dies and through her changing feelings as she tries to be a parent to her two younger brothers. In the end, she realizes that she must accept her father as he is, not as she would like him to be.

The Seven Treasure Hunts. Illustrated by Jennifer Barrett. HarperCollins, 1991. Target audience: grades 3-5; ages 7-10.

Jackson and his friend Goat make up a series of treasure hunts for each other to go on. The hunts provide both disastrous and hilarious results. This short book should appeal to those who are just confirming their ability to read chapter books.

The Summer of the Swans. Illustrated by Ted CoConis. Viking Childrens Books, 1970. Target audience: grades 3-5; ages 7-10.

Sara is not pleased with her skinny legs, enormous feet, and crooked nose. But she loves her beautiful older sister, her retarded younger brother, Charlie, and her aunt who is also the children's caregiver. Sara's 14th summer is difficult because she is attempting to find her own place in life. One day she takes Charlie to see the swans, but when she attempts to hurry him along he disappears. In the process of searching for Charlie, Sara comes to realize that a classmate she had suspected of stealing Charlie's watch is not really the villain she had made him out to be. When Charlie is found, hours later under some tangled underbrush, Sara realizes that she can see life more clearly.

The Two-Thousand-Pound Goldfish. HarperCollins, 1982. Target audience: grades 5-7; ages 10-12.

An enormous fish is Warren Otis's current favorite candidate to play one of his movie characters. Warren is a young boy who expects to become a famous producer of horror flicks. His fantasies are just a small part of his efforts to escape from the grief he has felt since his mother deserted him. She is an antiestablishment protester who has been involved in some crimes and is now on the run from the FBI. Warren and his older sister, Weezie, live with their maternal grandmother. Both Weezie and his grandmother attempt to convince him to give up his dreams that his mother will return one day. But Warren continues his dreams, filled with characters from monster movies and his own aspirations for his future.

Wanted—Mud Blossom. Illustrated by Jacqueline Rogers. Delacorte, 1991. Target audience: grades 3-5; ages 7-10.

If Junior has anything to say about it, Mud Blossom (the dog) will be tried for his crime. Junior Blossom suspects that Mud is responsible for the disappearance of the school hamster that was his responsibility for the weekend.

Author! Author!

Mavis Jukes

Mavis Jukes was born in Nyack, New York, and grew up in New York City and Princeton, New Jersey. After graduating from high school she earned a B.A. degree in elementary education from the University of California at Berkeley and taught for five years. Later she earned a law degree from Golden Gate University Law School and became a member of the California bar.

In the early 1980s she left her law career to become a full-time writer. Her husband, sculptor and painter Robert Hudson, converted an old pump house on their northern California farm into a writing office complete with computer. Each day, after her children go off to school, Mavis Jukes goes to her office to write. She says incidents involving her family and friends often appear in her books. Her husband's fear of spiders became part of the story in *Like Jake and Me,* and a fishing experience with her youngest daughter, Amy, became part of *Blackberries in the Dark.*

Mavis Jukes lives with her family in a rural area near Cotati, California. Surrounding their home are sheep, cows, and chirping birds. The Jukes have two daughters, River and Amy. Their family also includes Jukes's two adult stepsons, Cannon and Case.

From *Educator's Companion to Children's Literature, Volume 2: Folklore, Contemporary Realistic Fiction, Fantasy, Biographies, and Tales from Here and There.* © 1996. Libraries Unlimited. (800) 237-6124.

Mavis Jukes

Mavis Jukes was born on May 3, 1947, in Nyack, New York, and grew up in New York City and Princeton, New Jersey. She spent a lot of time playing outdoors with her brother Ken and her sister Caroline. Some of her most memorable childhood days were spent as a member of her brother's gang, even though she found out several years later that she was the only member—even her brother had quit. She jumped off the high end of the roof of the pig hut and dug in abandoned sites for box wrenches and gooseneck pliers. She wandered through burr-filled fields with the family poodle and dug holes—deep holes. By the time she was 11 or 12, Jukes could drive a Packard and fly a J-3 Piper Cub. She did not read much as a child except for comic books and the Montgomery Ward catalog.

Jukes did not always know she would be a writer; in fact, she says that she "grew up in the '50s when little girls didn't know that little girls could grow up and become anything."[2] But looking back, she says that there are two clues that she would become a writer. The first clue was that she loved to talk and she loved words. She told stories over and over, each time spicing them up a little bit more, eventually prompting someone to complain that Mavis was exaggerating again. The second clue was that she loved to pretend. And she believes that being able to pretend is an important element in being able to write.

After high school, Mavis Jukes earned a B.A. degree in elementary education from the University of California at Berkeley, and for five years she taught elementary school. In 1976 she married Robert Hudson and soon afterward entered law school at Golden Gate University. In 1979 she became a member of the California bar but decided to pursue a full-time writing career. Her first book was a book about her cat going to Nashville. It was 52 pages long and boring. She read it to her daughter, who fell asleep. In rewriting the book, Jukes replaced the cat with a dog who wears a hat—and no one goes to Nashville. Two years later, in 1983, the revised story became her first book, *No One Is Going to Nashville*. She says, "Every story has at least one idea from real life."[3] One day her husband, Bob, came into the house with an armload of wood. On his arm was a spider. He dislikes spiders, so when Mavis called attention to it, Bob hunched up his shoulders and edged his way outside so that the spider would not get loose in the house. This episode was spiced up and written into the story that became *Like Jake and Me*.

During a time when Jukes's stepson Cannon was still apprehensive about their relationship, she challenged him to get up on stage and tap dance in front of a full theater audience. He agreed to accept the challenge if she would go with him. She did, and it was the first time they held hands. That incident gave her an idea for a scene near the end of *Like Jake and Me*.

An episode involving Jukes and her younger daughter, Amy, and a trout fishing excursion inspired a scene Jukes wrote into the final pages of *Blackberries in the Dark*. The scene, which involves releasing a fish back into the water, symbolizes a young man's ability to let go of the grief over his grandfather's death.

Mavis Jukes's stories are often about what might be considered nontraditional families. Relationships with stepparents and grandparents are an important element in many of her stories. When asked why she so often writes about "broken families," she responds that she doesn't write about broken families, but about "mending families" and families that are starting their own traditions.[4]

Each day after her daughters go off to school, Jukes goes to her office to write. Her office is an old pump house, converted and furnished with desk, chairs, and a computer. If she has time, she occasionally writes on weekends. The time it takes her to write a book varies. It took her three years to write *Blackberries in the Dark* but only one week to write *Like Jake and Me*.

After writing several slim books of fiction, Jukes wrote a longer one, *Getting Even*, which features Maggie and her "crazy" friend Iris. Later, Iris became the chief protagonist in another of Jukes's books, this one dealing with child sexual abuse. *Wild Iris Bloom* was followed by a nonfiction title described as a book of sex instruction for teenage girls. That book, *Ladies' Business*, illustrated by Bonnie Timmons, was published by Knopf in 1994.

Jukes's family includes her husband, Robert Hudson; adult stepsons, Cannon and Case, and two daughters, River and Amy. Jukes lives with her family in Cotati, California, where their rural home is surrounded by green fields, sheep, cows, and chirping birds.

Books by Mavis Jukes

Blackberries in the Dark. Illustrated by Thomas B. Allen. Knopf, 1985. Target audience: grades 3-5; ages 7-10.
Austin has always spent summers with his grandfather and grandmother but this year his grandfather will not be there. Austin knows that some of the summer traditions cannot live on. Fly-fishing, picking blackberries in the dark, and coming home late for dinner will not be the same without Grandfather. Before the summer is over, Austin is able to let go of his grief and, with the help of his grandmother, is able to begin some new traditions. He discovers that there will always be memories, and now there will be a special relationship between the two of them—grandmother and grandson.

Getting Even. Knopf, 1988. Target audience: grades 5-7; ages 10-12.
Ten-year-old Maggie must tolerate an obnoxious classmate. Her parents, who are continuing their own personal two-year divorce war, and Maggie's "crazy" friend are all offering advice on how to deal with this classmate. But the advice is conflicting, and Maggie discovers that only she can bring an end to the irritating situation.

I'll See You in My Dreams. Illustrated by Stacey Schuett. Knopf, 1993. Target audience: grades 3-5; ages 7-10.
Skywriting, airplanes, and a terminal illness all play a part in this story of a young girl who is preparing to visit her seriously ill uncle in a hospital. During her time of preparation, she dreams of being a skywriter and flying over his bed with a message of love.

Lights Around the Palm. Illustrated by Stacey Schuett. Knopf, 1987. Target audience: grades 3-5; ages 7-10.
Seven-year-old Emma tries to convince her older brother that she is teaching their farm animals to read and speak English. Her mother thinks it is just a game. Bob, her older brother, thinks she is nuts. But Emma knows the animals can already talk, so why can't they read, too?

Like Jake and Me. Illustrated by Lloyd Bloom. Knopf, 1984. Target audience: grades 3-5; ages 7-10.
Alex and Jake, Alex's stepfather, have a fragile relationship at best. When Jake goes out to the woodpile to chop wood, Alex tags along hoping that he might be able to help. But Jake is reluctant to let Alex carry the sharpened ax and really does not need his help to cut the wood. But when Jake carries the wood into the house, Alex notices a wolf spider climbing up the back of Jake's neck. Jake does not like spiders, and as he eases outside, it is Alex who helps pull off his shirt, boots, and pants searching for the spider. After completely stripping, Jake is still not sure where the spider has gone—but Alex notices it on Jake's Stetson. The final episode shows Jake and Alex sharing a dance, which cements their new relationship.

No One Is Going to Nashville. Illustrated by Lloyd Bloom. Knopf, 1983. Target audience: grades 3-5; ages 7-10.
Sonia feels that she is destined to become a veterinarian when she grows up. In fact, she has even asked her father and stepmother to call her Dr. Ackley. So when the stray dog with the big ears enters their lives, Sonia just knows she is meant to have it. However, she already has a goose and an alligator lizard and her father sees no reason why she should have yet another animal. She finds that she has an unsuspected ally in her stepmother, Annette, who intercedes to prevent another family from taking the dog to their ranch.

Wild Iris Bloom. Knopf, 1992. Target audience: grades 5-7; ages 10-12.

Iris, Maggie's friend from *Getting Even*, is 11 now and staying with a sitter for six weeks while her parents are in France. But during the final few days, Iris manages to spend a day or two alone by convincing Mrs. Fuller, the sitter, that her parents are coming home. She spends the afternoon wandering the mall, and when she finally decides to head home, realizes it is dark. She foolishly accepts a ride from a shoe salesman, who on the way home pulls over and tries to kiss her. She bangs on the window to attract the attention of a boy who is a new neighbor. The man lets her out of the car, but she is shaken and does not want to tell her parents. Iris thought she could handle things herself but decides she should spend the night with Maggie. When she does, the story comes out, and even though Maggie has promised not to tell, she realizes she must. Maggie's parents help Iris realize that what has happened is not her fault and that her parents will need to be told when they arrive home. The story does not sidestep the fact that Iris made some poor decisions, but it also asserts that she did the right thing by taking action and telling someone. A great story.

Going Beyond

Books of realistic fiction allow many readers to identify with the characters they present. And the situations allow many opportunities for readers to look at their own lives and to assess the way they are handling various situations. Because most contemporary authors include many of their own experiences in their stories, sharing information about authors and their lives will help students realize that incidents from their own lives can provide the seeds for creating their own original stories. The following are some suggestions for other collaborative activities involving folk literature.

Contemporary Realistic Fiction Activity

- After reading the books by Mavis Jukes, show the video from Walt Disney Educational Media, *Writing Process: A Conversation with Mavis Jukes* (1989), in which Jukes shares some incidents from her life and tells how they found their way into her books.

- Mavis Jukes was known as a storyteller. When she told a story she spiced it up by adding details. Begin with a statement of something that happened in the classroom. As a group, reread the statement and then begin to add details. For example, the first statement might be "Jane went to the water fountain to get a drink." Continue by adding details: "Jane went down the hall to the water fountain to get a drink." Then: "After finishing her test Jane went down the hall to the water fountain to get a drink." Continue adding details, but keep the sentence realistic.

- Ask students to discuss a setting that represents the place where their story might take place. Then instruct readers to visit the library media center or the nearest public library and locate a book of realistic fiction that has a setting very similar to their own—for example, a large city apartment house or a single-family home in a midwestern city. After students have read the book, ask them to compare the setting with the facts as they know them to be.

- Invite parents or grandparents to come to school to tell a story from their own lives. After students listen to a story, have them discuss with the teller how the story would be told differently today. Rewrite the story using a contemporary setting.

Culminating the Focus on Contemporary Realistic Fiction

A culminating session need not be elaborate, it only needs to bring to closure the official classroom focus on realistic fiction. For ideas on culminating activities, see the suggestions discussed in chapter 1 (page 14). Roundtable discussions of great books that students have read might be an appropriate culmination to this focus. The discussions might focus on possibilities for using the book as the basis for a movie. Who would play the leading parts? Where should the film be shot? How would it rate as a money-maker?

The following four pages may be reproduced for student use.

Notes

1. Richard F. Abrahamson. "Reviews: Books for Adolescents, of Pinballs, Swans, and Families: An Interview with Betsy Byars." *Journal of Reading*. November (1986): 179.

2. Mavis Jukes. *The Writing Process: A Conversation with Mavis Jukes*. Walt Disney Educational Media Company, 1989. (Video)

3. Ibid.

4. Ibid.

Contemporary Realistic Fiction Reader's Journal

My Name: _____

Response Starter Suggestions

Your contemporary realistic fiction reader's journal is where you will record your ideas, your thoughts, your questions about vocabulary, and your questions and comments about the plot and characters in the book or chapter you have just read. Sometimes it is difficult to get started, so the following questions might give you an idea to help you begin. These questions are only suggestions; the journal is yours and should contain questions and comments about the parts of the book that interest you.

- What is the conflict or problem in this story?

- What do you know about the characters?

- What characteristics are like those that you possess or those that your friends possess?

- How do the events in the story reflect events in the real world?

- How is the characters' behavior similar to your behavior?

- Were there any surprises in the story?

- Is the action in the book realistic? Why or why not?

- The events in this book remind you of _____.

- The characters in this book remind you of _____.

- What other ways might the characters have dealt with the situation?

- How would this book be different if it had been set in a period of time 15 years ago?

Date each of your journal entries. Responses mean more later if you use complete sentences.

Have fun and enjoy your reading.

From *Educator's Companion to Children's Literature, Volume 2: Folklore, Contemporary Realistic Fiction, Fantasy, Biographies, and Tales from Here and There.* © 1996. Libraries Unlimited. (800) 237-6124.

Contemporary Realistic Fiction Books
I Have Read

Title	Author
1.	
2.	
3.	
4.	
5.	
6.	
7.	
8.	
9.	
10.	
11.	
12.	
13.	
14.	
15.	
16.	
17.	
18.	
19.	
20.	

Contemporary Realistic Fiction Books
I Want to Read

Title	Author
1.	
2.	
3.	
4.	
5.	
6.	
7.	
8.	
9.	
10.	
11.	
12.	
13.	
14.	
15.	
16.	
17.	
18.	
19.	
20.	

4
Books of Fantasy

My dear Noel, I don't know what to write to you today, so I shall tell you a story about four rabbits whose names were Flopsy, Mopsy, Cottontail and Peter. They lived with their mother in a sand bank under the root of a big fir tree.

—Beatrix Potter (1893)

With those words Beatrix Potter began a letter to a young friend—a letter that eventually became the text to Beatrix Potter's best-known book of fantasy, *The Tale of Peter Rabbit*. Six publishers rejected the manuscript before Potter decided to have it printed at her own expense. Those first privately printed copies were soon sold out, and Frederick Warne and Company asked to publish the book commercially. Seventy-five years later, more than 65 million copies had been sold in English, and *Peter Rabbit* had been translated into 16 languages, including Latin, Japanese, Icelandic, Afrikaans, and Braille. The language of imagination seemed to appeal to a great many readers.

In my childhood home I remember having only a volume of stories by Jacob and Wilhelm Grimm and a second volume of stories by Hans Christian Andersen. I spent hours during the cold Iowa winters reading those stories. It never occurred to me that while the Grimms' tales were part of the true folk tradition, the Andersen tales were in reality literary fairy tales—fantasies—spun from Andersen's own imagination. Both volumes seemed magical and took me away from the present and into a world populated by magical things and magical people. Years later, when reading tales to my own young children, I was introduced to the wonderful tales of Beatrix Potter. Only then did I begin to realize the common thread that ran through the stories of Potter and Andersen. The stories of each were spawned by the imagination of the author. The stories were fantastical tales of imaginary people, places, and animals that, nevertheless, seemed to live in a real world. My introduction to fantasy had taken place.

Books of Fantasy— Beyond the Introduction

Once readers recognize how many popular books are actually fantasy tales, they will realize that they have already read books in this genre. Most adults reading this book will recognize some of the major authors of fantasy: J. R. R. Tolkien, Kenneth Grahame, C. S. Lewis, Hans Christian Andersen, Beatrix Potter, Jane Yolen, Lloyd Alexander, Bruce Coville, Robin McKinley, Susan Cooper, Michael Bond, Rudyard Kipling, Robert Lawson, E. B. White, Margery Williams, A. A. Milne, Carlo Collodi, Carl Sandburg, Astrid Lindgren, Lewis Carroll, James Barrie, Madeleine L'Engle, Anne McCaffrey, and Monica Hughes. Reading books by these authors and thinking about the elements common among them will give readers a solid idea of the basic characteristics of fantasy books. For the most part the authors listed above are well known, creating such believable settings and characters that readers are able to suspend their belief long enough to enter that world.

Readers sometimes confuse contemporary realistic fiction with modern fantasy, because fantasy writers often attempt to build more reader identification with their plots, characters, and settings by creating those elements realistically before taking the text and readers into fantastical realms. Supernatural attributes, magic, unexplained events, and mysterious beings move the story from contemporary realistic fiction into the imaginary world of modern fantasy. The major and most definitive characteristic of fantasy is that the situations in fantasy stories are outside the realm of possibility. Problems in fantasy books are often solved through magical or supernatural power. Toys are personified; animals behave like people; and there are little people, supernatural beings, or real people who have supernatural experiences.

Some writers of fantasy, such as Hans Christian Andersen, have successfully mimicked the fairy-tale form and included familiar fairy-tale elements into their original work. Such stories, and those that resemble traditional folktales, are classified within the genre of fantasy fiction as literary folk or fairy tales.

Other writers tell stories that have religious themes or contain ethical allegories. There are quests, conflicts, supernatural immortals, evil dragons, and sources of unusual power. Modern fantasies include articulate animals and toys that come alive. Some feature preposterous characters and situations, curious and interesting worlds, little people, people with supernatural powers, spirits both friendly and frightening, time travel, and science.

Types of Fantasy

All types of fantastical stories can be found within the selections of books for various age levels of young readers.

Animals in Fantasy

Tales featuring articulate animals can be found in the books by Beatrix Potter, George Selden, and Robert Lawson. Potter's little books of Peter Rabbit, Tom Kitten, and other creatures were aimed at early readers, while George Selden (pseudonym for George Selden Thompson) courted readers from the middle grades with his Chester Cricket stories. His novels, *The Cricket in Times Square* (Farrar, 1960), *Tucker's Countryside* (Farrar, 1969), and *Chester Cricket's Pigeon Ride* (Farrar, 1981), follow Chester as he first finds himself in a subway station below Times Square and later must find a new home in the country. Older students move on to Robert Lawson's *Rabbit Hill* (Viking, 1944), a story that relates the effect humans have on the lives of animals, told from the point of view of the animals. What will happen to the animals when the mother of the house plants a garden and cultivates the fields to create a manicured lawn? And what if the family loves shotguns and traps? Other well-known fantastical animal tales include Beverly Cleary's *Mouse and the Motorcycle* (Morrow, 1965), *Ralph S. Mouse* (Morrow, 1982), and *Runaway Ralph* (Morrow, 1970). Cleary's tales and Kenneth Grahame's *Wind in the Willows* (Scribner, 1908; 1940) are popular with the middle grades (grades 3-5).

Fantasy in Mythical Worlds

Other writers create not only interesting characters but entire mythical worlds. One such world is the land of Prydain created by Lloyd Alexander. Alexander's mythical world is based on his memories of Wales, Welsh legends he first encountered while researching *Time Cat* (Holt, 1963), and childhood stories. In the Prydain chronicles, which begin with *The Book of Three* (Holt, 1964). Taran, an assistant pig-keeper, struggles against the evil forces that are attempting to destroy Prydain. Other books in the series are *The Black Cauldron* (Holt, 1965), *The Castle of Llyr* (Holt, 1966), *Taran Wanderer* (Holt, 1967), and *The High King* (Holt, 1968). Alexander invents a fantastical world populated by credible characters.

Connections for Readers—
Lloyd Alexander

Part of the credibility of Lloyd Alexander's fantasy tales comes from his sources. The dreams of the assistant pig-keeper in the Prydain Chronicles are like those Alexander had as a child. Alexander has said that he has been as fearful as Gurgi; he often clutches his poor tender head, just as some of his characters do; and that his wife, Janine, sometimes grumbles like Doli. Alexander's full novels appeal to the upper intermediate or middle school reader, but his fantastical tales of quests and battles of good against evil are more appropriate for slightly younger readers. Lloyd Alexander and his wife live in Drexel Hill, Pennsylvania, near Philadelphia. They share their home with many cats, which sometimes show up in Alexander's books.

Other writers include encounters with fantastical characters. John Bellairs's *The Spell of the Sorcerer's Skull* (Dial, 1984) is a story in which a professor disappears and a young boy is left to fight against the evil forces. Michael Patrick Hearn wrote a wonderful picture book tale of a quest for a magical potion in *The Porcelain Cat,* illustrated by Leo Dillon and Diane Dillon (Little, Brown, 1987). A servant boy is sent on a quest for a magical potion that will enable the porcelain cat to rid the surroundings of the many mice that run to and fro.

Time Travel Fantasies

Some titles combine a quest with time travel or some other element of fantastical fiction. In *The Ghost from Beneath the Sea* by Bill Brittain (HarperCollins, 1992), three friends, Tommy, Books, and Harry the Blimp, spend hours and a lot of energy attempting to save the historic Parnell House from destruction. Their quest for information is successful only when the original owner of the house travels forward in history (as a ghost) and assists the youngsters in proving the deed to the house is a fake.

The use of time travel is a common element that brings otherwise realistic fiction tales into the realm of fantastical fiction. For example, Virginia Hamilton brought Pretty Pearl down to earth to help former slaves journey from Georgia to Ohio in *The Magical Adventures of Pretty Pearl* (Harper, 1983). David Wiseman's *Jeremy Visick* (Houghton, 1981) tells the story of a contemporary Cornish boy who goes back in time to discover the location of a boy who was lost in a mine accident.

Fantasies for Every Age

Different levels of fantasy appeal to different levels of readers. The very young reader is able to deal quite well with talking animals who do things that only humans would normally do. A slightly older reader can move into dealing with friendly ghosts or spirits and animals who participate in adventures outside their immediate world. The plot, however, still needs to be quite closely aligned with the reader's own life experiences. As the reader moves into the intermediate grades, books of fantasy can take steps into other worlds through time travel, or into imaginary lands created especially for the characters. It is during this period that readers easily move from Michael Bond's Paddington stories (which are essentially stories of a talking toy animal) into a completely fantastical world such as in *Alice's Adventures in Wonderland* by Lewis Carroll (Macmillan, 1866; Knopf, 1984 facsimile edition), or to a time warp story as in Ruth Park's *Playing Beatie Bow* (Atheneum, 1982), in which a girl from Sydney, Australia, travels back in time to the 1870s.

But probably less time should be spent on attempting to categorize fantasy books according to set criteria than on actually reading the books and attempting to compare and contrast them with one's own ideas of what characteristics make certain stories similar or different. One might categorize Virginia Hamilton's *Magical Adventures of Pretty Pearl* primarily as a book of time travel, a ghost story, a book of historical fiction, or simply the story of a young girl who helps escaping slaves. Readers can distinguish between the fantastical elements in the story and the elements that are firmly grounded in reality.

As books are read, similarities will become apparent. A book written within the past 10 years might contrast with a plot and setting created by a writer decades before. The key here, as in other genres, is to encourage wide reading and to allow the readers to compare and contrast the plots, settings, characters, and other story elements. By comparing and contrasting, readers will come to make connections not only among books in the fantasy genre but to books in other genres as well.

Techniques Used in Writing Books of Fantasy

Realistic Context

Because fantasy writers are asking readers to suspend their belief in the reality of the laws and logic of the world as they know it, the writer must set up a situation where alternative laws and logic can become part of the reader's belief system. One technique for accomplishing this is to begin in a realistic context and then move into the realm of fantasy. For example, in Beatrix Potter's *The Tale of Tom Kitten* (Warne, 1907) she begins, "Once upon a time there were three little kittens, and their names were Mittens, Tom Kitten, and Moppet. They had dear little fur coats of their own; and they tumbled about the doorstep and played in the dust." Nothing unusual about these kittens—kittens often are named by their owners, have fur coats, and tumble about playfully. In fact, Potter's illustration even shows them without clothes and in a realistic setting.

It is only on turning the page that we begin to understand that these kittens may be outside our world of reality. "But one day their mother— Mrs. Tabitha Twitchit—expected friends to tea; so she fetched the kittens indoors, to wash and dress them, before the fine company arrived." Here Potter's illustration shows Mother in a lavender dress, standing upright on her two hind legs, in the doorway of a very fashionable house—a house that appears to be just the right size for a family of felines. Later Mrs. Tabitha (as she is referred to in the book) washes and combs her kittens, dresses them in clean pinafores and tuckers, and puts Tom in a fine blue suit. The rest of the story tells of the mischief the three naughty kittens get into once they are sent outside to wait for their mother's company. The antics of the kittens are not unlike the mischief that some young readers might have gotten into in a similar situation. So even as readers are asked to suspend some beliefs, the text also appeals to the readers' knowledge and their ability to identify with the action and characters in the newly constructed world.

Pam Conrad also used this technique in *Stonewords: A Ghost Story* (HarperCollins, 1990), a novel for older readers. A young girl, Zoe, has been left in the care of her grandparents by her mother. At first, the reader develops empathy for Zoe and feels that she is having a fairly normal childhood with her grandparents— until Zoe finds a playmate. Gradually an awareness comes over the reader that this playmate is really the ghost of a young girl who lived in the house in the 1870s and had perished in a fire that partially destroyed the house. The two girls develop the ability to travel between their two time periods. By then the reader has also moved into the fantastical nature of the story. A strong foundation of reality is laid down before readers are asked to enter the fantasy world. The author builds a logical framework, then develops characters' actions within that framework.

Language

Language is another tool authors use to build believability into the characters in fantasy stories. Animals, inanimate objects, or supernatural beings are routinely given human characteristics (personified). Humans are also placed in fantastical settings. In either case the characters must be presented in such a way as to seem believable in the situation. Elves are sometimes given poetic language to set them off as unique beings, noble and filled with a love of beauty. Other little people who are to be portrayed as cruder than elves might speak with more guttural sounds or at least in words or sounds that are less meaningful to the reader.

Language dialects, vocabulary, and speech rhythms can be used to suggest personalities of characters, a geographical setting, or a specific time period.

Setting

Creating a credible setting contributes to the ability of readers to acknowledge that anything might be possible in the setting described. The description must be thorough enough that the reader might be able to visualize, hear, and feel everything associated with the setting. In the world of *Charlotte's Web* by E. B. White (HarperCollins, 1952), readers are asked to visualize a rather normal farm and later a county fair inhabited by some very unusual animals. By helping us visualize the setting so completely, the author convinces us not only that the actions of the characters are perfectly normal in this realistic setting, but also that the entire plot is credible. Another example of using a realistic setting to set the stage for fantastical events is Jane Yolen's description of a 1940s death camp during the Holocaust, in *The Devil's Arithmetic* (Viking, 1988). The setting is so realistic that readers have little difficulty in following a contemporary girl back through time, through the doorway, and into the Jewish village where her adventure begins.

Point of View

Point of view is determined by the character the author chooses to tell the story. Different points of view can produce very different stories, so this is an important element to consider. Often a fantastical tale seems more believable if the story is told from the point of view of one of the fantastical characters (or a character in a fantasy situation) rather than someone who is looking in from the outside. However, Beatrix Potter successfully uses a storytelling technique that sometimes incorporates the comments of a narrator into the point of view of the main character. Such is the case in *The Tale of Peter Rabbit*. However, in *The Tale of Tom Kitten*, the story is told from the vantage point of a narrator. Thus, there is no hard rule about the point of view from which a story should be told. In the case of Potter's stories, the credibility lies with the narrator, who is pretending that the story is indeed true and is simply sharing the story with readers.

"Traditional" Fantasy

Mimicking the folk or fairy tales from many cultures told through many generations also provides some credibility to tales of fantasy. It is assumed that folklore is based in fact, so when the form is mimicked, the new tale becomes credible in much the same way that the folk literature is accepted as credible. Literary folk literature, by using elements found in traditional folk literature, finds its way into the realm of fantastical literature by virtue of its origin.

Connections for Readers— Elements of Folk Literature

The elements and motifs in traditional folk literature and literary folk literature are virtually in distinguishable. The main difference is that traditional folk literature comes from the oral tradition and cannot be traced to any single author or reteller. Literary folk literature mimics the oral tradition, but in fact can be attributed to a specific author, such as Beatrix Potter, Lloyd Alexander, or Hans Christian Andersen.

Science Fiction or Science Fantasy

One classification system breaks fantasy into six groups: imaginary kingdoms, animal fantasy, toys and dolls, little people, eccentric characters, and strange worlds. To those groups I would add literary folklore. Science fiction is sometimes considered part of the fantasy genre, but because science fiction is based on scientific principles and grounded in reality in terms of what is possible in the real world, I believe it should be considered a separate category. Science fiction often appeals to the more sophisticated and accomplished reader. In general, the appeal of science fiction is more firmly grounded in (and probably more appropriately aimed at) the middle school reader. Little true science fiction is available for the younger reader. Fantasy also appeals to the more sophisticated reader but is frequently also more accessible to the younger reader. In this chapter we will focus on fantasy, excluding for the most part science fiction, although some might argue that some of the titles listed are indeed science fiction. The line between science fantasy and science fiction is thin, and some titles could probably be classified as either. With regard to specific titles, the effort is hardly worth the distinction—but some may argue that point as well.

Beginning a Focus on Books of Fantasy

Serve chamomile tea and fresh bread with blackberry jam and begin this focus by reading aloud *The Tale of Peter Rabbit* by Beatrix Potter (Warne, 1901). Most children have some familiarity with this title, and it will create a discussion starter for examining the characteristics of a story of fantasy and the reality of a situation. If you prefer, select a chapter from a book of fantasy that you particularly enjoy and read it aloud as a discussion starter about the characteristics of fantasy.

Read-Alouds and Discussions

After the general introduction to the focus on fantasy, select a book of fantasy to read aloud. There is no one book that makes a best read-aloud title. Typically a successful read-aloud title will be fast-paced and will have enough action that one is able to hold the listeners' interest from day to day as the story progresses. Suggestions for read-alouds are given in the following section. The read-aloud book should be carefully chosen to interest listeners in reading more books of fantasy, such as those listed in the following section and on pages 83-85.

How the author created a sense of realism before pulling the reader into the fantasy world will be an important discusssion point, as well

as the fantastical elements and the reality elements of the story being read. Setting, behavior of characters, and plot structure should all be viewed in terms of fantasy versus realism.

During the read-aloud sessions, continue to discuss students' views of fantasy and realism. After group discussions and journal writing have been modeled to the whole class, break the class into smaller discussion groups as outlined in the "Reading Workshop Activities" and "Moving to Independent Reading" sections of chapter 1 (see pages 7-13).

Some Great Fantasies to Read Aloud

Armstrong, Jennifer. **Chin Yu Min and the Ginger Cat**. Illustrated by Mary Grandpré. Crown, 1993. Read-aloud audience: grades 3-5; ages 8-10.

A literary folktale, in picture book form, that shows the transformation of the widow Chin Yu Min from an arrogant tyrant to a humble friend. In a village of Kunming there lived an official, Secretary Chin. In the secretary's house were many fine objects: lacquer bowls, lettered scrolls, and many strings of cash. His wife, Chin Yu Min, felt that she deserved all this prosperity. She was proud and haughty and looked down on her servants, making them perform meaningless tasks only to establish her own sense of power. But when Secretary Chin fell out of a boat and drowned, his wife's days of idleness and luxury ended, and she began to realize that she could be a true friend—and that she needed to find her beloved ginger cat.

Bellairs, John. **The Mansion in the Mist**. Dial, 1992. Read-aloud audience: grades 5-8; ages 10-12.

Anthony Monday is invited to go along on a restful summer vacation with his friend, Miss Eells, and her brother, Emerson. The three of them plan to spend time in an old house on a desolate island. When Anthony begins to explore the house, he finds a large chest in a dusty bedroom. Upon opening the chest he discovers that the chest can transport him into another world—the world of Autarchs. That world is both frightening and exciting. Anthony always returns to his own world, but he begins to climb into the chest more and more frequently. Eventually Miss Eells and Emerson find themselves accompanying Anthony into the strange world in search of the logos cube—and the power of the Autarchs. It is that power that threatens to destroy the world.

Connections for Readers— John Bellairs

John Bellairs was born in Marshall, Michigan, a small town filled with strange and enormous old houses. His imagination makes strange things happen in those houses. He wrote a trilogy set in New Zebedee (Marshall): *House with a Clock in Its Walls* (Dial, 1973); *The Figure in the Shadows* (Dial, 1975); and *The Letter, the Witch, and the Ring* (Dial, 1976). Later when Bellairs moved to Haverhill, Massachusetts, near the White Mountains, the mountains provided him with another setting—one he used in many books, beginning with *The Curse of the Blue Figurine* (Dial, 1983). John Bellairs died in the early 1990s.

Brittain, Bill. **The Ghost from Beneath the Sea**. Illustrated by Michele Chessare. HarperCollins, 1992. Read-aloud audience: grades 5-7; ages 10-12.
The historic Parnell House is threatened with destruction until three friends—Tommy, Books, and Harry the Blimp—begin a successful campaign to save the mansion. Then Alonzo Peace steps forward and offers to finance a restoration project so that the town can use the mansion as a museum. Now the entire project is being threatened by Hiram Fixx's claim that his great-great-grandfather actually won the deed to the Parnell House years earlier in a card game on the ill-fated *Titanic*. Fixx intends to transform the historic grounds into an amusement park. If the three friends want to see the museum become

a reality, they must find a way to disprove Fixx's claim to the house.

Carris, Joan. **Howling for Home**. Illustrated by Judith Mitchell. Little, Brown, 1992. Read-aloud audience: grades 3-5; ages 7-10.
Written from the point of view of Beau, a Bernese mountain dog, this story recounts the displeasures Beau feels he must endure while living with his family. He doesn't have any real jobs, such as herding cattle or guarding the homestead. Instead he has to wear a noisy, nasty collar around his neck. Disgusted, Beau sets out to find his old home, but during his journey he begins to realize that his new home is really where he belongs. He returns home with sore feet and a newly developed sense of loyalty.

Conrad, Pam. **Stonewords: A Ghost Story**. HarperCollins, 1990. Read-aloud audience: grades 3-5; ages 8-10.
Zoe's grandparents surround her with love, but it doesn't seem to be enough, as she continually longs for the return of her mother. Soon some of the emptiness is filled by her new friend, Zoe Louise. At first Zoe's grandparents feel that the playmate is imaginary, but there is evidence that she actually exists. Zoe often refers to events that the grandparents recognize as events from the past. Soon it becomes clear that Zoe Louise does live in a time that has passed, and Zoe discovers that she has knowledge of what happened to Zoe Louise. Can Zoe stop the events of the past or is Zoe Louise's fate sealed in history?

Coville, Bruce. **Jennifer Murdley's Toad: A Magic Shop Book**. Illustrated by Gary A. Lippincott. Harcourt, 1992. Read-aloud audience: grades 3-5; ages 7-10.
In this book, the third in Coville's Magic Shop series, fifth-grader Jennifer Murdley purchases a talking toad that leads her into a series of extraordinary adventures. Earlier Magic Shop books include *The Monster's Ring* (Knopf, 1982) and *Jeremy Thatcher, Dragon Hatcher* (Harcourt, 1992), each of which got its start in Mr. Elive's Magic Shop.

Connections for Readers— Bruce Coville

Bruce Coville began writing the Magic Shop books when he created a short story, "The Monster's Ring," for the students he was teaching in Liverpool, New York. Over time the story was refined and polished until it was finally published. Later, Coville thought he would write a collection of short stories originating in Mr. Elive's Magic Shop, but the stories outgrew the short story format, and two have already been published as books.

Dicks, Terrance. **Sally Ann on Her Own**. Illustrated by Blanche Sims. Simon & Schuster, 1992. Read-aloud audience: grades 3-5; ages 7-10.

Mrs. Foster's Day Care Center is home to many stuffed animals. The newest addition is Sally Ann, a rag doll that arrives just in time to overhear two men tell Mrs. Foster that her day care center does not meet certain standards and she will have to close. The only other alternative is to spend a lot of money to bring the house up to the prescribed standards. It isn't long, however, before Mrs. Foster receives an offer to buy the old house. Sally Ann realizes that the two men are not really inspectors and that they hope to scare Mrs. Foster into selling her house cheap. Only when Sally Ann reveals that she can talk and tells Mrs. Foster of her suspicions is the plot uncovered and the day care center saved. All the toys cheer Sally Ann. Other titles about Sally Ann include *Sally Ann and the School Play* (Simon & Schuster, 1992) and *Sally Ann and the Mystery Picnic* (Simon & Schuster, 1993).

Greer, Gery, and Bob Ruddick. **Jason and the Escape from Bat Planet**. Illustrated by Blanche Sims. HarperCollins, 1993. Read-aloud audience: grades 3-5; ages 8-10.

This is the third intergalactic adventure of Jason, Cooper Var, and Lootna, who grapple with General Batso and his evil Demon Bats. The threesome began their adventures in *Jason and the Aliens Down the Street* (HarperCollins, 1991). In that tale, Jason follows his dog into his neighbor's yard and encounters an alien from space. Before he knows it, Jason is invited on a secret mission with Cooper "Coop" Vor and his pet, Lootna, Coop's talking cat. Coop is an Intergalactic Troubleshooter and needs an assistant. Other adventures of the three troubleshooters are told in *Jason and the Lizard Pirates* (HarperCollins, 1992).

Hildick, E. W. **The Case of the Weeping Witch**. Macmillan, 1992. Read-aloud audience: grades 5-7; ages 10-12.

Jack P. McGurk and his five buddies—Joey "Recorder-of-the-Truth" Rockaway, Willie "Sniffer" Sandowsky, Brains "Measurer" Bellingham, Wanda "Climber" Grieg, and Mari "Speaker" Yoshimura—belong to the McGurk Organization. They often meet to discuss what is going on in their community. During an investigation of life more than 300 years ago, the group of friends become involved in the story of witches and the witch hunts that were common at the time. The six have walkie-talkies capable of transporting the youngsters through time. Their first adventure is told in *The Case of the Dragon in Distress* (Macmillan, 1991). This second adventure takes them back 300 years to the days they have been studying. They become acquainted with 13-year-old Hester Bidgood, who is accused of being a witch. Master Peabody and his cohorts are determined to prove that she is a witch and to punish her, but he and his cronies had not counted on Hester receiving the help of the McGurk Organization and their walkie-talkies.

Lindbergh, Anne. **Three Lives to Live**. Little, Brown, 1992. Read-aloud audience: grades 5-7; ages 10-12.

Garet has lived with her Grandmother Atkins, "Gratkins," since she was just two. She arrived with a little ceramic piglet in her dress pocket. Things seem pretty normal until a girl just her age falls out of the laundry chute. Garet can't figure out what is going on, but Gratkins begins to tell everyone that Daisy is her twin sister. Slowly Garet begins to put the pieces together: Daisy has traveled through time via the laundry chute. Garet suspects that Daisy is actually

Gratkins when she was 13 years old and that she has traveled forward 50 years in time (1943-1993). Garet feels that all her problems will be solved if Daisy goes back in time, but when Daisy does leave, Garet begins to question her own origins.

Moving to a Multitude of Books

After listening to a fantasy read-aloud, the class will be ready to move on to reading workshops, discussed in "Moving to Independent Reading" (pages 10-13).

Two of the most popular fantasy writers are David Wisniewski and Betty Ren Wright. Wisniewski writes literary folktales, and Wright authors contemporary ghost stories. Either one of these authors would make an excellent subject for an author focus in connection with fantasy.

The books of Wisniewski can be used on several levels with a wide span of grade levels. Astrid Lindgren writes stories that will appeal to the early intermediate reader. Authors that might be considered for an author focus that will appeal to older intermediate and middle school readers include E. B. White, J. R. R. Tolkien, C. S. Lewis, Lloyd Alexander, Norton Juster, L. Frank Baum, William Sleator, Monica Hughes, and Robert C. O'Brien.

More Fantasies to Read

Amoss, Berthe. **Lost Magic**. Hyperion, 1993. Target audience: grades 5-7; ages 10-12.
Fourteen-year-old Ceridwen, abandoned as an infant, has supported herself as Wise Woman to the lord of the castle. She has learned the lore of herbs and their healing benefits but must continually ward off accusations of witchcraft. But then the plague comes and everyone and everything are threatened. Much real herb lore and knowledge of medieval life are included in this tale.

Banks, Lynne Reid. **The Magic Hare**. Illustrated by Barry Moser. Morrow, 1993. Target audience: grades 3-5; ages 8-10.

Ten stories feature a magic hare reminiscent of Br'er Rabbit and his trickster behavior and humorous ways. The hare shows both valor and kindness as he uses his magic to help people and animals.

Brennan, Herbie. **Emily and the Werewolf**. Illustrated by David Pace. Margaret K. McElderry, 1993. Target audience: grades 3-5; ages 7-10.
Emily is determined to keep Farmer Osboro from turning into a werewolf once again. Her plot to prevent him from doing so includes some help from her grandmother and a book on hypnosis. Fantasy and humor.

Brittain, Bill. **The Wish Giver**. Illustrated by Andrew Glass. HarperCollins, 1986. Target audience: grades 3-5; ages 7-10.
Four people make a visit to the county fair and buy a coupon for one wish from "the wish giver." As the three youngsters each attempt to cash in on their wish, they find that it is taken literally and its fulfillment brings great distress to them and their families. The only chance for the damage to be reversed is if the fourth wish can be used to correct the devastating situation. Literal interpretation of language is an important element in this tale.

Coville, Bruce. **Aliens Ate My Homework**. Illustrated by Katherine Coville. Minstrel, 1993. Target audience: grades 5-7; ages 10-12.
Rod is the older brother to twins. One day as he is babysitting his siblings, aliens crash-land in the papier-mâché he is using for a school project. The ensuing confusion involves Rod, the twins, and the local bully as the aliens attempt to track down an intergalactic fugitive.

Dicks, Terrance. **Sally Ann and the Mystery Picnic**. Illustrated by Blanche Sims. Simon & Schuster, 1993. Target audience: grades 3-5; ages 7-10.
The magical doll, Sally Ann, first introduced in *Sally Ann on Her Own*, comes alive once again. When her young owner gets into a dangerous situation on a river, Sally Ann is there to make the rescue.

Fleischman, Paul. **Graven Images**. Illustrated by Andrew Glass. HarperCollins, 1982. Target audience: grades 5-7; ages 10-12.
Three stories deal with what happens when people put their faith into graven images: a wooden boy, a copper saint, and a marble statue. Prim Miss Frye will lose her son to the sea and her secret to a servant. Nicholas, the apprentice cobbler, will be helped by his patron saint to pursue his courtship of errors. And the spirit of a dead man will show the too-proud stone carver Zorelli that he has feet of clay.

Hooks, William H. **Mean Jake and the Devils**. Illustrated by Dirk Zimmer. Dial, 1981. Target audience: grades 5-7; ages 10-12.
Three devils—Big Daddy Devil, Devil Junior, and Baby Deviline—are outwitted by Mean Jake. Each devil's struggle for power is featured in one of the three tales.

Hughes, Monica. **The Crystal Drop**. Simon & Schuster, 1993. Target audience: grades 5-7; ages 10-12.
The destruction of the ozone layer brings about a devastating drought to western Canada in the year 2011. And when the death of their mother leaves Megan and her little brother alone, the two of them set off across their ruined farm in search of their uncle and the community of Gaia—a fertile community that seems like utopia.

Irving, Washington. **Rip Van Winkle**. Illustrated by Gary Kelley. Creative, 1993. Target audience: grades 3-5; ages 7-10.
The classic tale of a man who falls asleep for 20 years and awakens to a strange new world. The illustrations aptly represent the dark gothic style of the Dutch settlers during the Revolutionary War era.

Jones, Diana Wynne. **Stopping for a Spell: Three Fantasies**. Illustrated by Jos. A. Smith. Greenwillow, 1993. Target audience: grades 5-7; ages 10-12.
These three short stories told with a bit of humor are connected through the theme of unwelcome guests. Included are an animated overstuffed armchair, four grannies undoing a magic spell, and some lively furniture that somehow is involved in "getting rid of Angus Flint."

Kipling, Rudyard. **Just So Stories**. Illustrated by Victor G. Ambrus. Rand McNally, 1982. Target audience: grades 3-5; ages 7-10.
A collection of classic tales in which Kipling explains how the rhinoceros got its tough skin, how the leopard got its spots, and how the bear got its stubby tail.

Koller, Jackie French. **A Dragon in the Family**. Illustrated by Judith Mitchell. Little, Brown, 1993. Target audience: grades 3-5; ages 7-10.
Darek is anxious to earn his father's respect by befriending the baby dragon, Zantor. But the villagers have traditionally viewed dragons as enemies and are not willing to give up fighting to destroy them. Zantor becomes part of Darek's family despite the apprehensions of the family's neighbors.

Lasky, Kathryn. **A Voice in the Wind: A Star-buck Family Adventure**. Harcourt, 1993. Target audience: grades 5-7; ages 10-12.
The Starbuck twins use their telepathic abilities during an adventure-filled trip to New Mexico. They encounter an Anasazi ghost and become entangled with a group of dangerous people who steal Native American artifacts.

Mazer, Anne. **The Oxboy**. Knopf, 1993. Target audience: grades 5-7; ages 10-12.
The offspring of a woman and an ox lives among humans, fearing the day that his ancestry will be revealed. This is an allegory that addresses how people view animals and how differences among humans can be the cause of sorrow and pain.

Nabb, Magdalen. **The Enchanted Horse**. Illustrated by Julek Heller. Orchard, 1993. Target audience: grades 5-7; ages 10-12.
A small toy horse transforms Irina's lonely life. Caring for the toy horse brings her repeated night-time visits from a wonderful live horse. Mystery, loneliness, absorbing love, the power of dreams, and the magical appeal of horses, all woven together, produce a moving winter fantasy.

Russell, Sharman Apt. **The Humpbacked Flute-player**. Knopf, 1994. Target audience: grades 5-7; ages 10-12.

May, 12 years old and homesick, arrives in Phoenix and visits some caves that were thought to have been inhabited by ancient people. When May touches a drawing of a humpbacked flute-player, she and a classmate, Evan, are transported through time into a parallel world. The two youngsters are kept as slaves by a tribe that is described as magical, harsh, and desert-dwelling. The youngsters become embroiled in the tribal struggle for control of the desert.

Scieszka, Jon. **Your Mother Was a Neanderthal**. Illustrated by Lane Smith. Viking Childrens Books, 1993. Target audience: grades 5-7; ages 10-12.

The Time Warp Trio returns in another adventure. This time they are stuck in the year 40,000 B.C. without their clothes, their magic book, or any of the modern gadgets they had intended to bring. Without those gadgets it is difficult to impress the cave people. Joe, Fred, and Sam manage to move from one entanglement to another. Four other titles feature this trio: *The Good, the Bad, and the Ugly* (Viking, 1992), *Not-So-Jolly-Roger* (Viking, 1991), *Knights of the Kitchen Table* (Viking, 1991), and *2095* (Viking, 1995).

Voigt, Cynthia. **Building Blocks**. Atheneum, 1984. Target audience: grades 5-7; ages 10-12.

A young boy plays in his room with building blocks, and as he crawls into the structure he has built, he finds himself transported back to the time when his father was his own age. Viewing his father in his childhood setting enables the boy to develop a more sympathetic view of his father's adult personality. When he is transported back to his own era, it is with renewed awareness and understanding.

Wrede, Patricia. **Calling on Dragons**. Harcourt/ Yolen, 1993. Target audience: grades 5-7+; ages 10-12+.

Morwen the witch attempts to prevent the wizards from keeping the power they have taken from the Enchanted Forest and from King Mendanbar's magic sword. Helping her accomplish the task are Kazul, the King of the Dragons; Princess Cimorene; Telemain the magician; Killer, a rabbit who is transformed into a blue donkey; and two of Morwen's nine sentient cats. Part of the Enchanted Forest Chronicles series.

Author! Author!

David Wisniewski

David Wisniewski was born in Middlesex, England, on March 21, 1953. His family followed his father, a member of the United States Air Force, to bases in Nebraska, Alabama, Germany, Texas, and finally to the Washington, D.C., area, where David enrolled at the University of Maryland. However, it wasn't long before Wisniewski decided he would rather go to clown college, so that is what he did. He spent three years touring with the circus before returning to Washington, where he interviewed for a job with a puppetry theater. He got the job and later married the woman, Donna Harris, who hired him. By 1980 the two had established their own troupe, the Clarion Shadow Puppet Theater, and toured the country from California to Florida, then back to Washington, D.C. The couple's daughter was born in 1981 and their son in 1985. Traveling around the country became more difficult, so David began to use the techniques he'd learned making puppet-show props and scenery to create book illustrations.

Wisniewski created his first book, *The Warrior and the Wise Man*, using silhouettes much like the shadows he created for the puppet plays. Later he began to create depth in his illustrations by using squares of foam behind some of the figures.

Before writing a book, Wisniewski thoroughly researches the culture where the book will be set, immersing himself in the stories, customs, and traditions of the region. Much of what he learns is incorporated into his stories. Thus far, he has set books in Japan, Iceland, West Africa (the Mali culture), Mexico (the Maya civilization), the Pacific Northwest (Tlinglit culture), and 16th century Prague.

David Wisniewski

David Wisniewski combines the art of paper cutting, popular in China for hundreds of years, and once fashionable silhouette art with meticulous research to create beautifully illustrated books of fantasy. He developed his technique creating background scenery and characters for the many shadow puppet shows he and his wife produced, first as employees of the Washington, D.C. Recreation Department, and later for their own Clarion Shadow Theater, which toured throughout the United States. They developed their research and writing skills to facilitate the creation of dramatic tales that would hold the attention of the audience. The intricate cut paper designs helped the couple tell their stories. Wisniewski's writing techniques, like his art, are basically self-taught.

Born in Middlesex, England, while his father was in the U.S. Air Force, David lived with his parents and brother on air bases in various parts of the United States and in England and Germany. The family finally settled in Washington, D.C., where Wisniewski entered high school and split his artistic interests between the visual and the performing arts. He entered the University of Maryland to study drama, but soon discovered that all of the "good" roles went to juniors and seniors. He was not willing to wait that long, so when a recruiter from the Ringling Brothers Circus came to the campus to talk about Clown College, David Wisniewski signed up.

For two years, David Wisniewski traveled with the Ringling Brothers Circus and then spent a year with Circus Vargas before returning to Washington, D.C. At the age of 22 he was hired for the park department's puppet theater troupe by Donna Harris. She taught him about different types of puppetry, and they began to specialize in shadow puppetry. Six months later, Donna Harris and Wisniewski were married, and in 1980 they founded their own shadow theater group, Clarion Shadow Theater, and toured throughout the United States. The preparation of scenery and puppets helped David develop the skills he later used to illustrate his

books of fantasy. More important is that as he wrote the plays the troupe performed, David became familiar with the legends, myths, and folklore from many different countries.

Eventually the Wisniewskis decided, as their daughter was entering school and after their second child was born, that constant traveling was not conducive to family life. Wisniewski did some jobs as a freelance illustrator until a friend suggested that he attend a seminar on children's books. An editor he met there suggested he take his art portfolio to New York City. Wisniewski wrote his first book, *The Warrior and the Wise Man*, just two weeks before he met editor Dorothy Briley, who liked his art and the story and offered to publish it.

Wisniewski always develops the story first and breaks it down to 14 sections; this is to be sure that the story can be contained within a picture book format. The first consideration is the point of the book, its moral. The next task is to identify a culture that will support that moral. The theme of *The Warrior and the Wise Man* was the superiority of wisdom over brute force. The medieval Japanese culture, with its wise and patient Buddhist monks and fierce samurai knights, seemed to be a good backdrop for that theme. By contrasting the actions of twin sons of the emperor—one a monk, the other a samurai knight—Wisniewski felt the strength versus patience and wisdom theme could emerge. Once the culture has been identified, Wisniewski researches the culture and develops a story that *could* have occurred in the chosen time and place.

Before he begins writing, Wisniewski spends an average of two to three months researching the background of the story. Once the story is developed and the illustrations sketched, he must do more research to help him flesh out the details of his illustrations. Wisniewski always begins his research in the children's section of the library. He finds that nonfiction for children is much easier to scan for focus areas than adult books. Later he moves to the adult section of the library and finally on to specialized libraries.

Because he lives near Washington, D.C., he is also able to visit the Smithsonian and consult with the cultural attachés of embassies. When he was researching the background of the Maya culture for *Rain Player,* Wisniewski consulted magazines such as *National Geographic* and *Scientific American* and read Maya folktales, and found that the Mayan gods were similar to Greek gods in that they interacted with humans and were fallible. In one Maya folktale, a servant got into trouble because he swept all the frogs (the god Chac's messengers) from the god's house. The servant also emptied water out of a gourd and flooded the whole earth. Wisniewski used each of these elements in *Rain Player*.

Wisniewski's illustrations fill in the gaps created when the reader or listener is unfamiliar with the culture surrounding the folktale. In other words, a storyteller from the original culture would assume the listeners knew what the characters wore and what games they played, because the stories come from a familiar time and place. But Wisniewski is telling stories to new cultures, so both his writing and his illustrations contribute to the audience's understanding of other cultures.

When David Wisniewski is not writing or working on illustrations, he enjoys visiting schools, reading, playing an occasional round of "X-Wing" (a Star Wars flight simulator game), and—if he is alone—playing the guitar.

Books by David Wisniewski

Elfwyn's Saga. Illustrated by David Wisniewski. Lothrop, 1980. Target audience: grades 3-5; ages 7-10.
Gorm the Grim puts a curse on Anlaf Haraldsson and his clan, which has settled in the lush green coastal valley of 10th-century Iceland. Gorm, a Viking warrior, wants the valley for himself and his men, but Anlaf's clan claims it first. The curse causes Anlaf's daughter, Elfwyn, to be born blind, but she is protected by the hidden folk of the valley. When Gorm delivers a large crystal to Anlaf and his clan as a peace gesture, only Elfwyn recognizes the gesture as an effort to bring stagnation and ruin to the clan. It is up to Elfwyn to destroy the crystal and bring reason

back to the clan. The story explains the origin of the northern lights.

The Golem. Illustrated by David Wisniewski. Clarion, 1996. Target audience: grades 3-5; ages 7-10.
The setting for this literary legend is 16th-century Prague. Wisniewski retells this tale from traditional sources adding his own embellishments to provide a thought-provoking tale of a supernatural force used to save an opposed people. More than 400 years ago, a Jewish teacher and scholar, Rabbi Loew, shaped a larger-than-life man of clay (a golem). When Rabbi Loew brought the golem to life, it was with the intent that he should protect the Jewish people from their enemies. When that task was completed, the Golem was returned to the earth and was not to return until the desperate need for justice comes again.

Rain Player. Illustrated by David Wisniewski. Clarion, 1991. Target audience: grades 3-5; ages 7-10.
Divinely inspired charts and calendars ruled the people of the ancient Maya culture, and those charts rule the characters in this tale. The charts have predicted a terrible drought, and all resign themselves to that fate—all except Pik, a young Maya boy, who challenges belief in the charts when he wagers the survival of the tribe on a game of pok-a-tok with the rain god, Chac. Pik struggles against the odds and succeeds in saving his people from the drought that is destroying their food supply.

Sundiata: Lion King of Mali. Illustrated by David Wisniewski. Clarion, 1992. Target audience: grades 3-5; ages 7-10.
This story is not a literary folktale; technically it is a biography of the 13th-century king Sundiata, who lived in western Africa. Because the history of this time and region was preserved through the stories of the griots (storytellers), much of what has been recorded has elements of fantasy. There is talk of spells, sorcerer kings who overthrow legitimate rulers, and unexplained recovery from severe physical handicaps. The tale is that of a powerful king, Sundiata, who despite his severe handicap is designated by his father to inherit the kingdom

of Mali. Sundiata is forced into exile, but when he reaches adulthood he is summoned back to his homeland to overthrow a sorcerer king. The author's note in this book, and a book by Patricia and Fredrick McKissack, *The Royal Kingdoms of Ghana, Mali, and Songhay: Life in Medieval Africa* (Holt, 1994), will help in the discussion of the elements of reality in this tale.

The Warrior and the Wise Man. Illustrated by David Wisniewski. Lothrop, 1989. Target audience: grades 3-5; ages 7-10.

A quest devised by the Japanese emperor will determine which of the emperor's twin sons will inherit the ancient kingdom. Tozaemon is the greatest warrior in the land. His brother, Toemon, is the wisest man in the land. The task before them is to retrieve the five eternal elements. The brother who returns first shall become the next emperor. One son retrieves the items by force and angers the armies of the land, while the other uses patience and kindness. The warrior returns first but the angry armies are at the gates demanding retribution for the damage he has done; they can be turned back only through the wisdom of the gentle and wise Toemon.

The Wave of the Sea-Wolf. Illustrated by David Wisniewski. Clarion, 1994. Target audience: grades 3-5; ages 7-10.

The setting for this book is the Tlingit culture of the Pacific Northwest coast of North America. Tlingit history and myth contributed facts and motifs for this story of the princess Kchokeen whose guardian spirit is the Sea-Wolf. The Sea-Wolf rescues Princess Kchokeen from drowning and later helps her summon a great wave and save her people from hostile strangers. Attacks by foreign traders on Native American peoples who attempted to resist their aggression are documented facts, as is the presence of *tsunami*, the huge tidal waves regarded by the Tlingit to be a manifestation of the spirits. The action and adventure in this story are, however, the fantastic creations of the author.

Author! Author!

Betty Ren Wright

Betty Ren Wright was only eight years old when she began her writing career by copying poems into a notebook with her name emblazoned on the cover. She continued writing through high school and college, when she began to submit articles to publishers. As an adult she began to work for Western Publishing Company as an editor and wrote children's books at night. In 1978 she began to write books full time. Since 1981, Wright has written a novel a year. Among her books are *The Dollhouse Murders*, *A Ghost in the Window*, *The Pike River Phantom*, and *The Ghost Comes Calling*.

Born in Michigan on June 15, 1927, Wright soon moved with her parents to Milwaukee, Wisconsin, where she grew up. She was only five when her father died. Her mother became a teacher and taught for 30 years. Two years before Betty Ren Wright became a full-time writer, she married George Fredericksen, and three grown stepchildren (with families of their own) became part of her family. The Fredericksens live in a house near Lake Michigan built in the late 1800s. They enjoy traveling, hiking, reading, and entertaining friends and family.

Betty Ren Wright

Betty Ren Wright was born in Wakefield, Michigan, on June 15, 1927, but her family soon moved to Milwaukee. Her father, a high school teacher, died suddenly when Betty was five years old. Betty's mother, while struggling to make ends meet, returned to college to earn a teaching degree; she taught fourth-graders for 30 years.

As a 14-year-old, Betty Ren Wright lost a year of school when she had to be put in a head-to-toe plaster cast to correct a spinal curvature. Later she attended Milwaukee-Downer College and graduated in 1949. Shortly after her graduation she became associated with the Western Publishing Company as a children's book editor. She spent her evenings writing. In 1976, at the age of 49, she married George Fredericksen and moved from her small city apartment to a 100-year-old house near Lake Michigan. Her small family grew to include three grown stepchildren and five (now eight) stepgrandchildren.

In 1978, two years after her marriage, Wright retired from her editor's position to become a full-time writer. At first she thought she would write adult books, but once she tried writing a children's novel she became hooked. Her first book, *Getting Rid of Marjorie*, was based on situations she felt could have happened had her new family been anything but warm and welcoming.

The plot in *The Dollhouse Murders* developed from her experiences on two different afternoons. She spent the first afternoon with a friend who was cleaning a dollhouse. The friend's dollhouse was an exact miniature of her grandparents' Victorian home. As they cleaned and dusted the house and its furnishings, Wright's friend shared many of her memories. Wright concluded that if the house held so many memories, it must also hold ghosts. During the second afternoon, Wright observed two brothers—one of whom was mentally handicapped—sharing a picnic lunch at a roadside park. This relationship was the subject of several short stories Wright wrote, but she wanted to deal with the topic in a full-length novel. The two afternoons contributed to the plot of *The Dollhouse Murders*.

The Fredericksens enjoy fishing for muskellunge (pike) in the waters of northern Wisconsin. Sometimes they do manage to catch the "big one"—the giant fish mentioned in *A Ghost in the Window* actually hangs on one of the walls in their house. Between novels, in addition to fishing, Wright enjoys working on other writing projects, traveling, and gardening. Together the Fredericksens hike (they live at the end of a country road with trees and fields all around them), do a lot of reading, and play with their pets, a dog and a cat. When Wright is writing, her husband, a painter, is often at his easel. At times they take their breaks together and discuss how their work is going—and sometimes if it isn't going so well they continue their break and go outside for a while. The Fredericksens' home is near Kenosha, Wisconsin.

Books by Betty Ren Wright

Christina's Ghost. Holiday, 1985. Target audience: grades 3-5; ages 7-10.
When Christina goes to spend the summer with her grandmother, she takes ill and must stay in an isolated Victorian house with her grumpy uncle Ralph. There are no children nearby to play with, her uncle seems to dislike her, and she is miserable. It isn't long, though, until Christina sees the ghostly figure of a small boy. Before she can talk to him he disappears. Christina is convinced that the ghost has something to do with the murders that took place in the house 30 years earlier. What she discovers in the attic is so chilling that even Uncle Ralph gets involved in the ghost hunt. Two very different people become friends in this suspenseful tale of the supernatural.

The Dollhouse Murders. Holiday, 1983. Target audience: grades 3-5; ages 7-10.
Amy and her mentally handicapped sister discover a strange dollhouse in their aunt's attic. Soon the girls discover that the dollhouse holds

more than play furniture. In the middle of the night it is filled with a ghostly light and the girls find that the dolls have moved about. The strange occurrences help Amy and her sister discover the mystery that surrounded the grisly murders that took place years before.

A Ghost in the Window. Holiday, 1987. Target audience: grades 3-5; ages 7-10.
Meg, whose dreams have been coming true, fears her nightmare will as well. It seems that a man who died in a car crash after allegedly stealing $50,000 from a bank tries to communicate with the family through Meg's dream. Sequel to *The Secret Window*.

The Ghost of Ernie P. Holiday, 1990. Target audience: grades 3-5; ages 7-10.
When Ernie P. Barber moves from Los Angeles to Treverton, he is trouble waiting to happen. He chooses Jeff as his best friend without Jeff having much choice in the matter. Ernie P. was always promising to cut Jeff in on his "T.S.P."— his top secret plan. But when Ernie P. has been in Treverton just three months, a freak accident takes his life, and he comes back to haunt Jeff. Newspaper clippings mysteriously appear, and Jeff becomes convinced that Ernie P. wants him to carry out the T.S.P. alone. But Jeff doesn't even know what the plan really is, and he doesn't find out until he faces a dangerous situation and gets the courage to stand up to the ghost of Ernie P.

The Ghost of Popcorn Hill. Illustrated by Karen Ritz. Holiday, 1993. Target audience: grades 3-5; ages 7-10.
Martin and Peter live on top of Popcorn Hill. They long for a dog and find that their cabin is haunted by a lonely ghost. They get a lively and active dog, Rosie, but she is not as desirable as the big sheepdog that roams about outside the cabin. Soon, however, the boys find out that the sheepdog is a ghost. Since the dog seems as lonely as the ghost they had encountered earlier, they bring the ghosts together and in the process learn to appreciate their own dog. A short chapter book.

Ghost Witch. Illustrated by Ellen Eagle. Holiday, 1993. Target audience: grades 3-5; ages 7-10.
Jenny and her mother have inherited a house that is said to be inhabited by a ghost of a previous occupant, and Jenny encounters the ghost several times. Eventually an encounter on Halloween brings Jenny and the ghost to a resolution. The ghost will relocate, and Jenny and her mother will continue to live in the house.

Ghosts Beneath Our Feet. Holiday, 1984. Target audience: grades 3-5; ages 7-10.
During a summer in an old abandoned mining town, Katie must deal with her rebellious stepbrother—and with ghosts that seem to be literally beneath their feet. Katie is terrified and puzzled when a crippled ghost-girl appears in an abandoned mine. Katie and her stepbrother team up to probe the past to discover why the ghosts are in the mine.

The Ghosts of Mercy Manor. Scholastic, 1993. Target audience: grades 3-5; ages 7-10.
Gwen, an orphan, intends to remain aloof but finds that she is beginning to like her foster family in spite of herself. But she remains disturbed about the ghostly figures she and Tessie continue to encounter. Gwen senses that her foster mother knows something about the figures, but she evades the subject each time Gwen brings it up. A suspenseful fantasy.

Haunted Summer. Scholastic, 1996. Target audience: grades 3-5; ages 7-10.
Left alone with her older brother and a babysitter, nine-year-old Abby discovers that their house is haunted by a ghost. The ghost is attempting to reclaim a stolen music box.

Nothing but Trouble. Drawings by Jacqueline Rogers. Holiday, 1995. Target audience: grades 3-5; ages 7-10.
Vannie's parents must travel to California in search of work, and Vannie and her pet dog, Muffy, must stay with a cranky great-aunt on an old farm in Ohio. Vannie attempts to make the best of things, but there is nothing but trouble.

Out of the Dark. Scholastic, 1995. Target audience: grades 3-5; ages 7-10.

The nightmares begin when Jessica moves to her grandmother's childhood home and makes friends with the handicapped girl next door. The nightmares take Jessica to the old schoolhouse in the woods; she is puzzled why the dreams include the old schoolhouse and why she is the one having the nightmares.

The Pike River Phantom. Holiday, 1988. Target audience: grades 3-5; ages 7-10.

Thirteen-year-old Rachel and her cousin Charlie become linked to the mysterious ghost of a fierce old woman when Charlie realizes that the woman is eerily involved in the dreams Rachel has been having about the upcoming Sunbonnet Queen contest. Miserable because he has been tagged a troublemaker (his father is an ex-convict), Charlie considers running away to California but changes his mind when he realizes that he must try to save Rachel from the strange and mad phantom.

Rosie and the Dance of the Dinosaurs. Holiday, 1989. Target audience: grades 3-5; ages 7-10.

Rosie has only nine fingers but finds that there are situations where nine fingers are a positive attribute. She is a pianist who must cope with her physical handicap as well as deal with her father's absence when he leaves the family to find a new job in a distant city.

The Scariest Night. Holiday, 1991. Target audience: grades 3-5; ages 7-10.

Erin Lindsay delights in being the much-loved only child of schoolteacher parents. Everything is just how she wants it until nine-year-old Cowper moves in. Cowper, whose parents were killed in a car accident, is a musical prodigy, and Erin's parents become his adoptive parents. Erin's parents seem to be obsessed with making Cowper happy and have little time left for Erin. In fact, the family is spending the summer in an apartment in Milwaukee so that Cowper can take piano lessons at the conservatory. Erin is away from her friends, bored, and jealous—but all that changes when she meets a senior citizen and medium, Molly Panca. Erin's experiences give her the "scariest night of her life."

The Secret Window. Holiday, 1982. Target audience: grades 3-5; ages 7-10.

Meg is disturbed by her dreams, which seem to be coming true. She needs help to understand that her extrasensory perception is a gift that can help others. And she does learn that her ability to see into the future can be useful. *A Ghost in the Window* is a sequel to this title.

Going Beyond

Fantasies will often attract the more able readers, those who can imagine the magical settings created by fantasy writers. It is critical that readers are not only able to read the words in books of fantasy but are also able to conceptualize the images and situations presented. Fantasy provides many opportunities for readers to go beyond what they know and to combine new ideas with old. For example, the Frog and Toad titles by Arnold Lobel are effective introductions to fantasy, because young readers identify with the animal characters and do not regard them as such. Intermediate readers, who enter the genre by reading the tales of James Howe, *Bunnicula: A Rabbit-Tale of Mystery* (Atheneum, 1979) and *Hot Fudge* (Morrow, 1990), regard them as talking animal tales, seeming to reserve the label "fantasy" for such titles as those by John Bellairs, who writes of ghosts, spirits, and magical time clocks. Time machines and fantastical animals clearly signal the fantasy genre to most readers. Some readers (especially young readers, and those who deal most successfully with concrete elements) will regard anything they read as being something that *could* happen. Some suggestions for activities that will focus on the real versus the imaginary follow.

Fantasy Activity

- Read a chapter from a book of fantasy and make two parallel lists, one of events from the story that *could* actually happen and one of things that could not happen in the world as we know it.

- Discuss the type of fantasy book the book being read is: talking animal, literary folktale, time warp, etc.

- As a class, create an imaginary world inhabited by imaginary characters. Create a society for the characters, establish living units (will they live in family groups as we know them or perhaps they will live in like age groups), and propose a setting. Integrate the book into other areas of the curriculum by devising a structure of government and creating a numerical system (ours is a base 10, computers use base 2).

- Create a fantasy museum. In the museum include objects from some of the stories, such as the "monster ring" from Bruce Coville's *The Monster's Ring*, the hard round ball used in Pik's pok-a-tok game from David Wisniewski's *Rain Player*, or the dollhouse from Betty Ren Wright's *The Dollhouse Murders*.

- Establish a fantasy club. Hold regular meetings and either read books of fantasy or tell fantastic stories. Children should practice their presentations before sharing them with the class. The club should be more of a performance opportunity than a "show-and-tell."

Culminating the Focus on Fantasy

A culminating session need not be elaborate; it only needs to bring to closure the official classroom focus on fantasy. General ideas for culminating activities are discussed in chapter 1 (page 14). A first meeting of the Fantasy Club could provide the culmination to the focus, or perhaps just some time to share fantasy books spontaneously. A few students might wish to read nonfiction books on magic and to culminate the focus with a magic show. The following four pages may be reproduced for student use in conjunction with this focus on fantasy.

Fantasy
Reader's Journal

My Name: _____

Response Starter Suggestions

Your fantasy reading journal is intended for your ideas, your thoughts, your questions about vocabulary, or questions and comments about the plot and characters in the book or chapter you have just read. Sometimes it is difficult to get started, so the following questions might provide you with an idea to help you begin. These questions are only suggestions; the journal is yours and should contain the questions and comments about the parts of the book that you are interested in.

- How did the author make you feel as if the book were realistic?
- At what point did you think that the book might be one of fantasy?
- What techniques did the author use to make the story credible?
- What elements in the story were fantastical—for example, the setting, characters, actions?
- How is the characters' behavior similar to your behavior, or how is their behavior fantastical?
- Explain how the setting is based in reality or how it is fantastical.
- Does the author describe the setting in a realistic or accurate way?
- Describe the point of view from which the story is told. Is that point of view consistent with the details, sights, feelings, and physical reactions to the actions in the plot?
- Did the author foreshadow any events to come?
- If the book includes animal characters, describe the balance between reality and fantasy by identifying the human characteristics and the animal characteristics attributed to each of the animals.
- What does this story make you think of?
- Thinking about the characters in the story, do any of them make you think of someone you know?

Date your journal entry each time you write in it. Responses mean more later if you use complete sentences.

Have fun and enjoy your reading.

Fantasy Books I Have Read

Title	Author
1.	
2.	
3.	
4.	
5.	
6.	
7.	
8.	
9.	
10.	
11.	
12.	
13.	
14.	
15.	
16.	
17.	
18.	
19.	
20.	

Fantasy Books I Want to Read

Title	Author
1.	
2.	
3.	
4.	
5.	
6.	
7.	
8.	
9.	
10.	
11.	
12.	
13.	
14.	
15.	
16.	
17.	
18.	
19.	
20.	

Biographies

> I began early trying to figure out what my life would be like if I were someone else.
> I think I've been doing that ever since, which explains why
> I write biographies and why I think it's important for everyone to
> imagine themselves in the shoes of other people.
>
> —Jean Fritz (1987)

Biographies allow young readers to explore the lives of other people and the times in which they lived—in a small way, to walk in the shoes of another person. The best biographies present characters honestly, showing both their strengths and their frailties. They do not resort to negative stereotyping based on gender, race, ethnicity, or physical ability. Although the historical setting and the style in which the book is written are important, the primary focus of a biography must be on its subject and the people who influenced him or her.

Biography— An Introduction

Although historical figures are often the subject of biographies, interesting or noteworthy contemporary figures from current events and fields of endeavor, as well as well-known figures from the worlds of entertainment, politics, and history are also the subjects of biographies. Biographies are not limited to famous individuals; good biographies may be written about anyone who has done something of interest or has made a significant contribution to the world or the lives of individuals. For example, Kate Shelley is the subject of two biographies: *Kate Shelley and the Midnight Express* by Margaret K. Wetterer (Carolrhoda, 1990) and *Kate Shelley: Bound for Legend* by Robert D. San Souci (Dial, 1994). Shelley was only a young girl when she risked her life crawling across a dangerous railroad trestle to alert a station master

that a bridge was out. Her heroic actions saved a trainload of passengers and presented Shelley as a model of courage and unselfishness. It was Shelley's influence on others that made her an appropriate biography subject.

Other biographies focus on people who became famous for their accomplishments. Subjects of successful biographies range from artists to politicians to inventors to many others. Biographies about notable subjects generally fall into two categories: those that cover the entire life of the subject from birth to death (or birth to present), and those that focus on accomplishments, giving little information about the subject's youth or private life. For example, a biography of Abraham Lincoln such as Ingri and Edgar Parin d'Aulaire's *Abraham Lincoln* (Doubleday, 1939) deals with his childhood, his years as a lawyer in Illinois, and his presidency. In contrast, Russell Freedman's *Lincoln: A Photobiography* (Clarion, 1987) deals primarily with Lincoln's years as president.

There are also two types of biographical subjects: those whose influence and accomplishments will endure through generations, and those whose major claim to fame is their present popularity or notoriety. For example, Eleanor Roosevelt, the subject of Russell Freedman's photobiography, *Eleanor Roosevelt: A Life of Discovery* (Clarion, 1993), was the first presidential wife to have a public life and a career of her own. She is a woman whose accomplishments have stood through several generations. On the other hand, another first lady, Barbara Bush, the subject of Arleen McGrath Heiss's *Barbara Bush* (Chelsea, 1992), was an interesting subject and a strong literacy advocate during her husband's presidency, but interest in her has diminished since the end of her husband's presidency. Other subjects of fleeting interest are often movie stars, sports figures, popular musicians, politicians, and people who, for one reason or another, make national news.

Historical Fiction or Biography?

There is sometimes some confusion as to what is fiction, especially historical fiction, and what is biography. While there are elements common to both historical fiction and biography, there are also some distinct differences. Both historical fiction and biographies of historical figures help readers experience the past and empathize with the hardships, dangers, joys, and conflicts of another time. For example, we can read about the Civil War and memorize the battles, the dates, and the statistics. But we need to put ourselves in the place of someone who actually lived during those times to see the human costs of the war and develop a deeper understanding of historical events.

Historical fiction and biography also help readers understand the effect historical figures have or have had on the destiny of others and on future events. Readers are able to compare the past with the present, to recognize past errors in judgment, and to better appreciate the struggles and interdependence of all people.

The confusion between historical fiction and biography comes when authors use accurate historical facts, as do James Lincoln Collier and Christopher Collier, but create fictional characters to carry the story. While the characters in historical fiction are based on real people, most never actually lived. Dialogues might be accurate in spirit but are not verifiable using authenticated sources. On the other hand, biographies use real characters, and while most biographers no longer construct dialogue, some do. The line between the genres becomes more blurred as authors of historical fiction strive to become as accurate as possible and as authors of biographies attempt to create the most readable story possible—often approaching the style of a completely narrative text carried by dialogue.

Jean Fritz has at times referred to those biographies that include constructed dialogue as "old-fashioned," and she does not invent dialogue. She uses dialogue only when she can document it. Present-day standards no longer tolerate those who surmise facts or who make up dialogue for the sake of the narration. Fritz says that if the subject is interesting enough and worthy of being a biographical subject, readers will not need "facts dressed up in fictional trimmings." Today's biographies demand total truth and accuracy. Dialogue must be based on actual records of the subjects' lives and activities. Quotes must be used only when they are verifiable through primary sources such as letters, diaries, historical documents created at the time of the event, or recorded conversations and dialogues.

There is at least one recent and notable exception to the "no invented dialogue rule." Andrea Davis Pinkney created dialogue for her biography of *Alvin Ailey* (Hyperion, 1993). To alert readers to that fact, she inserted a disclaimer, which reads: "*Alvin Ailey* is a biographical narrative history based on the actual events that occurred during Alvin Ailey's lifetime. The individuals, places, dates, and dance numbers cited throughout are real. Dialogue has been created to weave the story together." And although the Library of Congress Cataloging states that the book must carry a 792.8 call number (the Dewey decimal category for dance), the subject headings included also indicate that the book is biography. Although some might argue that *Alvin Ailey* would be more accurately classified as historical fiction, it received outstanding reviews from *Booklist*, *Publishers Weekly*, *School Library Journal*, and the *New York Times Book Review*. However, this biography's treatment of dialogue is an exception to current trends favoring complete authenticity.

Terms and Techniques in Biography Writing

Characterization

The ability to characterize the biographical subject is perhaps the most important requirement for creating a good biography. Characterization enables the reader to empathize with the feelings and thoughts of the subject and learn who the person really was or is.

Historical Accuracy

Much research must go into the writing of a book of biography, whether it is written for children or for adults. Errors in children's biographies, according to Ann W. Moore,[1] fall into three basic categories: factual errors such as dates and names, which can easily be checked in basic reference sources; statements that misrepresent the facts—often due to the author's efforts to simplify the information; and blatantly false or incorrect information. Moore stresses the need for biography writers to be accurate in their writing.

During speeches to librarians and teachers, Russell Freedman speaks frequently of the extensive research he conducts prior to writing about a subject. And in her autobiography, *Surprising Myself* (Richard C. Owen, 1992), Jean Fritz tells about her research efforts to find information relating to James Madison before writing *The Great Little Madison* (Putnam, 1989). She went to James Madison's home in Virginia and took notes on everything she saw. She climbed the same steps where Madison once stood and looked out over his plantation. Whenever she writes about a person, Fritz travels to places where they lived or visited.

Biographers must be aware of the many reference books available to verify facts, because everything—including weather, dates of birth, and other significant events—must be verified. For example, in Iowa any weather-related information since 1953 can be found in a periodical publication, *Climatological Data for Iowa*. Prior to 1953, information about weather could be located in newspapers of the times, many of which have been preserved on microfilm and can be accessed quite readily in local libraries. Many other specialized reference books are available in larger public libraries or college research libraries. Primary sources such as journals, diaries, letters, and other such documents are often collected in research libraries. But if the subject of the biography is not so famous (or infamous), such documents might be in the possession of private parties who might allow the author access to them. Producing an accurate manuscript demands that authors make every effort to locate all available information.

Accuracy in biographies goes beyond the mere verification of dates, facts, and events. Omissions can also make a biography less than truthful. For instance, many of the earlier biographies of Benjamin Franklin failed to mention that Franklin had a son before he married Deborah Read. Even early editions of the *World Book Encyclopedia* make no mention of the fact that Franklin had another son by a mistress (though no one seems to know who the woman was), and other biographers do not even mention the existence of this son. Jean Fritz included information about the son in the author's notes she included at the end of *What's the Big Idea, Ben Franklin?* (Coward, 1976). In their Caldecott Award-winning *Abraham Lincoln* (Doubleday, 1939), Ingri and Edgar Parin d'Aulaire ignored totally Lincoln's assassination. The final page of the book shows Lincoln sitting in a rocking chair with his son, Tad, at his side. The text on the opposite page tells about the end of the Civil War and concludes, "Then he sat down on his rocking chair to rest. He had done what he should do. He had held together the great nation brought forth upon this continent by his forefathers." No mention is made that Lincoln's life ended a short time later by assassination. Such omissions leave readers with a less-than-complete picture of the subject's life.

Language or Dialect

Language or dialect in a biography must be consistent with the time and place in which the subject lived and the subject's education and background. These criteria would determine whether a small stream running through a field would be referred to as a "creek" or a "crick" and whether bacon is cooked in a "frying pan" or "skillet." However, sometimes an author must simplify the dialect or language to make it more accessible to readers.

Honesty

In his Newbery acceptance speech for *Lincoln: A Photobiography* (Clarion, 1987), Russell Freedman spoke of the changes in the way biographies are written. He noted that in the early part of the 1900s, biographers often avoided revealing the misdeeds or misdirected motives of their subjects. "The hero worship of the past has given way to a more realistic approach, which recognizes the warts and weaknesses that humanize the great."[2] The change seemed to come in the late 1960s and early 1970s. Along with exposing those "warts and weaknesses," today's biographers attempt to tell their stories without fictionalization and "adhere as closely to documented evidence as any scholarly work. And the best of them [biographers] manage to do so without becoming tedious or abstract or any less exciting than the most imaginative fictionalization."[3]

Equal Representation

Also changing is the ratio of biographies about women and minorities to those about men. Biographers often presented subjects that they believed were moral examples for young readers; not only did they protect the children from the subjects' weaknesses and misdeeds, but they also chose only those subjects whose accomplishments they deemed worthy. The achievements and lives of most women and minorities were not generally valued as much as the lives of the men who dominated the social and political world. Nonwhite people were, for the most part, considered too unimportant and too controversial to be viable subjects for a biography for children. In an effort to change those outdated attitudes, many authors are beginning to focus on women and minorities. However, many of the accomplishments of minorities do not appear in written records, and it is sometimes difficult to locate enough accurate and factual information to warrant a biography about a single subject. Collective biographies allow authors to group several short biographies in a thematically connected collection. Examples of collective biographies include *Mistakes That Worked* by Charlotte Foltz Jones (Doubleday, 1991), which includes a biographical chapter about George Crum, a Native American chef who created the potato chip while trying to please a difficult customer, and *Famous Asian Americans* by Janet Nomura Morey and Wendy Dunn (Cobblehill, 1992).

Biographies for Every Age

Many experts in children's literature observe that the ability to read and comprehend biographies closely correlates with the general stages of reading. Early primary readers are learning the conventions of reading (reading from left to right, attaching the same sound to the same word), learning to decode words, and later confirming their ability to decode. Intermediate readers begin to read for information, and middle school readers begin to read with a view toward a world or global view of the material. Similar stages are evident as children read biographies. Primary-age children are characteristically egocentric, and if they are able to relate at all, they relate best to characters and experiences closely connected to their own world—that is, to children their same age or to events in the present. They do not easily put themselves into the lives, time periods, or situations that ask them to identify with adult concerns and perceptions. At about the age of eight, readers begin to look beyond themselves and can begin to understand and identify with subjects of biographies if the subjects are people who interest them and if the biographies are interestingly written and have a direct connection to their own lives. Students in the intermediate grades begin to explore other perspectives and situations in terms of time periods, cultures, history, and beliefs. Once students enter middle school and junior high, their interest in a person's life and what motivates that person increases. Reading stages should be considered when choosing biographies for young readers.

Again, biographies of contemporary subjects are more comprehensible to younger readers. If they can connect to situations and events that are part of their world, they can better understand the lives of the subjects. As readers move into other reading stages—reading for information and reading for a worldview—they also move into those same stages in connection with the reading of biographies.

Beginning a Focus on Biographies

Introduce the focus on biography by reading aloud from one of the shorter recommended biographies in the following section. Explain that a biography is a book written (graphy) about a person's life (bio). An autobiography is a book written about oneself (auto). In most school libraries and in many small public libraries, biographies are cataloged in a unique manner. In the Dewey decimal system they are technically considered a 900 book since they deal with the history of people. Most of these books are given a numerical call number with an author designation below. Often that author designation would be the first three letters of the author's last name. However, most readers who wish to locate a biography or autobiography are more interested in the subject of the biography, so the Dewey decimal classification has been modified to remove biographies and autobiographies from the 900s and to place them in a special section with a "B" designation. The second line of the call number is the first three letters of the subject's last name. Thus, all the biographies about Benjamin Franklin would be shelved together by *Fra*. Collective biographies (that is, a collection of chapters about individuals whose lives have a common connection) are

still shelved in the 900 area of the library media center.

Read-Alouds and Discussions

Carefully select a biography to read aloud to the entire class. Introduce the biography by providing tantalizing glimpses into the life of the subject and sharing some information about his or her accomplishments. The subject's life must be of enough interest that you will be able to capture the interest of the listeners as the book progresses chapter by chapter over a series of days. Several suggestions for novel-length selections are given in the following section.

The general procedures for using a read-aloud title to initiate and model discussions are outlined in chapter 1 (see pages 5-6). After group discussion and journal writing have been modeled to the whole class, using the common read-aloud, break the class into smaller discussion groups as outlined in the "Reading Workshop Activities" and "Moving to Independent Reading" sections of chapter 1 (see pages 7-13). Students might be interested in reading books about people who lived during the same era or biographies about the same person written by different authors. The many books by Jean Fritz profiling Revolutionary War figures are good examples of books that might be read from the same era.

Some Great Biographies to Read Aloud

Adler, David A. **A Picture Book of Rosa Parks**. Illustrated by Robert Casilla. Holiday, 1993. Picture Book Biography series. Read-aloud audience: grades 3-5; ages 7-10.
It was Rosa Parks who, by refusing to give up her seat on a Montgomery, Alabama, bus, became the catalyst for the bus boycott considered by many to be the beginning of the modern-day civil rights struggle. Parks's role in the boycott and her later work for African Americans' civil rights are included in this biography. Titles in Adler's series feature Frederick Douglass, Anne Frank, Benjamin Franklin, Thomas Jefferson, Martin Luther King Jr., and others.

Connections for Readers— Rosa Parks

Rosa Parks now lives in Detroit, Michigan, where she continues to work with the Rosa & Raymond Parks Institute to achieve equality for all people. Anyone wanting to know more about Parks's work in this area may contact the Rosa & Raymond Parks Institute at 65 Cadillac Square, Detroit, MI 48226.

Ferris, Jeri. **Native American Doctor: The Story of Susan LaFlesche Picotte**. Carolrhoda Books, 1991. Trailblazers series. Read-aloud audience: grades 5-7; ages 10-12.
Susan LaFlesche Picotte was an Omaha Indian who became one of the first Native Americans to earn a medical degree when women doctors were few and Native American doctors were even fewer. Picotte lived and worked among her people, the Omahas, on the reservation until her own health forced her to resign as reservation doctor. Later she was instrumental in having a hospital built on the reservation.

Fritz, Jean. **The Great Little Madison**. Putnam, 1989. Read-aloud audience: grades 5-7; ages 10-12.
James Madison became the fourth president of the United States and was instrumental in the framing of the United States Constitution and in making it work. He was a contemporary of Aaron Burr and George Washington and was a close friend of Thomas Jefferson. He was president during the British march on the White House. James's wife, Dolley, is given credit for saving a valuable painting of George Washington when the White House was set on fire by the British.

Giblin, James Cross. **George Washington: A Picture Book Biography**. Illustrated by Michael Dooling. Scholastic, 1992. Read-aloud audience: grades 3-5; ages 7-10.
A birth-to-death biography of our nation's first president. Washington's childhood, his early years at Mount Vernon, and his success as a farmer are covered. In his early 40s, when the

American Revolution began, Washington was asked to serve as commander-in-chief of the colonies' militia. Eventually Washington became the first president of the United States, serving two terms before retiring to Mount Vernon, where he died in 1799.

Connections for Readers— James Cross Giblin

James Giblin uses extensive notes at the end of the picture book text to give us added details about George Washington. Included in the "More About George Washington" section are a map of the United States in 1797; important dates in George Washington's life; information dispelling the tale about George and the cherry tree; Washington's rules of behavior; monuments to George Washington; and information about Washington's estate, Mount Vernon. When Mount Vernon was on the brink of decay and ruin, a group of women formed the Mount Vernon Ladies' Association and raised enough money to purchase the property and restore it. To this day the association still maintains Mount Vernon with the admission fees collected from thousands of visitors; no federal or state government funds are used.

Lucas, Eileen. **Jane Goodall, Friend of the Chimps**. Illustrated with photographs. Millbrook, 1992. Gateway Biography series. Read-aloud audience: grades 3-5; ages 7-10.
Jane Goodall made her mark in Kenya, where she has spent decades observing and studying the life habits of the chimpanzee. She was the first to document that chimpanzees eat meat (they were thought to be vegetarian) and that they use tools. Goodall spent her lifetime working with the chimpanzees in the African rain forest.

Say, Allen. **El Chino**. Houghton, 1990. Read-aloud audience: grades 3-5; ages 7-10.
Bong Way Wong was the first Chinese American to become a famous bullfighter in Spain. He

grew up in Arizona and dreamed of being a professional basketball player. Because of his height "Billy" abandoned his dream and studied engineering. When he took his first vacation to Spain, he became interested in the sport of bullfighting. He never returned to his engineering career.

Connections for Readers— El Chino

Although many of Allen Say's stories come from his own experience living and growing up in Japan, he first became acquainted with the *El Chino* story when Billy Wong's story was published in a Sunday newspaper supplement, *California Living*. The story intrigued him and he became even more interested when he met a Jewish woman with the surname Wong. Since that was rather unusual, he struck up a conversation and discovered that she was a sister-in-law of Billy Wong. That connection gave him the opportunity to obtain information from primary sources and helped him develop the story.

St. George, Judith. **Dear Dr. Bell-Your Friend, Helen Keller**. Illustrated with photographs. Putnam, 1992. Read-aloud audience: grades 5-7; ages 10-12.
At the age of 19 months Helen Keller was stricken with an illness that left her deaf and blind. Her inability to communicate contributed to her angry, outrageous behavior. The day she locked her mother in a pantry convinced her parents to get help for her.

Turner, Robyn Montana. **Faith Ringgold**. Little, Brown, 1993. Portraits of Women Artists for Children series. Read-aloud audience: grades 3-5; ages 7-10.
Faith Ringgold is the author/illustrator of several books for young readers. Her first title, *Tar Beach* (Crown, 1991), was based on the Harlem adventures of Cassie. The story was originally told in a story quilt. Later the story and the illustrations were reworked to fit into a picture book format. Ringgold has told several more stories and continues to create story quilts and to exhibit in prestigious art museums throughout the United States.

Connections for Readers— Faith Ringgold

Faith Ringgold's biography features her story quilts, which have become the basis for several books. *Tar Beach* (Crown, 1991) tells about the dream adventures of eight-year-old Cassie, who recalls events that took place in Harlem in 1939. The tar beach was actually the tar roof of her family's apartment building. Faith Ringgold linked the history of the Underground Railroad and Harriet Tubman with fantasy in *Aunt Harriet's Underground Railroad in the Sky* (Crown, 1992). "The Dinner Quilt," another quilt featured in the biography, inspired *Dinner at Aunt Connie's House* (Hyperion, 1993). That book tells the story of 12 African American women who were influential and inspiring during their time. Ringgold's illustrations are lush and brilliant oil paintings, each inspired by her story quilts.

Weidt, Maryann N. **Mr. Blue Jeans: A Story About Levi Strauss**. Illustrated by Lydia M. Anderson. Carolrhoda, 1990. Creative Minds Biographies series. Read-aloud audience: grades 5-7; ages 10-12.
Löb Strauss was a native of Bavaria, who emigrated to the United States with his mother and two sisters to join Löb's stepbrothers, Louis and Jonas, who had emigrated earlier. When Löb Strauss arrived in the United States, government workers misunderstood his first name and he became Levi. First peddlers of household wares on the East Coast and later dry goods retailers out west during the days of the Gold Rush, the Strauss brothers created a business empire that became famous for its production of heavy denim jeans—now known the world over as Levis.

Wisniewski, David. **Sundiata: Lion King of Mali**. Illustrated by David Wisniewski. Clarion, 1992. Read-aloud audience: grades 3-5; ages 7-10.

The picture book format of this book makes it appropriate for even younger readers. But because of its time period and its basis in legend, or oral history, as preserved by the ancient African *griots* (storytellers), this biographical tale also appeals to more sophisticated audiences. Despite Sundiata's childhood physical handicap, his father, the king of Mali, designated him as his successor. After his father's death and due to a number of political circumstances, Sundiata and his mother were exiled from Mali. During that time his people were ruled by a sorcerer king. Eventually Sundiata was summoned by his people to return and claim his father's throne. He gathered together an army, and his return was a triumph for the common citizens of Mali. He became known as the "Lion King" and ruled the country successfully for many years.

Connections for Readers— Africa

Africa's history did not begin with slave ships. The continent boasts some of the world's earliest civilizations and had thriving trade centers. Between A.D. 500 and A.D. 1600, three medieval kingdoms of West Africa flourished: Ghana, Mali, and Songhay. The *griots* (storytellers) were responsible for maintaining the oral history of the kingdoms. Wisniewski used those stories to construct the biography of Sundiata. Patricia McKissack and Fredrick McKissack also used the oral histories of the Malinke and Soninke *griots*, as well as archeological reports and Arabic texts, to put together a rich and fascinating history of the three kingdoms in their book for middle school readers, *The Royal Kingdoms of Ghana, Mali, and Songhay: Life in Medieval Africa* (Holt, 1994).

Moving to a Multitude of Books

After listening to a biography being read aloud, the class will be ready to move on to reading workshops, discussed in "Moving to Independent Reading" (pages 10-13).

Two of the most popular biographers are Jean Fritz and Russell Freedman. Either one of these authors would make an excellent subject for an author focus in connection with biography. Each of these writers focuses on the middle-grade reader. Other authors that might be considered for an author focus include David A. Adler, Nathan Aaseng, Robyn Montana Turner, and James Cross Giblin.

More Biographies to Read

Demarest, Chris L. **Lindbergh**. Illustrated by Chris L. Demarest. Crown, 1993. Target audience: grades 3-5; ages 7-10.

The focus of this biography is Lindbergh's childhood and youth. Illustrations are lively, detailed watercolors that complement the informative text.

Everett, Gwen. **John Brown: One Man Against Slavery**. Illustrated by John Lawrence. Rizzoli, 1993. Target audience: grades 5-7; ages 10-12.

Bold and graphic illustrations help evoke the powerful emotions that are part of John Brown's story, told here in a first-person narrative from the viewpoint of Brown's daughter, Annie. The narrative is brief but aptly tells the story of John Brown's raid on Harper's Ferry.

Fisher, Leonard Everett. **Gutenberg**. Illustrated by Leonard Everett Fisher. Macmillan, 1993. Target audience: grades 5-7; ages 10-12.

The story of the creator of movable type and the printer of the Gutenberg Bible is well told in this carefully researched biography. Details of the 15th-century setting and the development of the printing press are linked with the biographical information.

Lasky, Kathryn. **The Librarian Who Measured the Earth**. Illustrated by Kevin Hawkes. Little, Brown, 1994. Target audience: grades 3-5; ages 7-10.

A highly illustrated biography of Eratosthenes, a Greek boy, who lived more than 2,000 years ago. Eratosthenes grew up to become the chief librarian at the cultural center of Alexandria and to write the first complete geography book. He also discovered the first accurate way to measure the circumference of the Earth.

Marzollo, Jean. **Happy Birthday, Martin Luther King**. Illustrated by J. Brian Pinkney. Scholastic, 1993. Target audience: grades 3-5; ages 7-10.

A sensitively written biography of a man whose work sparked the emergence of the peaceful protests that brought about movement toward equality and civil rights for all Americans.

McKissack, Patricia, and Fredrick McKissack. **African-American Scientists**. Millbrook, 1994. Proud Heritage series. Target audience: grades 5-7; ages 10-12.

Well-documented, interestingly written portraits of well-known scientists, such as Benjamin Banneker and George Washington Carver, and lesser-known scientists including women, all of whom made significant contributions to science. Black-and-white photographs and artwork illustrate the volume.

Mohr, Nicholasa. **Nicholasa Mohr: Growing Up Inside the Sanctuary of My Imagination**. Illustrated with photographs. Messner, 1994. Target audience: grades 5-7; ages 10-12.

The author of *Felita* (Dial, 1979; Bantam, 1990) and *El Bronx Remembered* (HarperCollins, 1975; Arte Público Press, 1985) tells of the strength of her family and her growing-up years in the Puerto Rican barrio of Spanish Harlem. She describes the prejudice and insensitivity she encountered in school and outside the barrio. This autobiography is a memoir that will help students develop a greater understanding of other cultures.

Connections for Readers— Nicholasa Mohr

Many of Nicholasa Mohr's fiction books are drawn from her life. *Felita* is about an incident in her life. In the story, Felita's family is hassled and harassed in their new all-white neighborhood until they have to move back to their old neighborhood because of fear for their well-being. In real life, Nicholasa has said, "We too were beaten, harassed, and had to move out of an all-white ethnic neighborhood and return to our old neighborhood." But just like Felita's family, Nicholasa's family survived. Her high school years were marred by lack of encouragement. She was told that she should not plan on going to college; she should study domestic science so she would not be a burden on society. Instead she became a visual artist whose work was collected by many patrons of the arts. Her works were displayed in many art museums. Nicholasa Mohr, a poor Puerto Rican girl from the barrio, was eventually awarded an honorary degree of Doctor of Letters by the State University of New York.

Morris, Ann. **Dancing to America**. Photographs by Paul Kolnik. Dutton, 1994. Target audience: grades 3-5; ages 7-10.

The story of Anton Pankevich, a gifted 16-year-old student of the American Ballet in New York City. As an immigrant from Russia, everything about his life in New York is new to him except for the ballet. The biography follows his acclimatization into the American culture, his dancing, and his progress in his new country.

Moutoussamy-Ashe, Jeanne. **Daddy and Me: A Photo Story of Arthur Ashe and His Daughter, Camera**. Illustrated with photographs. Knopf, 1993. Target audience: grades 3-5; ages 7-10.

Arthur Ashe's widow uses black-and-white photographs and her daughter's perspective to tell of the relationship between Camera and her father, who died of AIDS. The text aptly shows the support and love between daughter and father and the life-affirming activities that are possible even when one must deal with a long-term illness. Arthur Ashe's death is not part of the story.

Roop, Peter, and Connie Roop, eds. **Capturing Nature: The Writings and Art of John James Audubon**. Illustrated by Rick Farley. Walker, 1993. Target audience: grades 5-7; ages 10-12.

The Roops have edited the century-old diary of Audubon. The diary entries reflect thought processes from years ago and describe a country and countryside that seem timeless. Audubon's description of his struggles and doubts gives readers fascinating insight into a past culture.

Stanley, Diane, and Peter Vennema. **Charles Dickens: The Man Who Had Great Expectations**. Illustrated by Diane Stanley. Morrow, 1993. Target audience: grades 5-7; ages 10-12.

In this pictorial biography of the famous author of *A Christmas Carol* and other classics, Dickens's life is presented as the basis for many of his famous writings. Dickens is shown to be a lively, ambitious person.

Turner, Robyn Montana. **Dorothea Lange**. Little, Brown, 1994. Portraits of Women Artists for Children series. Target audience: grades 3-5; ages 7-10.

Dorothea Lange was a photographer who lived during the early 1900s and photographed wealthy San Franciscans. During that time she began to feel confined by having to pose her subjects in her studio, so she began to take her camera to the city streets. There she recorded candid images of people affected by the Depression. Other subjects in this series include Rosa Bonheur, Mary Cassatt, Frida Kahlo, Georgia O'Keeffe, and Faith Ringgold.

Author! Author!

Russell Freedman

Born on October 11, 1929, Russell Freedman grew up in San Francisco, California, where his father, one of the first publishing representatives to call on librarians, managed the San Francisco office of Macmillan Publishing. Russell often accompanied his father as they made their way to every library west of the Rockies and "grew up thinking that librarians were the salt-of-the-earth." He still spends a lot of time in libraries. When he identifies a biographical subject, he begins by making a list of the available contemporary books written about that person. Then he begins reading, taking notes, and locating information about sources of photographs.

After his library research, Freedman conducts field research. Then comes the actual writing of the manuscript. Finally, Freedman locates the photographs to accompany the text. Freedman writes in the study of his Manhattan apartment. He spends most of each day there, and sometimes after an afternoon walk and dinner, he works into the evening. He often works simultaneously on writing one manuscript, checking another, and collecting material for yet a third book. His goal for all of his writing is that it be informative and fun to read.

Russell Freedman continues to live and work in New York City's Upper West Side.

Russell Freedman

Russell Freedman was born October 11, 1929, and grew up in San Francisco. He graduated from the University of California at Berkeley and later served in the United States Army during the Korean War. After his service with the army's Second Infantry Division, Freedman worked for the Associated Press as a reporter and editor. Later he worked as a publicist for several network television shows.

In the late 1950s Freedman read an article in the *New York Times* about the 16-year-old boy who, although blind, had invented a Braille typewriter. As remarkable as that seemed, Freedman was impressed even more with other information he found in the article. The Braille system itself, as used today all over the world, was invented by another blind 16-year-old. That boy was Louis Braille, who lived in France more than 150 years ago. That newspaper article sparked Freedman's curiosity, and after weeks of research, he discovered a surprising number of people who had earned places in history before they turned 20. The article and the research inspired Freedman's first book, *Teenagers Who Made History*. Since that time he has been a full-time writer and a member of the Writing Workshops faculty at the New School for Social Research.

Freedman lives and works in a large Manhattan apartment filled with books, plants, and an endless procession of visiting relatives and friends. Every morning he goes to his study, where he spends most of the day working on his latest project. Later in the afternoon, in all seasons, he will often take a long walk through Riverside Park or through the busy Upper West Side neighborhood streets. If he is working against a deadline, Freedman will often work after dinner and late into the night. But when he is not so pressured, he enjoys the company of friends and "the incredible variety of films, plays, concerts, restaurants, and street life that New York offers." Freedman also travels a great deal to research material for his books, to speak to children in schools, to attend conventions, and to see the world.

During some of his presentations, Freedman describes his great joy in writing nonfiction books for young people. It gives him, he says, the chance "to explore subjects that excite my curiosity, my enthusiasm, or my concern—preferably all three." His book ideas seem to come from anywhere, from a personal experience or from something he's seen or read or overheard. His subjects have ranged from American history to animal behavior.

Russell Freedman, Newbery Award winner for his photobiography of Abraham Lincoln, *Lincoln: A Photobiography* (Clarion, 1987), spent months visiting original sites and studying original materials while researching the book. In a 1991 presentation at the University of Iowa Festival of Children's Books, Freedman said, "I think of myself as a storyteller but I do not make up things." He says that he has "a pact with the reader to stick to the facts" but that "facts do not rule out art and imagination." His work is based on solid research but reads with a narrative carefully crafted from the facts. Freedman wants to keep the reader turning the page and he does so by creating vivid detailed scenes. He dramatizes but keeps the information factual.

Freedman's research helps him develop a subject's character. For example, Freedman learned that Lincoln said things like "Howdy" and "Stay a spell," and that he wore carpet slippers to greet dignitaries. At a White House reception, he referred to his wife as "Mother." On the evening Lincoln was assassinated, he had with him his glasses in a velvet case; a handkerchief with "A. Lincoln" stitched on it in red; and a red silk-lined, brown leather wallet with a five-dollar Confederate bill and a newspaper clipping praising him.

In a 1988 interview Freedman discussed his research for *Abraham Lincoln: A Photobiography*. "While writing my biography of Abraham Lincoln, I visited all the important historical sites, from his log-cabin birthplace in Kentucky to Ford's Theatre in Washington, D.C. But the biggest thrill was stepping into a temperature-controlled bank vault at the Illinois State

Historical Library in Springfield, in the company of Tom Schwartz, curator of the Lincoln Collection. Tom showed me the original documents written in Lincoln's own hand—letters to his wife, drafts of speeches, notes scrawled on scraps of paper during long-ago trials in country courthouses. Each document had been treated with a special preservative that removed all traces of acid from the paper. Pointing to one of Lincoln's courtroom notes, Tom said, 'This will last a thousand years.'

"I'll never forget that afternoon. I already knew a great deal about Lincoln, yet there's something magic about being able to lay your eyes on the real thing. Looking at those original documents, I could feel Lincoln's presence as never before—almost as though he had reached out to shake hands."

Freedman's research for a biography of Franklin Delano Roosevelt revealed that, as a child, if he did not feel like practicing the piano, he would tell his governess that his hand hurt and if going to church was not something he wanted to do, he said he had a headache. Roosevelt was a great admirer of Lincoln, and despite their differences in background and style, there were many connections between the two presidents. One of FDR's speech writers was also a playwright who won an award for a play about Lincoln. Lincoln is often characterized as a poor backwards boy, born in a log cabin with a dirt floor. He didn't smoke, drink, or swear. Roosevelt was a pampered child in a household employing several servants. He breezed through life drinking martinis and using language said not to be fit for a family newspaper. Yet, both Lincoln and Roosevelt were skilled politicians, and each could be ruthless.

Freedman remembers seeing newsreels showing Franklin D. Roosevelt bathing in the stream in Hot Springs and greeting kings and queens. People seemed to either love or hate him. Freedman remembers that on the day Roosevelt died, school was let out early. One junior high teacher was overheard to say, "Thank God that awful man is dead." Others cried.

Serendipity played a role in Freedman's research for the Roosevelt biography. One day, while working on the book, Freedman made a routine visit to his attorney and learned he could connect him with one of FDR's grandsons, Curtis D. Roosevelt. Curtis grew up in the White House close to his grandparents and had in fact often tumbled on the presidential bed. Another time, a visit to a physician led to an interview with an 80-year-old retired doctor who had been with Roosevelt at Hot Springs. After the book was published, Freedman was signing books in a Cincinnati library when an elderly gentleman approached and announced his picture was on page 167 of the book. He had been a member of the secret service for Roosevelt. He told Freedman that FDR's hacking cough had been described by the head of the secret service the day before he died as "no cough; that's a death rattle." As Freedman left the library, the secret service agent continued to sign Freedman's books—on page 167.

Freedman's research technique has no set format, no set time span, no predetermined level of complexity. It all depends, he says, "on how much I know." First, he compiles a bibliography of the most recent books about the subject, then he begins to read. After extensive reading and note taking, he begins his field research. His collective biography *Indian Chiefs* was written entirely from library research, but other books require both on-location visits and in-person interviews with those who had some connection to the subject. After reading and researching, Freedman's third step is to identify and locate photographs. For every 90 to 100 photographs used in his books, he locates and identifies approximately 1,000 photos from libraries, museums, and archival holdings, after which he must obtain permission to reproduce them and, if necessary, negotiate a fee for doing so.

Freedman often works on more than one project at a time. He focuses on one book while finishing others. For example, while working on his manuscript for the biography of Eleanor Roosevelt, he was checking material for *Indian Winter* and collecting material for his next book.

In 1988 Russell Freedman was awarded the Newbery Award for *Lincoln: A Photobiography*. Since he began writing in the 1960s, he has written more than 35 nonfiction books for young readers. He presently lives and works in New York City.

Books by Russell Freedman

Eleanor Roosevelt: A Life of Discovery. Clarion, 1993. Target audience: grades 5-7; ages 10-12.
The first presidential spouse to lead a public life of her own and to retain her career is the subject of this sensitive biography. More than 100 black-and-white photographs portray Eleanor Roosevelt at every age.

Franklin Delano Roosevelt. Clarion, 1990. Target audience: grades 5-7; ages 10-12.
A comprehensive biography of the only president to serve four terms. Known as FDR, Roosevelt was a pampered child in a home that employed a butler, a maid, and a governess. As an adult he endured the physical effects of polio which left him unable to stand or walk unaided. But he was a ruthless politician who did not like to lose. At his side through all this was his wife, Eleanor.

Indian Chiefs. Illustrated with photographs. Holiday, 1987. Target audience: grades 5-7; ages 10-12.
A collective biography that details the lives and involvement of six Native American chiefs who, when faced with invasion by non-native pioneers, had to decide to cooperate (give them the land) or fight. Chapters are included on Red Cloud, Satanta, Quanah Parker, Washakie, Chief Joseph, and Sitting Bull.

Lincoln: A Photobiography. Illustrated with photographs. Clarion, 1987. Target audience: grades 5-7; ages 10-12.
A biography that focuses primarily on Lincoln's presidential years and his impact on the nation through his stand on the Civil War and the issue of slavery. This well-researched and comprehensive text is illustrated with dozens of photographs. Our 16th president's impact on the nation is aptly demonstrated.

Teenagers Who Made History. Portraits by Arthur Shilstone. Holiday, 1961. Target audience: grades 5-7; ages 10-12.
A collective biography of several teenagers who made their mark on history before they reached the age of 20. One of the most notable is Louis Braille, who at the age of 16 invented the Braille system of reading and writing still in use today.

The Wright Brothers: How They Invented the Airplane. Illustrated with photographs by Wilbur and Orville Wright. Holiday, 1991. Target audience: grades 5-7; ages 10-12.
This biography details the childhood of the two brothers whose ingenuity and curiosity brought them to experiment with machines that fly. Orville and Wilbur Wright not only developed the airplane but also photographed each stage of its development.

Author! Author!

Jean Fritz

Jean Fritz was born in China and lived there until she was a teenager. She went to school with children from several other countries, including England. She often found herself having to defend America's actions during the Revolutionary War.

Surrounded by people from different cultures with different ideas, Jean Fritz often wondered what it would be like to be someone else. She always liked to write but did not begin to write books until she was married and had children. She and her husband, Michael, moved to Dobbs Ferry, New York, where she began to volunteer at the local library, which did not have much to offer young readers. Fritz was asked to help create a children's room, so for two years she read a lot of children's books. The reading helped her realize that she would like to write books for children. Her first published book, *The Cabin Faced West,* was based on a family story about how George Washington had had supper with Fritz's great-great-grandmother, Ann Hamilton. Later Fritz turned to writing biographies and became known for her superb stories of John Hancock, Benjamin Franklin, and other figures of the Revolutionary era. Her most recent books are about Harriet Beecher Stowe and Elizabeth Cady Stanton.

Jean Fritz still lives and writes in Dobbs Ferry, New York.

From *Educator's Companion to Children's Literature, Volume 2: Folklore, Contemporary Realistic Fiction, Fantasy, Biographies, and Tales from Here and There.* © 1996. Libraries Unlimited. (800) 237-6124.

Jean Fritz

Jean Fritz, winner of the 1986 Laura Ingalls Wilder Award, was born on November 16, 1915, in Hangkow, China, 500 miles up the Yangtze River. She lived in China with her missionary parents until she was 13, and spoke Chinese before she spoke English. In 1928, the family returned to the United States. As a child in China, Fritz often found herself defending America and its actions from the Revolution on.

In a 1988 interview Jean Fritz explained her interest in writing biographies by saying, "As a child in China, I brushed against so many different cultures, with different problems that I began early trying to figure out what my life would be like if I were someone else. I think I've been doing that ever since which explains why I write biographies and why I think it's important for everyone to imagine themselves in the shoes of other people. I can't imagine not reading books and writing them too! And I travel as much as I can so that I can meet new people who may show me how they look at life."

Jean Fritz always wanted to write. But she did not start writing for publication until she was married and had children, and then she wrote for adults. When Jean, her husband, Michael, and their two children, David and Andrea, moved to Dobbs Ferry, New York, in the early 1950s, Jean found the local library had no children's program and few books. She started a story hour and later was asked to plan and open a children's room. For the next two years, Fritz immersed herself in children's literature, reading constantly. This concentration and the ongoing experience of reading aloud gave her a sense of story and helped convince her that writing for children was what she wanted to do.

As a child in China, Jean Fritz always felt different from the rest of the children. She longed for "home," even though she had never been there. When the family did return to the United States and settled in Connecticut, the other children referred to her as "that kid who was born in China." Years later when she began to write for children, Fritz turned to American history, in part, she believes, "in an effort to find her roots." Her first book, *The Cabin Faced West* (Putnam, 1958), came from a family story about how George Washington had eaten supper with Fritz's great-great-grandmother, Ann Hamilton. Fritz later turned to writing biographies because she found that what really happens in life is generally more surprising than stories people make up. She enjoys researching an authentic biography. She reads books others have written about the subject. She also reads old newspapers and original letters that she finds in libraries and historical societies. Research is like being a detective, a treasure hunter, a puzzle solver, and an eavesdropper—all things Jean Fritz has enjoyed doing.

Jean Fritz chooses to write about people who are no longer living, because one doesn't "know the full story of a person who is still alive and doing things." Fritz will only choose subjects whose lives she thinks make good stories with plenty of ups and downs. And she likes to choose complicated subjects. For example, on the outside, Civil War Confederate general Stonewall Jackson appeared to be a flamboyant show-off, but inside he was hungry for approval. Fritz also likes to choose subjects students will meet in their required history courses. She wants readers to be able to imagine Benjamin Franklin signing the Declaration of Independence, and she wants readers to be able to "see" him being knocked out at the electrical picnic he gave.

Fritz writes her biographies with extreme care and strives for accuracy. She uses no dialogue unless she has records to support what was actually said. And when she cannot verify a supposition, she qualifies it by writing "must have," "perhaps," and "may have." When Fritz wrote *And Then What Happened, Paul Revere?* she wanted to include the name of Revere's horse but she could not locate it. Weeks after the book was published, she found the name, Brown Beauty. The omission of the name did not diminish the accuracy of the text, but if she'd known in time, Fritz would have asked the illustrator to change the color of the horse on the jacket illustration. Margot Tomes had made the horse a dapple gray.

For several years Jean Fritz wrote biographies about men, specifically men during the Revolutionary War era. However, she has also written about Theodore Roosevelt and about Abraham Lincoln's Gettysburg Address. In a 1981 interview with Elaine Edelman for *Publishers Weekly*,[4] she was asked why she had not yet written a biography for children about a woman. She answered that she was "not a sociologist." She continued that she really wrote for herself and if it helped children, that was fine. However, she did modify that statement to discuss her efforts to give children a more realistic picture of Christopher Columbus, who had been "so wrongly portrayed to children." After the Columbus biography she wrote a story about Benedict Arnold and one that explored her own years in China. And recently she has written about three women: *George Washington's Mother* (Putnam, 1992); *Harriet Beecher Stowe and the Beecher Preachers* (Putnam, 1994); and *You Want Women to Vote, Lizzie Stanton?* (Putnam, 1995).

Jean Fritz's daughter, Andrea Fritz Pfleger, took most of the photographs that appeared in Fritz's autobiography, *Surprising Myself* (Richard C. Owen, 1992). Andrea and her husband, Frank, live on a lake in New York state with four house cats and three barn cats. Fritz's son, David, is married to Carmela and they have two sons, Dan and Michael Scott. Jean Fritz and her husband, Michael, still live in Dobbs Ferry, New York, where they enjoy visits from their family. They will often travel to a place that appears in the manuscript Jean is working on, and every year they spend three weeks in the Caribbean on the island Virgin Gorda. While they are gone Jean Fritz leaves her manuscript in the safest place she can think of—the refrigerator.

Books by Jean Fritz

Can't You Make Them Behave, King George? Illustrated by Tomie dePaola. Coward, 1977. Target audience: grades 3-5; ages 7-10.

A biography of George the Third, king of Great Britain at the time of the American Revolution. He was a ruler who was determined to be a good king but felt that anyone who did not agree with his viewpoint was a "traitor or a scoundrel."

The Double Life of Pocahontas. Illustrated by Ed Young. Putnam, 1983. Target audience: grades 5-7; ages 10-12.

This book about Pocahontas is described as being about "a famous American Indian princess, emphasizing her life-long adulation of John Smith and the roles she played in two very different cultures." This biography has been called into question regarding its authenticity, point of view, and sensitivity.[5]

George Washington's Mother. Illustrations by DyAnne DiSalvo-Ryan. Putnam, 1992. All Aboard Reading series. Target audience: grades 3-5; ages 7-10. All Aboard Reading series.

Describes the life of Mary Ball Washington and her relationship with her children, including George, the first president of the United States.

The Great Little Madison. Putnam, 1989. Target audience: grades 5-7; ages 10-12.

The fourth president of the United States and close friend of Thomas Jefferson, James Madison played a large role in the writing of the United States Constitution. He was a sickly child with a weak voice, but he grew up to become president during the British march on the White House. The biography includes Madison's wife, Dolley, who refused to leave the burning White House until she rescued a painting of George Washington. Because the painting's frame was mounted on the wall and would have been too bulky to carry, she cut the painting from the frame and carried it under her coat.

Harriet Beecher Stowe and the Beecher Preachers. Putnam, 1994. Target audience: grades 5-7; ages 10-12.

Stowe's preacher father would have preferred to have had sons instead of daughters. Sons could have become preachers and followed in his footsteps. But Stowe's father had a profound influence on her life—he instilled in her a strong hatred of slavery.

Make Way for Sam Houston. Illustrations by Elise Primavera. Putnam, 1986. Target audience: grades 3-5; ages 7-10.

Sam Houston was known first as a soldier who led the fight for Texas's independence from Mexico. Later he gained notoriety as a governor and senator who opposed secession during the Civil War.

The Man Who Loved Books. Illustrated by Trina Schart Hyman. Putnam, 1981. Target audience: grades 3-5; ages 7-10.

Saint Columba was an Irish saint who was known for his love of books and his missionary work throughout Scotland. He lived from A.D. 521 to 597.

Stonewall. Illustrated by Stephen Gammell. Putnam, 1979. Target audience: grades 5-7; ages 10-12.

General Stonewall Jackson was a Confederate leader during the Civil War. A master of strategic maneuvers, he was known as one of the best generals in the war. Fritz's biography portrays a man who was both strange and great.

Surprising Myself. Illustrated with photographs by Andrea Fritz Pfleger. Richard C. Owen, 1992. Meet the Author series. Target audience: grades 3-5; ages 7-10.

In this autobiography, Fritz describes her daily life, the way she researches and writes, and her annual trip to the Caribbean Islands. Photographs show her at work, in the Caribbean, and with her family.

Traitor: The Case of Benedict Arnold. Putnam, 1981. Target audience: grades 5-7; ages 10-12.

During the Revolutionary War, Benedict Arnold was a brilliant general who was lured by money to the British side. As a deserter and a loyalist he was considered a traitor. Fritz examines Arnold's life and character.

What's the Big Idea, Ben Franklin? Illustrated by Margot Tomes. Coward, 1976. Target audience: grades 3-5; ages 7-10.

Ben Franklin was a statesman and a patriot who helped shape the United States by participating in the Constitutional Convention. As a printer, inventor, and statesman he played an influential role in the early history of the United States.

Where Do You Think You Are Going, Christopher Columbus? Illustrated by Margot Tomes. Putnam, 1980. Target audience: grades 3-5; ages 7-10.

Discusses the voyages of Christopher Columbus, who was intent on being the first to reach India by sailing west. The story brings out Columbus's pigheadedness, egotistic nature, and false notions. No one, it seems, could convince him that he had not found the route to India.

Where Was Patrick Henry on the 29th of May? Illustrated by Margot Tomes. Coward, 1975. Target audience: grades 3-5; ages 7-10.

From planter to statesman, Patrick Henry became an important figure in the Revolutionary War. Fritz shares both the good and less desirable characteristics of Henry and includes unusual and humorous facts as well.

Why Don't You Get a Horse, Sam Adams? Illustrated by Trina Schart Hyman. Target audience: grades 3-5; ages 7-10.

Although most other men of the time rode horses, Samuel Adams did not. This biography tells of his active role in the early history of the United States and how he was finally persuaded to learn to ride a horse.

Will You Sign Here, John Hancock? Illustrated by Trina Schart Hyman. Coward, 1976. Target audience: grades 3-5; ages 7-10.

The first signer of the Declaration of Independence is profiled in a tale that outlines all that he did for himself as well as what he did for Massachusetts and his new nation.

You Want Women to Vote, Lizzie Stanton? Illustrated by DyAnne DiSalvo-Ryan. Putnam, 1995. Target audience: grades 5-7; ages 10-12.

Tells the story of one of the nation's leading suffragists, Elizabeth Cady Stanton, who lived from 1815 to 1902. Stanton, an outspoken advocate for women's rights, including the vote, was considered a feminist even in her time.

Going Beyond_____

In this focus on biography, students will read many books about the lives of others. These biographies present well-researched information that tells an intimate story of history and people. Background and additional information regarding the specific time period can be researched in the library media center. Many topics within a book of collective biography can be an expansion topic for wide reading. For example, after reading Freedman's *Indian Chiefs,* the reader might wish to read some of Virginia Driving Hawk Sneve's First Americans series, including *The Hopi: A First Americans Book* (Holiday, 1995); *The Iroquois: A First Americans Book* (Holiday, 1995); *The Navajos: A First Americans Book* (Holiday, 1993); *The Nez Percé: A First Americans Book* (Holiday, 1994); *The Seminoles: A First Americans Book* (Holiday, 1994); and *The Sioux: A First Americans Book* (Holiday, 1993).

Similarly, a reader who enjoys Robyn Turner's biography of Faith Ringgold may wish to read Ringgold's picture books to further explore her work. The reader may also wish to correspond with the curators of museums that exhibit her work and search for additional information about her work. Reading a biography of John Muir may lead to an inquiry into national parks or specifically those parks established, in part, through Muir's efforts. A travel brochure or tourist booklet might be developed so that other students may become familiar with the locations of the parks. A reader who reads Jean Fritz's *Where Do You Think You're Going, Christopher Columbus?* may wish to read Francine Jacobs's *Tainos: The People Who Welcomed Columbus* (Putnam, 1992) and then compare the two authors' characterizations of Columbus. Milton Meltzer's book, *Columbus and the World Around Him* (Franklin Watts, 1990), will supplement the information in Jacob's book and will help balance the representations in other more general biographies of Columbus.

Activities related to historical topics can help integrate critical thinking skills, history/geographical topics, and other curriculum content.

Biography Activities

- Build a focus on the period during which the subject lived. Make a list of things about the period that we know and that we want to know. After further reading, make a list of things we have learned. (This technique is commonly known as the KWL method—What we know, want to know, and what we have learned.) Create a trivia game based on facts about the specific period or location.

- Read widely in the subject's time period. Search for collaborative reading titles and make the entire selection available to students. Be sure to include a wide range of picture books, historical fiction, information books, and, of course, biographies. Set up a center with videos, books, posters, artifacts—immerse yourself in the time period.

- Use any piece of information learned from a wide-reading activity and devise some method of displaying that knowledge. Those who read *Keep the Lights Burning, Abbie* by Peter Roop and Connie Roop (Carolrhoda, 1985), a biography about a young girl who operated a lighthouse in the absence of her father, may wish to explore information about lighthouses. A good start would include *Beacons of Light: Lighthouses* by Gail Gibbons (Morrow, 1990).

- Get involved in the life of the subject. In addition to eating the foods the person ate, play the games the person might have played, learn in a classroom typical of the period, and read books the children of the period read. For subjects who lived in relatively recent times, the reading activity takes on a different perspective since many books should be available. The Newbery Award titles will provide suggestions to get started. *Adventures with Social Studies (Through Literature)* by Sharron L. McElmeel (Teacher Ideas Press, 1991) includes a chapter, "A History of the Newbery Books: A Capsule View of the Changing Character of American Society" (pages 121-138), that views the Newbery Award books, first awarded in 1922, from a historical perspective.

- Considering the many biographies of men of European ancestry, identify some men of non-European ancestry and some women and members of minorities they feel might be interesting topics for biographies. Send the suggestions to the children's book marketing directors of the major publishing houses.

Culminating the Focus on Biography

The purpose of a culminating activity is to bring closure to a specific focus. General ideas for culminating activities are discussed in chapter 1 (page 14). If you can schedule enough time, one culmination for a biography unit is to ask students to select a subject from within their family to interview and use for a biography that the student writes. Review the characteristics of a well-written biography—accuracy, interesting facts, and anecdotes—and generate basic questions one will need to ask. Then, each child should make arrangements for a person-to-person interview, if possible. If that is not possible, a phone interview or an interview conducted by mail will suffice. If the interview is by phone or in person, the student may wish to tape-record the interview to help ensure accuracy. Once the biographies have been written and collected into individual books, the reading and writing unit might share a culmination by inviting the subjects of the student-written biographies to a "bioreception." If this writing activity culmination is not appropriate, consider adapting a suggestion from chapter 1 or from the biography activities on the preceding pages.

The following four pages may be reproduced for student use.

Notes

1. Ann W. Moore. "A Question of Accuracy: Errors in Children's Biographies." *School Library Journal* 31 (February 1985): 34-35.

2. Russell Freedman. "Newbery Medal Acceptance." *The Horn Book* (July/August 1988): 447.

3. Ibid.

4. Elaine Edelman. "PW Interviews: Jean Fritz." *Publishers Weekly* (July 24, 1981): 77.

5. Beverly Slapin and Doris Seale. *Through Indian Eyes: The Native Experience in Books for Children* (Philadelphia: New Society Publishers, 1992), pp. 156-157.

Biography Reader's Journal

My Name: _____

Response Starter Suggestions

Your biography reader's journal is where you will record your ideas, your thoughts, your questions about vocabulary, and your questions and comments about the plot and the people involved in the book or chapter you have just read. Sometimes it is difficult to get started, so the following questions might give you ideas to help you begin. These questions are only suggestions; the journal is yours and should contain questions and comments about the parts of the book that interest you.

- What information do you already know about the subject?

- What new information is the author giving you about the subject?

- What kind of person is the subject of the biography?

- What are the credentials of the author for writing about this person?

- How did this person influence the people around her or him?

- What about this person has made her or him someone you want to know more about?

- Does this biography deal with all stages of the subject's life, or does it focus on a specific period?

- How does the biography's depiction fit with your prior image of this person? How has your image changed?

- Does the author describe the setting in a realistic or accurate way?

- Describe the point of view from which the story is told.

Date each of your journal entries. Responses mean more later if you use complete sentences.

Have fun and enjoy your reading.

Biographies I Have Read

Title	Author
1.	
2.	
3.	
4.	
5.	
6.	
7.	
8.	
9.	
10.	
11.	
12.	
13.	
14.	
15.	
16.	
17.	
18.	
19.	
20.	

Biographies I Want to Read

Title	Author
1.	
2.	
3.	
4.	
5.	
6.	
7.	
8.	
9.	
10.	
11.	
12.	
13.	
14.	
15.	
16.	
17.	
18.	
19.	
20.	

6
Tales from Here and There

High adventure and bright dreams,
Books are mightier than they seem,
Words that follow leaning stars,
Words that tell of strange bazaars.
Mysteries hide within the chapters—all knowing,
Characters that ride where winds are blowing,
Books of fiction, books of wind and weather,
Non-fiction books—taken altogether.
Books are really magic carpets for would-be vagabonds.

—D. S. Tejmms (1994)

A vagabond is someone who wanders from place to place. Readers who read in a variety of genres will also wander from place to place. Readers of Gloria Skurzynski's survival adventure, *Trapped in the Devil's Desert* (Lothrop, 1982), will become acquainted with the deserts of the American Southwest: the climate, the terrain, the plants, and the animals. Readers of Lloyd Alexander's *Time Cat* (Holt, 1963) will travel through time with Jason and his magic cat to nine different places in the world. Joan Carris's *Hedgehogs in the Closet* (Lippincott, 1988) is set in England and gives readers a feel for that country. In *Katie John and Heathcliff* (HarperCollins, 1980) and other books featuring Katie John, Mary Calhoun writes of days spent in 1940s Keokuk, Iowa. After reading only the four books just described, readers will have wandered through and learned about more than a dozen countries. However, while one visit to a new location can give the visitor a good idea about the place and its people, many more trips are required to learn all there is to know. The same is true of books. One book will provide a taste of the location, but as more books are read, the reader gains additional information and insight. The total impression a reader has of a place is a combination of four basic areas in varying degrees: 1) reading fictional stories about people and events in specific settings; 2) reading nonfiction information about the same setting; 3) visiting the location to experience it firsthand; and 4) gathering information from others who have been to the location. This chapter focuses on fictional stories set in specific geographical settings.

Books and Places

Because the books cited here were chosen for their settings, they will represent a variety of genres. The setting influences the action in many stories. Many discussions of folklore emphasize setting, but less common is the use of setting to help readers understand the plot twists and actions of characters in other genres. Identify books from a variety of settings to create an awareness among students of both the obstacles and benefits of life in other cultures and geographical settings. For a young reader living in New York City, life in a small town in the Midwest might seem completely foreign. Yet readers should be able to explore and learn about life in places that they have never seen.

It is fairly obvious that a mystery set in the Hispanic barrio of New York City would include details quite different from those in a mystery with a similar plot that takes place in a rural midwestern farming community. Being able to empathize with characters in a variety of situations will help young readers develop understanding and empathy for people whose different beliefs and expectations have been influenced by their environment. It is important that students read books set in locations both similar and dissimilar to their own.

Settings—Their Influence on Story

Setting is generally the location of a story in time and place. If a story is set in an identifiable period of time or in an identifiable geographical location, the details of that setting must be accurate even if the story is fiction. The plot and characters must support the setting in that their actions and the story line must be consistent with the location and time period. However, settings should also wrap around the characters and events. For example, Patricia MacLachlan's *Sarah, Plain and Tall* (Harper-Collins, 1985) presents the essence of the prairie visually: "She came through green grass fields that bloomed with Indian Paintbrush, red and orange, and blue-eyed grass." But MacLachlan also presents the prairie through other senses when she speaks of picking the wildflowers, hearing meadowlarks sing, and sliding down a haystack dune.

A good example of a story that uses the setting as an integral part of the story, while keeping the plot and characters in full view, is *Julie of the Wolves* (HarperCollins, 1972). While researching the book, Jean Craighead George spent a summer studying wolves and the Arctic tundra, so she was able to write accurately about the life of a wolf and the survival skills of an Eskimo girl. George was able to provide an almost perfect blending of story and setting as she wrote about Julie's trek across the trackless stretches of snow. The harsh setting contributes to the tension in the story, which does not lift until the final pages of the book.

In some stories, understanding the setting is integral to the progression of the story line. In other stories, the setting is simply a backdrop for the tale. Some settings are so well known that a mere suggestion of the setting can conjure an image in the mind of the reader. Fairy tales are perhaps the best example of this. The words "Once upon a time" bring to mind an era when magic and transformation were possible, when there were beasts large and small, and when kingdoms consisted of beautiful castles and dark, gloomy forests.

Settings also help set the mood of stories. Few scary stories take place in the bright sunlight. And few warm family stories take place in haunted castles. Babbling brooks, trees with full green branches, and meadow flowers among the grass are places that produce settings filled with magic. An expansive parking lot, devoid of trees or vegetation, would not seem to be the place for that same magic. Storms generally bring conflict or evil, while sunshine brings good tidings.

In many tales of adventure, when the story's plot pits a person against society or nature, the setting is an antagonist. Most, if not all, of Jim Kjelgaard's stories, stories of survival in hostile, snowy, northern lands, fit into this category. Other settings are the antagonist because of prevalent attitudes. Stories such as Mildred Taylor's *Roll of Thunder, Hear My Cry* (Dial, 1976) show conflicts arising from the beliefs and prejudices common to the setting. The conflict in this story would simply not have happened in an environment without those underlying beliefs and prejudices. As we read other books set in the same general location, we are able to draw some conclusions about life in that area of the country. We are also able to question the motivation behind and the value of the actions of other people in other circumstances.

Accurate Details and Settings

A folklore unit used in our schools a number of years ago stated that the Paul Galdone retelling of *Little Red Riding Hood* (McGraw-Hill, 1974) had "no setting." What I think the writer of this unit actually meant was that the setting was not significant to the story in terms of location or mood. In fact, every book must have a setting; often more than one, depending on the scenes and action in the book. Galdone's tale takes place in a nondescript location; there is nothing significant or unusual about the woods that she travels through, and the grandmother's little wooden hut at the edge of the woods is not glamorous. On the other hand, Trina Schart Hyman's version of *Little Red Riding Hood* (Holiday, 1983) has an elaborate setting with a lot of details. The kitchen of the little girl's home is quaint and charming, the woods include lush vegetation, and Grandmother's home is comfortable in appearance. The setting resembles the beautiful wooded areas near Hyman's New England home. The depiction of the setting can change from one of simplicity to one of complexity and elaborate details.

Geographical locations must be represented accurately. In modern-day settings, small bits of information, such as the fact that many homes in the southern United States are built without basements, while many of the homes in the Midwest have full basements, play an important part in certain tales. For example, a mystery in which one of the characters hides in the basement would surely be more realistic set in the Midwest than in the South. But to represent a location accurately, the author must know it intimately. What the author does not know firsthand must come from extensive research; minute details make the setting credible.

Some stories have distinct settings that actually set the tone for the story. *Sarah, Plain and Tall* by Patricia MacLachlan is set in two distinct locations: the prairie and the state of Maine (in the 1800s). These two settings are quite different. One is marked by prairie grass and few trees, the other by coastal waters and cool breezes. Those settings are an integral part of both the story and the characters.

Settings also help create moods for various scenes in the book. Patricia McKissack used a setting of time and place to establish a mood that contributed to the effectiveness of the tales she tells in *The Dark-Thirty: Southern Tales of the Supernatural* (Knopf, 1992). The gentle family setting of Cynthia Rylant's many stories set deep in the Appalachians helps develop the aura of a happy, loving family.

To be an effective component of a story, the setting must be carefully developed to increase readers' interest and to move the plot and the actions of the characters along. And settings with a specific geographical location will help readers learn about their own and other environments.

The tales from here and there cited in the following sections are all set in an identifiable geographical location. Familiar settings bring quick reader identification, and less familiar settings introduce readers to new locations, allowing them to see the streets, gardens, towns, special landmarks, and other features.

Beginning a Focus on Tales from Here and There

Introduce the unit focusing on settings by reading aloud a picture book that has an identifiable setting. For example, many of Cynthia Rylant's books are set in the Appalachians where she spent her early childhood. Patricia Polacco sets her many stories in basically two locations: the Oakland, California, neighborhood where she lived with her mother and the small town in Michigan where she spent summers with her father. Select a book to read aloud where the listener can experience the setting through various senses, not just through the pictures. Discuss the effect the geographical location has on the plot of the story. How, if at all, would the story have changed if the story had been set in a different geographical location?

Read-Alouds and Discussions

Select a book set in an interesting setting to read aloud. Show the geographical location of the story on a large map and invite those who are reading other books to pinpoint the location of their books on the map as well if their book has a definite geographic setting.

The general procedures for using a read-aloud title to initiate and model discussions are outlined in chapter 1 (see pages 5-13). During the read-aloud sessions, continue to discuss details of the setting described in the book. A bulletin board can be dedicated to new locations. Use the new words and settings to move into a discussion of the writer's techniques for identifying the settings and the effect setting has on the plot.

After group discussion and journal writing have been modeled to the whole class using the common read-aloud, break the class into smaller discussion groups as outlined in the "Reading Workshop Activities" and "Moving to Independent Reading" sections of chapter 1. Students who read books set in the same general location may wish to compare the descriptions and events that are influenced by the setting as presented in each book. Those who are reading books from varying settings will be able to compare and contrast the type of influence the setting has on the action in each of their books.

Some Great Tales from Here and There to Read Aloud

Corcoran, Barbara. **Wolf at the Door**. Atheneum, 1993. Read-aloud audience: grades 5-7; ages 10-12. Setting: Rocky Mountain states (Montana).
Sibling rivalry plagues Lee as she feels she is always in the shadow of her beautiful and talented younger sister. As an avoidance Lee turns to caring for a wolf pack that needs protection from cattle ranchers who believe the wolves are attacking their livestock.

DeClements, Barthe, and Christopher Greimes. **Double Trouble**. Viking, 1987. Read-aloud audience: grades 3-5; ages 7-10. Setting: Pacific Coast states (Washington).
Faith and Phillip, twins, are separated when their parents and older sister are killed in a crash. The older sister had helped the two of them develop their psychic powers, which prove to be both a help and a danger. Portions of the story are set in Seattle, while the sections told from Faith's point of view are set in Lake Stevens, Washington.

DeVito, Cara. **Where I Want to Be**. Houghton Mifflin, 1993. Read-aloud audience: grades 5-7; ages 10-12. Setting: Southwestern states (Arizona).
Her father has died and her mother left her years ago, so 14-year-old Kristie finds herself living in a small Arizona town trying to sort out her feelings about her older half-brothers and the situation in which she finds herself.

Dygard, Thomas. **Wilderness Peril**. Morrow, 1995. Read-aloud audience: grades 5-7; ages 10-12. Setting: Midwestern states (Minnesota).
Two young men, Todd and Mike, decide to take one last canoe trip to the Boundary Waters canoe area in northern Minnesota before they set off for college. As they embark on their trip they hear of an airplane hijacking in which the hijacker parachutes into the very area where they are headed. During the next days their lives become intertwined in the life of the hijacker.

Fox, Paula. **How Many Miles to Babylon?** Illustrated by Paul Giovanopoulos. Bradbury, 1967; 1980. Read-aloud audience: grades 3-5; ages 7-10. Setting: Middle Atlantic states (New York).
Ten-year-old James is struggling to survive in a Brooklyn ghetto. But trouble comes when he skips school to go to his secret place, a deserted house, where he is found by three teenage boys who force him to join their dognapping ring.

Gilson, Jamie. **It Goes eeeeeeeeeeeeee!** Clarion, 1994. Read-aloud audience: grades 5-7; ages 10-12. Setting: Midwestern states (Illinois).

Patrick is the new boy in class and not particularly popular. In an effort to make friends, he causes trouble in the classroom. Richard and the others in the class are not particularly impressed by Patrick's antics. But attitudes begin to change when Patrick begins work on a science project that includes bats. An idyllic setting in a rural environment.

Guback, Georgia. **Luka's Quilt**. Greenwillow, 1994. Read-aloud audience: grades 3-5; ages 7-10. Setting: Pacific Islands (Hawaii).
Luka's grandmother makes a traditional two-color Hawaiian quilt for her, but they disagree about which colors the quilt should include. The traditions of Hawaii play an important part in this picture book story.

Hahn, Mary Downing. **Daphne's Book**. Clarion, 1983. Read-aloud audience: grades 3-5; ages 7-10. Setting: Southern states (Maryland).
This book is set in a town much like the author's hometown of Columbia, Maryland. Daphne is the new girl in school, and she looks and acts different. Jessica and her popular friends are not eager to make friends with Daphne, but when their teacher pairs Jessica with Daphne for a school assignment, Jessica finds that she must choose between pleasing her friends and doing what she knows is right. She decides to work with Daphne, who she finds is not only a friend, but a friend with a secret. Jessica learns that being a friend is more important than conformity.

Hurwitz, Johanna. **Hooray for Ali Baba Bernstein**. Illustrated by Gail Owens. Morrow, 1989. Read-aloud audience: grades 3-5; ages 7-10. Setting: Middle Atlantic states (New York).
The humorous adventures of Ali Baba Bernstein (originally known as David Bernstein) involve a lost library card and a meeting with the "real" Santa Claus. Set in New York City.

Irwin, Hadley. **The Original Freddie Ackerman**. McElderry, 1992. Read-aloud audience: grades 3-5; ages 7-10. Setting: New England states (Maine).
Trevor Frederick Ackerman has an original mother, an "other dad Charlie," an "other dad Norman" who came before Charlie, and an original father who is married to Freddie's "other mother Daphne." When Freddie's mother and Charlie take a trip to Bermuda, Freddie is sent to stay with his great-aunts on Blue Isle, Maine. The setting promises nothing but boredom until Freddie discovers the ads on the back pages of his aunts' magazines. Before he knows it he is receiving the most mail of anyone on the island. It isn't long before he finds himself in the middle of a stakeout for smugglers, a search for a valuable book, and a friendship with Ariel. He learns that there are family secrets to keep and that the out-of-the-way island is not as boring as he first thought.

Kimmel, Eric A. **One Good Tern Deserves Another**. Holiday, 1994. Read-aloud audience: grades 5-7; ages 10-12. Setting: Pacific states (Oregon).
As if it weren't enough that his stepfather has died, 14-year-old Floyd's mother insists on moving from Oklahoma to the Oregon coast. Floyd wishes for his former home until he makes friends with a beautiful young bird-watcher. He gets a job at a marine aquarium and eventually begins to adjust to life in Oregon and to the possibility of a new stepfather.

Konigsburg, E. L. **T-Backs, T-Shirts, COAT, and Suit**. Atheneum, 1993; Hyperion, 1995. Read-aloud audience: grades 5-8; ages 10-12. Setting: Southern states (Florida).
Twelve-year-old Chlöe is spending the summer with her stepfather's sister, who operates a meals-on-wheels service, and Chlöe helps her aunt. Through a series of events the two become involved in a controversy surrounding the wearing of T-back bathing suits on Florida beaches.

Paterson, Katherine. **Jacob Have I Loved**. Crowell, 1980. Read-aloud audience: grades 5-8; ages 10-12. Setting: Southern states (Maryland and Virginia).
Twin sisters are as different as day and night. One is beautiful and smart, and one is plain and average. The competition between the two of them bring conflict and sibling rivalry. This first-person narrative is told from the vantage point of the less favored daughter. Set in the Chesapeake Bay area of Maryland and Virginia.

Waters, Kate, and Madeline Slovenz-Low. **Lion Dancer: Ernie Wan's Chinese New Year**. Scholastic, 1990. Read-aloud audience: grades 3-5; ages 7-10. Setting: Middle Atlantic states (New York).

With his family and schoolmates, Ernie Wan prepares for the Chinese New Year celebration. This will be Ernie's first public performance of the lion dance. This book contains wonderful images of traditions that are still part of life among Chinese Americans in New York City.

Moving to a Multitude of Books

After listening to a read-aloud book, the class will be ready to move on to reading workshops, discussed in "Moving to Independent Reading" (pages 10-13).

More Tales from Here and There

While many authors set their books in exotic locations, others locate their stories in close-to-home settings. But any setting becomes important if it provides information to the reader about a new place and opens new horizons. Whereas the other chapters in this book have suggested author focuses for the genres being studied, this chapter suggests that readers engage in wide reading. If an author routinely writes books set in the same general location, students who read only books by that author will not necessarily continue to expand their geographical horizons. On the other hand, even if an author writes books with many different settings, reading books by that one author would not be any more valuable than reading books by a variety of authors. It also doesn't allow readers to compare various authors' descriptions of the same places. Thus, the titles listed in this section cover a variety of settings and a variety of authors. In this way, the focus on settings can be emphasized. An index of authors and titles by location is also provided.

A Booklist and Reader's Connections

Avi. **Windcatcher**. Simon & Schuster, 1991. Target audience: grades 5-7; ages 10-12. Setting: New England states (Connecticut).

Tony Souza is not looking forward to spending the summer at his grandmother's house at Swallow's Bay, off the coast of Connecticut. But when his parents offer to buy him a 12-foot sailboat, the summer suddenly looks more interesting. But sailing was to be only one of the adventures Tony would have. A search for a payroll ship (with a million dollars or more onboard), thought to have sunk in the waters surrounding the Thimble Islands in Swallow's Bay, brings adventure, suspense, and mystery.

Connections for Readers— Avi

Avi's images of New England have come from firsthand knowledge. He was born in Manhattan, grew up in Brooklyn, and after attending graduate school in the Midwest at the University of Wisconsin, he settled in New England. For many years he lived in Providence, Rhode Island, but is presently living in the Midwest.

Ballard, Robert D. **Lost Wreck of the Isis**. Scholastic, 1994. Target audience: grades 5-7; ages 10-12. Setting: Europe (Mediterranean area/Italy).

The search for a Roman shipwreck and the investigation of an active underwater volcano provide the interest for this nonfiction story of adventure and discovery, while the Mediterranean Sea and the shores of Italy provide the backdrop.

Connections for Readers— Sunken Ships

Robert Ballard has discovered several sunken ships and has written about their rescue. The rescue sites are located in different places but are similar in that each is underwater. *Exploring the Titanic* (Scholastic, 1988) and *Exploring the Bismarck* (Scholastic, 1991) provide other visions of beneath-the-sea settings, as does Gail Gibbons's title, *Sunken Treasure* (Crowell Jr. Books, 1988), which tells of the rescue of a ship, *Atocha,* that sank off the coast of Florida in 1622.

Branscum, Robbie. **Cameo Rose**. Harper, 1989. Target audience: grades 5-7; ages 10-12. Setting: Southern states (Arkansas).
Cameo Rose is a 14-year-old girl with an insatiable curiosity. When a local ne'er-do-well is murdered, Cameo Rose knows that there is more to the situation than her taciturn neighbors in the Arkansas hills would like anyone to know.

Brenner, Barbara. **Wagon Wheels**. Illustrated by Don Bolognese. HarperCollins, 1993. Target audience: grades 3-5; ages 7-10. Setting: Midwestern states (Kansas).
Shortly after the Civil War, a black family travels to Kansas to take advantage of the free land offered through the Homestead Act. The family—three sons and a father—settle in the black community of Nicodemus, Kansas. Later the father moves several hundred miles farther west to search for a better farming location. When he decides he has found the right spot, he sends a message to his three young sons (none yet in his teens) to follow his map to their new home. They set out and eventually find their father, after a most remarkable journey.

Bryson, Jamie S. **The War Canoe**. Alaska Northwest Books, 1990. Target audience: grades 5-7; ages 10-12. Setting: Alaska.
A young Tlingit Indian, Mickey, is a troublemaker in his small Alaskan village. His demeanor changes when he discovers his heritage through the help of several interested adults, who help him build a traditional war canoe to honor his discovery.

Carlson, Nancy. **A Visit to Grandma's**. Illustrated by Nancy Carlson. Viking, 1991. Target audience: grades 3-5; ages 7-10. Setting: Southern states (Florida).
When Tina and her parents go to Florida to visit Grandmother in her condominium, they find that she is different from when she lived on the farm.

Cherry, Lynne. **The Armadillo from Amarillo**. Illustrated by Lynne Cherry. Harcourt, 1994. Target audience: grades 3-5; ages 7-10. Setting: Southwestern states (Texas).
A whimsical tale of a wandering armadillo who sees some of the cities, historical sites, geographic features, and wildlife of Texas. In this book the plot is the setting.

Connections for Readers— Fun Animal Titles

Lynne Cherry has written a book that focuses directly on the setting. Writing a similar tale about an animal visiting another location, perhaps in your state, could help students appreciate the importance of researching a setting. The trick may be finding an animal that rhymes with a location where that animal would live. However, an alliterative title might also work. Perhaps "A Lizard from Laredo," "A Pig from Palo" (Iowa), "A Cow from Council Bluffs" (Iowa), "A Bug from Boca Raton" (Florida), and so forth.

Clifford, Eth. **Will Someone Marry My Sister?** Houghton Mifflin, 1992. Target audience: grades 5-7; ages 10-12. Setting: Middle Atlantic states (New York).
Although the characters are definitely center stage in this book, the setting is important and very metropolitan. Abel lives with his grandmother and two older sisters in a small apartment over Grandmother's bakery and coffee shop. Because the apartment is cramped, Abel

longs for his older sister, the one studying to be a doctor, to get married so that he will get a room of his own.

Coerr, Eleanor. **Mieko and the Fifth Treasure**. Putnam, 1993. Target audience: grades 5-7; ages 10-12. Setting: Asia (Japan).
Ten-year-old Mieko has been staying with her grandparents ever since the United States dropped the bomb on Nagasaki, Japan. Mieko feels that the happiness in her heart has been taken forever. Because of this sadness Mieko feels that she will no longer be able to produce a beautiful drawing for the contest at school. This historical fiction is set in Japan during World War II.

Connections for Readers— Sadako and the Thousand Paper Cranes

Eleanor Coerr is the author of the book *Sadako and the Thousand Paper Cranes: An Illustrated Storybook*, illustrated by Ed Young (Putnam, 1993). Sadako Sasaki (1943-1955), who lived in Japan during World War II, suffered from leukemia believed to have been caused by the atom bomb the United States dropped on Hiroshima. Legend has it that folding 1,000 paper cranes will make a sick person healthy, so while in the hospital, Sadako raced against time in an attempt to fold 1,000 paper cranes. But Sadako died before completing the task. Friends and schoolchildren across Japan joined in a campaign to finish folding the thousand paper cranes after her death. Today, the paper crane has become a symbol of world peace. Sadako Sasaki's headstone features a paper crane in memory of the young girl who believed in tradition and in peace.

Cooney, Caroline B. **Flash Fire**. Scholastic, 1995. Target audience: grades 3-5; ages 7-10. Setting: Pacific Coast states (California).
As fire sweeps through a Los Angeles canyon, teenagers Donna and Hall Press and a number of other children whose parents are not around must work together to save themselves.

Connections for Readers— Tikvah Means Hope

Patricia Polacco has illustrated a story, *Tikvah Means Hope* (Doubleday, 1994), that recounts a true incident that occurred while the fires ravaged Oakland, California, in the early 1990s. The story incorporates a Jewish tradition into the story of the devastating fire.

Corcoran, Barbara. **Stay Tuned!** Atheneum, 1991. Target audience: grades 5-7; ages 10-12. Setting: New England states (New Hampshire).
Fourteen-year-old Stevie is on her way to stay with a relative she has never seen. Feeling abandoned, she joins up with three other young people with no place to live, and together they take a detour into the New Hampshire woods. There Stevie hopes to start a new life.

Cruise, Beth. **Silver Spurs**. Collier Books, 1994. Saved by the Bell series. Target audience: grades 3-5; ages 7-10. Setting: Southwestern states (New Mexico).
When the "Saved by the Bell" gang decide to go to a New Mexico dude ranch for the weekend, they become involved in unexpected events. The complications begin when Zack is mistaken for a rodeo star and Jessie becomes suspicious of the ranch owner's past.

dePaola, Tomie. **Bonjour, Mr. Satie**. Illustrated by Tomie dePaola. Putnam, 1991. Target audience: grades 5-7; ages 10-12. Setting: Europe (France).
Sophisticated Uncle Satie (a cultured feline) returns from a voyage to Paris to visit his midwestern niece and nephew. During the visit he tells the children about a Paris salon encounter between Pablo Picasso and Henri Matisse. Younger readers will enjoy the colors of Picasso's blue period and the boldness of Matisse's work, but older readers will recognize

the parodies of the famed artists' work. They will also be drawn to read biographies of the characters portrayed in the book, particularly Alice B. Toklas and Gertrude Stein.

Connections for Readers— Bonjour, Mr. Satie

Although the main characters in Tomie dePaola's *Bonjour, Mr. Satie* (Putnam, 1991) are feline, the book is otherwise populated by Mr. Satie's friend, a rat, and all the "in" people in Paris society just before and after World War I. The inclusion of the notable people of the 1920s will recommend this story to older readers, who can appreciate the parodies of the artists' works, the social interaction of the well-known personalities of the time, and the setting (both time and place). Many notable people are pictured in a scene set in the legendary salon of Gertrude Stein and Alice B. Toklas. DePaola has taken some literary (or artistic) license by including in one scene people from different periods of Stein and Toklas's lives. In addition, U.S. president Calvin Coolidge may have known Stein's and Toklas, but there is no evidence that he ever visited them in France. Other people included in the major salon scene are Sylvia Beach, James Joyce, Edith Sitwell, Isadora Duncan, Stephen Spender, Mabel Dodge, George Gershwin, Calvin Coolidge, B. Top, Josephine Baker, Olga Pound (Rudge), Pablo Picasso, Ezra Pound, Ernest Hemingway, Zelda Fitzgerald, Paul Robeson, Claude Monet, and Virgil Thomson.

Edwards, Michelle. **Eve and Smithy: An Iowa Tale**. Illustrated by Michelle Edwards. Lothrop, 1994. Target audience: grades 3-5; ages 7-10. Setting: Midwestern states (Iowa).
Eve spends all her time gardening and painting pictures of Iowa. Her neighbor and friend, Smithy, tries to think of a gift for her.

Foreman, Michael. **War Boy: A Country Childhood**. Arcade, 1990. Target audience: grades 5-7; ages 10-12. Setting: British Isles (England).
Young children suffered many hardships growing up in England during World War II. This book details one boy's experiences in a wonderfully illustrated retelling of his childhood.

Friedman, Ina R., and Allen Say. **How My Parents Learned to Eat**. Illustrated by Allen Say. Houghton Mifflin, 1984. Target audience: grades 3-5; ages 7-10. Setting: Asia (Japan).
An American soldier meets a Japanese woman and they fall in love. As a surprise for each other, they attempt to learn how to eat using the other's traditional utensils. This picture book depicts one small element of a culture and shows how a member of another culture attempts to respect it.

Connections for Readers— Allen Say

Allen Say, the illustrator of *How My Parents Learned to Eat* (Houghton Mifflin, 1984), was born in Japan and spent his early years there. Say's mother was born in America, but her parents were Japanese. Say's father was Korean. As a teenager, Say traveled to America, much as his grandfather had done two generations before. His grandfather's story (combined with elements from his own journey) was told by Say in the 1993 Caldecott Award book *Grandfather's Journey* (Houghton Mifflin, 1993).

Fritz, Jean. **Homesick: My Own Story**. Illustrated by Margot Tomes. Putnam, 1982. Target audience: grades 5-8; ages 10-12. Setting: Asia (China).
Fritz has vivid memories of her childhood in Hankow, China. She recalls the sights and sounds of the city and the surrounding countryside. However, her story is more than the smells, sights, and feel of the place; she writes a compelling

story of growing up in an environment where she is surrounded by children of other cultures and beliefs. The teeming life of the city comes alive as Fritz recounts her days as a child.

Connections for Readers— China

In *Homesick: My Own Story,* Jean Fritz vividly describes her childhood home of Hangkow, China. Readers come away with visions of the muddy Yangtze River: elderly women praying on its banks to the River God, other women washing clothes, and coolies hauling water on their backs and shoulders. She brings visions of crowded houseboats filled with people, chickens, and pigs. And her streets are filled with beggars. To the reader who has never been to China, this vision will need to be balanced against a more modern vision of China. It is important to realize that the China described by Fritz is the China of her childhood, more than 70 years ago. If there are international companies in your community, find out if any of their personnel travel to China. If so, ask a representative to speak to the class so students can learn what China is like today. Alternatively, research in the library media center will provide secondhand information regarding modern China.

Gibbons, Faye. **King Shoes and Clown Pockets**. Morrow, 1989. Target audience: grades 5-8; ages 10-12. Setting: Southern states (Alabama).
Rural Alabama is the setting for this story about two 10-year-old boys and their friendship. Each has his own personal problems, but together they face the changes in their lives.

Hahn, Mary Downing. **Look for Me by Moonlight**. Clarion, 1995. Target audience: grades 5-7; ages 10-12. Setting: New England states (Maine).

A tale with vampires, ghosts, stepfamilies, hotels, and motels. While staying at a remote and reportedly haunted inn run by her father and pregnant stepmother, 16-year-old Cynde feels increasingly isolated from her father's new family. In her loneliness, she finds comfort in the attention of a charming but mysterious guest.

Hall, Lynn. **Dagmar Schultz and the Green-Eyed Monster**. Scribner, 1991. Target audience: grades 5-8; ages 10-12. Setting: Midwestern states (Iowa).
Thirteen-year-old Dagmar attempts to draw attention away from the pretty and popular new student. With humorous results Dagmar succeeds, for a time.

Connections for Readers— Lynn Hall

Lynn Hall was born in Illinois but grew up in Des Moines, Iowa, where she lived until her mid-20s. She always loved animals and dreamed of having some of her own. Deciding to write full time gave her the freedom to move to more rural areas in Iowa. She now lives near Elkader, Iowa, in a stone house she designed and had built (although she did much of the work herself). Many of her books are set in the Iowa countryside and feature some of her favorite animals— horses and dogs.

Hamilton, Virginia. **The Bells of Christmas**. Illustrated by Lambert Davis. Harcourt, 1989. Target audience: grades 3-5; ages 7-10. Setting: Midwestern states (Ohio).
Springfield, Ohio, is the site of an 1890 Christmas that leaves 12-year-old Jason with wonderful memories. This snow-filled, magical holiday story gives readers a new perspective on the traditions of the day.

Connections for Readers— Virginia Hamilton

Virginia Hamilton and her husband, Arnold Adoff, live and work in their home in Yellow Spring, Ohio, on land that was settled by Hamilton's ancestors, who were born slaves and fled to freedom across the Ohio River.

Jakobsen, Kathy. **My New York**. Illustrated by Kathy Jakobsen. Little, Brown, 1993. Target audience: grades 3-5; ages 7-10. Setting: Middle Atlantic states (New York).

Through a series of letters, a young New Yorker writes to a friend in the Midwest, Martin, to tell him about the things they will see in the city when he comes to visit. Some pages fold out to show a panoramic view of New York.

Connections for Readers— Kathy Jakobsen's New York

Kathy Jakobsen is a folk artist who paints from her studio in rural Connecticut. She paints farmlands and horses as easily as she does curbsides and hansom cabs. The scenes in *My New York* present New York at its best—children and their parents visit the seals at Central Park Zoo and watch the fireworks from New York Harbor.

Keller, Holly. **Grandfather's Dream**. Illustrated by Holly Keller. Greenwillow, 1994. Target audience: grades 3-5; ages 7-10. Setting: Asia (Vietnam).

After the Vietnam war, the wetlands of the Mekong Delta are virtually destroyed and the beautiful large cranes are gone. A young boy's grandfather dreams of restoring those wetlands and seeing the cranes return.

Krisher, Trudy. **Spite Fences**. Delacorte, 1994. Target audience: grades 5-7; ages 10-12. Setting: Southern states (Georgia).

A young girl with a troubled relationship with her mother is drawn into violence, hatred, racial tension, and plenty of mistrust in the small Georgia town where she is living in the 1960s.

Kroll, Steven. **Patrick's Tree House**. Illustrated by Roberta Wilson. Macmillan, 1994. Target audience: grades 3-5; ages 7-10. Setting: New England states (Maine).

A surprise awaited nine-year-old Patrick when he arrived at his grandparents' home in Maine— a tree house. But Patrick soon finds that he must deal with two troubled boys who have taken over the tree house.

Kroll, Virginia. **Sweet Magnolia**. Illustrated by Laura Jacques. Charlesbridge, 1994. Target audience: grades 3-5; ages 7-10. Setting: Southern states (Louisiana).

Denise visits her grandmother, a wildlife rehabilitator in the Louisiana bayou country, and helps her heal and free an injured grackle baby.

Lawlor, Laurie. **Gold in the Hills**. Walker, 1995. Target audience: grades 5-7; ages 10-12. Setting: Rocky Mountain states (Colorado).

Ten-year-old Hattie and her brother are left behind with relatives while their father goes prospecting for gold in the Colorado mountains. To make their lives bearable while he is gone, the children depend on the friendship of an elderly recluse who lives nearby.

Lawson, Julie, reteller. **The Dragon's Pearl**. Paintings by Paul Marin. Oxford, 1992. Target audience: grades 3-5; ages 7-10. Setting: Asia (China).

A picture book retelling of a traditional Chinese legend. During a terrible drought, a cheerful, dutiful son finds a magic pearl that forever changes his life and the lives of his mother and neighbors.

Martin, Jacqueline Briggs. **Grandmother Bryant's Pocket**. Illustrated by Petra Mathers. Ticknor & Fields, 1996. Target audience: grades 3-5; ages 7-10. Setting: New England states (Maine).

After her dog dies in a fire, a young girl has nightmares. When she goes to live at her grandmother's Maine home, she learns about life and living.

Connections for Readers—
Jacqueline Briggs Martin

Jacqueline Briggs Martin was born in Maine and grew up there. The setting is one that is very familiar to her and comes from her childhood memories. Many of Martin's books mention stone fences (very common in Maine), piney woods (which are not always pine trees), and other details characteristic of the New England landscape.

Naylor, Phyllis Reynolds. **Beetles, Lightly Toasted**. Atheneum, 1987. Target audience: grades 3-5; ages 7-10. Setting: Midwestern states (Iowa).

When a Cedar Rapids, Iowa, radio station (WMT) promotes a contest challenging listeners to come up with nutritious new food sources, fifth-grader Andy decides to enter. With his cousin, Andy makes up recipes using unusual food sources and tests them on unsuspecting friends and family.

Connections for Readers—
Phyllis Reynolds Naylor

Phyllis Reynolds Naylor's *Beetles, Lightly Toasted* is set in Iowa. Naylor's grandparents had a farm near Waverly, Iowa, where she spent time during the summer, often listening to the radio. When she was writing *Beetles*, Naylor read about station WMT in a *National Geographic* article in which a farmer said he liked the station because it soothed the cows. So Naylor used the call letters in her book. Only later did she realize that it was the same radio station she had listened to on her grandfather's farm.

Neville, Emily Cheney. **The China Year: A Novel**. HarperCollins, 1991. Target audience: grades 5-7; ages 10-12. Setting: Asia (China).

A New York City teenager, Henrietta Rich, travels to Beijing where her father has accepted a teaching position. This is Henrietta's account of her year-long sojourn in China.

Petersen, P. J. **Liars**. Simon & Schuster, 1992. Target audience: grades 5-7; ages 10-12. Setting: Pacific Coast states (California).

Alder Creek, an isolated town in California, is a boring place for eighth-grader Sam and his friends. That is, until Sam's newly discovered ability to tell when a person is lying involves him in a series of mysterious events.

Pinkney, Gloria Jean. **Back Home**. Illustrated by Jerry Pinkney. Dial, 1992. Target audience: grades 3-5; ages 7-10. Setting: Southern states (North Carolina).

When eight-year-old Ernestine visits relatives on the North Carolina farm where she was born, she finds out much about herself and the place.

Rand, Gloria. **Prince William**. Illustrated by Ted Rand. Henry Holt, 1992. Target audience: grades 3-5; ages 7-10. Setting: Alaska.

An oil spill on Prince William Sound in Alaska is the cause of damage to the coast and to many animals living in the sound. Denny rescues a baby seal that is hurt by the oil spill and watches as it recovers at a nearby animal hospital.

Connections for Readers—
Comparing Settings

To see how setting influences the story grammar of Rand's story, read and compare it to Jacqueline Briggs Martin's *Birdwashing Song: The Willow Tree Loon*, illustrated by Nancy Carpenter (Macmillan, 1995). It is the story of a loon that is caught in an oil spill, found, treated, washed, and released. The oil spill is caused when a barge hits a bridge. The book tells the story of many volunteers who give up their time to scrub and rehabilitate injured birds. This tale is set in the Atlantic coastal area and will provide some contrasts to the setting of the Rand title, which is a continent away in Alaska.

Ruby, Lois. **Steal Away Home**. Macmillan, 1994. Target audience: grades 5-7; ages 10-12. Setting: Midwestern states (Kansas).
Parallel stories: An 1850s Quaker family in Kansas operates an Underground Railroad station. Almost 150 years later, 12-year-old Dana moves into the same house and finds the skeleton of a black woman who helped the Quakers.

Say, Allen. **El Chino**. Illustrated by Allen Say. Houghton Mifflin, 1990. Target audience: grades 3-5; ages 7-10. Setting: Southwestern states (Arizona) and Europe (Spain).
High-school basketball star Billy Wong realizes that he won't be a star in college basketball, so he gives up his dream of being a sports hero. Instead he studies engineering and saves his money for a trip to Spain. While in Spain he falls in love with the sport of bullfighting and after much work, he becomes the first Chinese bullfighter—El Chino.

Connections for Readers— The Chinese Matador

Allen Say first learned about El Chino when he met a Jewish woman whose last name was "Wong." It turned out that she was Billy Wong's sister-in-law. When Billy Wong's eldest sister saw the first photographic illustration in the book—a picture of her parents and their six children—she cried. The story of the Chinese Matador was, according to Say, originally published in a Sunday newspaper supplement, *California Living*.

Schlein, Miriam. **The Year of the Panda**. Illustrated by Kam Mak. Crowell, 1990. Target audience: grades 3-5; ages 7-10. Setting: Asia (China).
A starving baby panda is rescued by a Chinese boy, who in the process of caring for the panda, learns why pandas are endangered and what the government is doing to save them.

Seabrooke, Brenda. **The Bridges of Summer**. Cobblehill, 1992. Target audience: grades 5-7; ages 10-12. Setting: Southern states (South Carolina).
When she reluctantly goes to South Carolina to stay with her grandmother on a small island, 14-year-old Zorah gradually learns to accept her grandmother's Gullah traditions and different way of life.

Shannon, George. **Climbing Kansas Mountains**. Illustrated by Thomas B. Allen. Bradbury, 1993. Target audience: grades 3-5; ages 7-10. Setting: Midwestern states (Kansas).
A young boy and his father share the magic of climbing the "Kansas Mountains." It is a bonding experience in the Kansas countryside.

Skurzynski, Gloria. **Goodbye, Billy Radish**. Bradbury, 1992. Target audience: grades 5-7; ages 10-12. Setting: Middle Atlantic states (Pennsylvania).
In 1917, as the United States enters World War I, 10-year-old Hank sees changes all around him in the western Pennsylvania steel mill town where he lives. Hank feels that his older Ukrainian friend, Billy, is drifting away from him.

Connections for Readers— Gloria Skurzynski

Gloria Skurzynski was born in Duquesne, Pennsylvania, on July 6, 1930. Her growing-up years were filled with images from books and movies and stories her father told about his own childhood. A book she wrote the year before he died, *The Tempering* (Clarion, 1983), is a story of that childhood. The story tells of Karl Kerner, who can hardly wait until he can quit school and get a real job in one of the town's steel mills. The dreadful scene where Karl's foot is burned with molten lead actually happened. *Good-Bye, Billy Radish* is a story that came out of other experiences during World War I.

Stolz, Mary. **Coco Grimes**. HarperCollins, 1994. Target audience: grades 3-5; ages 7-10. Setting: Southern states (Florida).

First introduced in *Go Fish* (HarperCollins, 1991), Thomas is now 11 years old and intent on talking his grandfather into driving across Florida to meet Coco Grimes. Grimes, now an old man, remembers Negro League baseball. Thomas's meeting with Grimes is bittersweet.

Turner, Ann Warren. **Grasshopper Summer**. Macmillan, 1989. Target audience: grades 5-7; ages 10-12. Setting: Midwestern states (South Dakota).

In 1874, 11-year-old Sam and his family move from Kentucky to southern Dakota territory. During a particularly dry and harsh growing season, a plague of hungry grasshoppers threatens the family's survival.

Uchida, Yoshiko. **The Happiest Ending**. Atheneum, 1985. Target audience: grades 5-7; ages 10-12. Setting: Pacific Coast states (California).

Yoshiko tells of an incident from the World War II era when 12-year-old Rinko learns that a neighbor's daughter is coming from Japan to marry a stranger twice her age. Rinko sets out to change this arrangement and gains new insight into love and adult problems.

Connections for Readers— Yoshiko Uchida

Yoshiko Uchida was born on November 24, 1921, in Alameda, California. Her parents were natives of Japan, and the entire family was put in concentration (internment) camps during World War II. Yoshiko's father, Dwight Takashi Uchida, was a San Francisco businessman, and her mother, Iku Uchida, wrote poetry. For many years the family lived in Berkeley in a small house where her mother cooked traditional Japanese foods. Yoshiko and her sister sometimes wore kimonos for special programs at school. They celebrated Dolls Festival Day (March 3) and held tea parties in their honor. The family was forced to the camp at Tanforan Race Track. They were held there for five months and then sent to a guarded camp, Topaz, in the Utah desert. Yoshiko Uchida incorporates some of her experiences into her many books about the Japanese experience in America—and while doing so she shares much of life in the Pacific Coast states. Among her books are *The Best Bad Thing* (McElderry, 1983), *A Jar of Dreams* (McElderry, 1981), and *Journey to Topaz: A Story of the Japanese-American Evacuation* (Creative Arts, 1985). These stories are historical fiction and, as such, give us valuable insight into what was happening on the West Coast in the 1940s. Compare and contrast the information in this book with information readers' parents or grandparents might convey about life in other parts of the United States (or in other countries) during World War II.

Wallace, Bill. **Blackwater Swamp**. Holiday, 1994. Target audience: grades 5-7; ages 10-12. Setting: Southern states (Louisiana)

The Witch of Blackwater Swamp is a woman who is really unknown by most of the residents in the area. Ted, a fifth-grader, comes to know the true nature of the woman and must decide whether or not to come to her aid when she is accused of the thefts taking place in his small Louisiana town.

Wisniewski, David. **Sundiata: Lion King of Mali**. Written and illustrated by David Wisniewski. Clarion, 1992. Target audience: grades 5-7; ages 10-12. Setting: Africa (Mali).

Biography of a 13th-century king in western Africa. Despite Sundiata's severe handicap, he is his father's heir to the kingdom of Mali. Sundiata is forced into exile, but when he reaches adulthood, he is summoned back to his homeland to overthrow a sorcerer king.

Connections for Readers—
Sundiata: Lion King of Mali

This tale seems to be part biography and part legend, but because the African *griots* keep their history alive through oral stories, this biography appears to be within that tradition. Sundiata lived during medieval times in the area of Africa now known as Mali. The setting is important to the account of Sundiata's life, as the struggle was for control of a specific country—now Mali. More information about the ancient kingdom of Mali may be found in Joan Joseph's *Black African Empires* (Watts, 1974) and *Mali in Pictures* by Thomas O'Toole (Lerner, 1990), and the more recent *The Royal Kingdoms of Ghana, Mali, and Songhay: Life in Medieval Africa* by Patricia McKissack and Fredrick McKissack (Holt, 1994).

Because many readers tend to view all parts of Africa as one and the same, efforts should be made to give readers views of other parts of Africa.

If one wishes to focus on an author during a discussion of setting, David Wisniewski would make an appropriate choice. Each of his five books is singular in that the author draws upon thorough research of distinctive settings to build his literary folktales. Author focus information about David Wisniewski can be found in chapter 4.

Yolen, Jane. **Let Swift Water Go**. Illustrated by Barbara Cooney. Little, Brown, 1991. Target audience: grades 3-5; ages 7-10. Setting: New England states (Massachusetts). Sally Jane and the changing times around her are recounted in this tale—a tale of the drowning of Swift River towns in western Massachusetts to form the Quabbin Reservoir and provide a viable water supply to Boston.

Going Beyond

In this focus on tales from here and there, students will read many works of fiction, nonfiction, and biography. If authors accurately represent the geographical locations in their books, readers will learn to appreciate the different conditions in a variety of locations that affect events and actions of people who live there. The information provided on these settings either comes from the author's firsthand knowledge of the geographical location or is the result of extensive research.

Activities related to settings can help integrate critical thinking skills, geography, and other curriculum content. The list on page 138 has suggestions for collaborative activities.

Culminating the Focus on Books from Here and There

The purpose of a culminating activity is to bring closure to a specific focus. General ideas for culminating activities are discussed in chapter 1 (page 14).

As a culminating activity, readers might be asked to select a passage from their book that would give clues to the geographical setting of the books they have read. Reading aloud the selections and attempting to use the clues to pinpoint the geographical setting on a world map might provide a final culminating activity or a read-and-feed session (children read the books and eat snacks) featuring food that might have been eaten in each of their settings. For example, if the book is set in Iowa, corn chips or popcorn might be appropriate; southern Georgia might inspire eating peanuts as a snack; and orange juice might represent a book set in Florida.

Pages 139-142 may be reproduced for student use.

Focus Activity:
Geography and Books

- Brainstorm a 10-point list of "Things I Know About _____ "(setting). Each point should be verified using an acceptable reference source.

- Map the setting. Draw the neighborhood, city, or other area where the story is set. Mark streets, landmarks, woods, houses, and so forth, so the action in the story can be followed through the map.

- Create a 3-D map of the setting.

- Make a list of facts included in the book concerning the setting. Then research to verify the accuracy of those facts. For example, in Phyllis Reynolds Naylor's *Beetles, Lightly Toasted,* Naylor mentions several towns in Iowa, all but one of which actually exist in Iowa. Locating these towns on an Iowa map indicates that these towns are within the listening range of the radio station WMT, mentioned as the promoter of the food contest.

- Use the following list to categorize books from similar areas:

    Middle Atlantic states: New Jersey, New York, Pennsylvania.

    Midwestern states: Illinois, Indiana, Iowa, Kansas, Michigan, Minnesota, Missouri, Nebraska, North Dakota, Ohio, South Dakota, Wisconsin.

    New England states: Connecticut, Maine, Massachusetts, New Hampshire, Rhode Island, Vermont.

    Pacific Coast states: California, Oregon, Washington.

    Rocky Mountain states: Colorado, Idaho, Montana, Nevada, Utah, Wyoming.

    Southern states: Alabama, Arkansas, Delaware, Florida, Georgia, Kentucky, Louisiana, Maryland, Mississippi, North Carolina, South Carolina, Tennessee, Virginia, West Virginia.

    Southwestern states: Arizona, New Mexico, Oklahoma, Texas.

    Other states: Alaska, Hawaii.

    Countries: List by continent then by country, such as Africa (Mali) or Asia (China).

- Rewrite a scene or episode by changing the setting and the elements of the story that would be affected if the setting were changed.

- If the time element of the setting is significant, make a timeline indicating significant events that occurred in the world during the same period.

Tales from Here and There

Reader's Journal

My Name: _____

From Educator's Companion to Children's Literature, Volume 2: Folklore, Contemporary Realistic Fiction, Fantasy, Biographies, and Tales from Here and There. © 1996. Libraries Unlimited. (800) 237-6124.

Response Starter Suggestions

Your reader's journal for tales from here and there is where you will record your ideas, your thoughts, your questions about vocabulary, and your questions and comments about the plot and the people involved in the book or chapter you have just read. Sometimes it is difficult to get started, so the following questions might give you ideas to help you begin. These questions are only suggestions; the journal is yours and should contain questions and comments about the parts of the book that interest you.

- What part does the setting play in this book?

- What is the setting? (Note: There may be more than one.)

- How does the author make the setting an integral part of the story?

- How does the author's description of the setting agree or disagree with your knowledge of the area?

- How does the setting influence the actions of the characters?

- How does the setting influence the development of the plot?

- Is the action in the book realistic? Why or why not?

- What does the setting in this book remind you of?

- How would this book be different if it had been set in a different geographical location?

- What facts in this book identify the geographical location?

Date each of your journal entries. Responses mean more later if you use complete sentences.

Have fun and enjoy your reading.

Tales from Here and There I Have Read

Title	Author
1.	
Setting:	
2.	
Setting:	
3.	
Setting:	
4.	
Setting:	
5.	
Setting:	
6.	
Setting:	
7.	
Setting:	
8.	
Setting:	
9.	
Setting:	
10.	
Setting:	

Tales from Here and There I Want to Read

Title	Author
1.	
Setting:	
2.	
Setting:	
3.	
Setting:	
4.	
Setting:	
5.	
Setting:	
6.	
Setting:	
7.	
Setting:	
8.	
Setting:	
9.	
Setting:	
10.	
Setting:	

Index of Authors and Titles by Location_____

New England States (Massachusetts)
Yolen, Jane. *Let Swift Water Go* (p. 137)

New England States (New Hampshire)
Corcoran, Barbara. *Stay Tuned!* (p. 130)

Other States (Alaska)
Bryson, Jamie S. *The War Canoe* (p. 129)
Rand, Gloria. *Prince William* (p. 134)

Other States (Hawaii)
Guback, Georgia. *Luka's Quilt*. Read-aloud list. (p. 127)

Pacific Coast States (California)
Cooney, Caroline B. *Flash Fire* (p. 130)
Petersen, P. J. *Liars* (p. 134)
Uchida, Yoshiko. *The Happiest Ending* (p. 136)

Pacific Coast States (Oregon)
Kimmel, Eric A. *One Good Tern Deserves Another*. Read-aloud list. (p. 127)

Pacific Coast States (Washington)
DeClements, Barthe, and Christopher Greimes. *Double Trouble*. Read-aloud list. (p. 126)

Rocky Mountain States (Colorado)
Lawlor, Laurie. *Gold in the Hills* (p. 133)

Rocky Mountain States (Montana)
Corcoran, Barbara. *Wolf at the Door*. Read-aloud list. (p. 126)

Southern States (Alabama)
Gibbons, Faye. *King Shoes and Clown Pockets* (p. 132)

Southern States (Arkansas)
Branscum, Robbie. *Cameo Rose* (p. 129)

Southern States (Florida)
Carlson, Nancy. *A Visit to Grandma's* (p. 129)
Konigsburg, E. L. *T-Backs, T-Shirts, COAT, and Suit*. Read-aloud list. (p. 127)
Stolz, Mary. *Coco Grimes* (p. 136)

Southern States (Georgia)
Krisher, Trudy. *Spite Fences* (p. 133)

Southern States (Louisiana)
Kroll, Virginia. *Sweet Magnolia* (p. 133)
Wallace, Bill. *Blackwater Swamp* (p. 136)

Southern States (Maryland)
Hahn, Mary Downing. *Daphne's Book*. Read-aloud list. (p. 127)

Southern States (Maryland and Virginia)
Paterson, Katherine. *Jacob Have I Loved*. Read-aloud list. (p. 127)

Southern States (North Carolina)
Pinkney, Gloria Jean. *Back Home* (p. 134)

Southern States (South Carolina)
Seabrooke, Brenda. *The Bridges of Summer* (p. 135)

Southwestern States (Arizona)
Say, Allen. *El Chino* (p. 135)
DeVito, Cara. *Where I Want to Be*. Read-aloud list. (p. 126)

Southwestern States (New Mexico)
Cruise, Beth. *Silver Spurs* (p. 130)

Southwestern States (Texas)
Cherry, Lynne. *The Armadillo from Amarillo* (p. 129)

Index

About the Author

The books that Sharron McElmeel read most often as a child were collections of stories by the Grimm Brothers and Hans Christian Andersen. She still enjoys folklore and literary tales told by Andersen, David Wisniewski, Paul Goble, and the many others who mimic the folklore form. In her teenage years she savored the turnabout endings in the work of O. Henry and later read about his life. From there she developed an interest in learning more about people who accomplished things she admired. One book always led to another. Now in the course of a year, she reads a multitude of books as part of her research for the many reference books and periodical articles she writes.

In addition to her writing, Sharron is a library media specialist in the Cedar Rapids (Iowa) Community School District. She earned her B.A. in education from the Northern University of Iowa and her M.A. in library science from the University of Iowa. She has been named Iowa Reading Teacher of the Year and is frequently asked to speak at state and national conferences. Her columns, articles, and reviews on books and authors appear regularly in *Library Talk*, *Mystery Scene Magazine*, *School Library Journal*, *The Iowa Reading Journal*, and several other publications.

Sharron is the author of the best-selling Author a Month series and the Bookpeople albums published by Libraries Unlimited/Teacher Ideas Press. Her books dealing with curriculum integration include *My Bag of Book Tricks*, *Adventures with Social Studies (Through Literature)*, and *McElmeel Booknotes: Literature Across the Curriculum*. Her newest releases are *The Latest and Greatest Read-Alouds*, *Great New Nonfiction Reads,* and the companion volume to this title, *Educator's Companion to Children's Literature, Volume 1: Mysteries, Animal Tales, Books of Humor, Adventure Stories, and Historical Fiction.*

The author lives with her husband in a rural area north of Cedar Rapids, Iowa, where their home is frequently filled with friends and family—and several hundred books.